CONTENDING FOR THE FAITH

Contending
for the Faith

Southern Baptists
in New Mexico, 1938–1995

DANIEL R. CARNETT

UNIVERSITY OF NEW MEXICO PRESS

ALBUQUERQUE

To my father,
Charles B. Carnett,
whose love of history and interest in
this subject inspired me to undertake
the project and bring it to fruition,
even though he was unable
to see its completion.

© 2002 by the University of New Mexico Press
All rights reserved.
First edition

Library of Congress Cataloging-in-Publication Data

Carnett, Daniel Richard.
    Contending for the faith: Southern Baptists in New Mexico, 1938–1995 /
    Daniel Carnett.
        p.   cm.
    Includes bibliographical references and index.
    ISBN 0-8263-2837-7 (alk. paper)
    1. Baptist Convention of New Mexico—History—20th century.
    2. Southern Baptist Convention—New Mexico—History—20th century.
    3. New Mexico—Church history—20th century. I. Title
BX6462.4N6C37 2002
286'.1789—dc21
                                                                2002008743

All figures courtesy of the Baptist Convention of New Mexico,
Historical Archives, Albuquerque, New Mexico.

DESIGN: Mina Yamashita

Contents

Preface

For anyone interested in the study of religion in America, the state of New Mexico offers unparalleled opportunities. It is a microcosm of the nation. Within the state's borders, one finds Native Americans practicing their ancient beliefs alongside adherents to Islam. A short distance away, Sikhs congregate at their temple. Although Roman Catholics and Protestants dominate the religious landscape, various forms of Eastern mysticism and New Age thought also abound. They have roots traceable to the "health seekers" who followed the Santa Fe Trail looking for alternative methods of healing involving the mind as well as the body.

New Mexico, therefore, is an ideal place to undertake a study examining paradigm shifts in American religious history. Originally, my idea had been to study the effects of alternative religions on mainline Protestantism. But my academic colleagues helped me to steer the project into more manageable waters. Instead, I chose one group, the Southern Baptists, to examine for possible adaptations to a pluralistic environment.

Before World War II, the Southern Baptists in New Mexico were a small denomination struggling for their existence. Two decades later, they were the largest Protestant body, and second only in size to the Roman Catholic Church in New Mexico. Given the background of Southern Baptists and the nature of New Mexico, the study posed an interesting academic question. How did a Southern form of evangelical religion, which was culturally, racially, and geographically homogeneous, rise to prominence in a state noted for its pluralism and diversity?

This study begins in 1938 with the employment of Harry Stagg as the new corresponding secretary for Southern Baptists in New Mexico. Under his administration the Southern Baptists' state convention achieved its phenomenal growth. Fortunately, Stagg was still living at the time this book was written and agreed to be interviewed. The study concludes in 1995, when the Baptist Convention of New Mexico went through a second reorganization, in an attempt to position itself for the twenty-first century. Such an event provided a natural point of demarcation. A brief epilogue on the 1996–2000 period brings their story up to the present.

Interestingly, soon after the project began, it became apparent that Southern Baptist numbers in New Mexico had plateaued. Now, the focus of the study changed. I searched not only for factors that had caused them to grow, but also those contributing to a possible decline. Examining expansion and stagnation would allow me to understand better the Southern Baptist journey in New Mexico, illuminating any paradigm shifts in their theology and practice.

Such an inquiry required a different method of analysis, one that would juxtapose the two conditions. For this purpose, I chose to study the three areas of church function: theology, structure, and fellowship. The interplay among these elements over time would reveal the nature of any alteration in Baptist practice, thus providing answers to why this reversal occurred and under what circumstances.

The study is divided into five sections. Chapters 1 and 2 provide a historical backdrop, starting with Baptist beginnings in England up to the present, as well as a survey of Baptists in New Mexico from 1849 through 1937. Chapters 3 through 5 concentrate on the Stagg years and include the building of the Southern Baptist Convention's western conference grounds at Glorieta. The tumultuous 1960s receive attention in chapters 6 and 7. Baptist adjustments to the post-1960s era comprise chapters 8 through 10. Finally, chapter 11 seeks to answer the two questions that framed the study: What factors allowed Southern Baptists to grow to prominence in New Mexico and why are they now beginning to decline?

Attempting to write about Southern Baptists presents a unique set of problems. They are a noncreedal, nonhierarchical, fiercely independent people. In fact, in the seventeenth century, both the English government and the Anglican Church considered Baptists to be anarchists. This tradition continues to the present day. Indeed, "the" Baptist church does not exist. One can be a member of "a" Baptist church, and Baptist churches may come together for fellowship or to conduct specific work, usually evangelism and missions, yet each is totally autonomous. One must be aware then, that general statements about Baptists refer to trends or patterns. Such tendencies do not necessarily apply to a specific Baptist church. Therefore, readers are encouraged to turn to the appendix before beginning to read this book to acquaint themselves with Baptist beliefs. Foy Valentine, who for many years directed the Christian Life Commission of the Southern Baptist Convention, sums up the problem this way:

> A resolution at a meeting of the Southern Baptist Convention, a state Baptist convention, or a Baptist association will be generally

understood by most Baptists as having issued from an assembly or a body which never existed before and which will never exist again, which is endowed by neither God in heaven nor Baptists on earth with any authority whatsoever over them, and which in their opinion did not in all likelihood say the right things in the right way at the right time anyway. Because Baptist polity prevents any meeting, assembly, or convention from having any authority, formal or informal, over any individual Baptist or over any other individual Baptist body . . .[1]

The Southern Baptist experience in New Mexico is in many ways the story of the Southern Baptist Convention in miniature during the post-World War II era. Rapid expansion after the war brought that body into direct contact with pluralism, diversity, and secularization. As the vanguard for this territorial growth, the Baptist Convention of New Mexico felt the brunt of this encounter more than any other state convention. Attempting to address these new conditions altered Southern Baptists. In addition, as the largest evangelical denomination in the country, their experience in New Mexico provides useful insights into the direction of that movement in the latter half of the twentieth century.

જ઼

No book is the product of one person's efforts, and this one is no exception. Special thanks go to my dissertation committee. Andrew Burgess and Donald Sullivan provided invaluable comments on the text along with suggestions for improvements. Richard Etulain's radical editing made the manuscript look like a literary version of Sherman's "march to the sea," moving it forward as a suitable work for publication. The award for patience and fortitude goes to Frank Szasz, who suffered through draft after draft, never tiring in his efforts to see this work brought to fruition. To him goes much of the credit for whatever contribution this book will make to the literature on religion in the American West.

No researcher could ask for more cooperation and assistance than that provided by the Baptist Convention of New Mexico's staff, pastors, and laypeople. Their time, records, facilities, and in some cases, even their homes, were open to me as I pursued the project. So many people were involved that space does not permit listing all who participated, but their contributions are recorded in the endnotes and in the interview section of the bibliography. Special note must be made of a few, however, for without their continued support the project could not have been sustained. From the beginning,

Executive Secretary Claude Cone put the convention's full resources behind the project. Whether taking time out for interviews, opening doors for new areas of inquiry, or discussing details over lunch, his assistance helped push the project along. A note of gratitude must also go to Hoyt Welch, because as chair of the convention's history committee, he was invaluable not only in directing me to resources, both human and documentary, but his knowledge of events helped me to clarify many issues. A special thanks belongs to Dale and Betty Danielson. Because of them, this book could be written. That the Baptist Convention of New Mexico even has historical archives is due solely to their efforts. Many an hour was spent in their basement poring over documents and newspaper clippings. Their knowledge, especially of the formative years of Baptist development in New Mexico, proved to be invaluable.

Finally, I am very grateful to my wife, Peggy, for all the time and effort she invested in putting up with me as I neglected her, the family, and all other forms of responsibility, while hiding behind the excuse of needing to finish the book. Actually, Peggy did much more. She was at times co-researcher, troubleshooter, document tracer, appointment maker, and chief foil for my ideas on structure, content, and interpretation during those long drives across New Mexico to conduct interviews. To her I owe a debt that can never be repaid, although she has given me some hints on where to start.

CHAPTER I

An Overview of Baptist History

The English separatist tradition provided the ferment from which a people that would later be called Baptists emerged during the early years of the seventeenth century.[1] Early records of a group with identifiable Baptist beliefs center on an English minister by the name of John Smyth who led a small congregation to Holland in 1607. Smyth soon left the congregation, however, to join the Mennonites whose views he found more suited to his growing radicalism. Upon his departure, Thomas Helwys assumed the leadership of the church and brought it back to England in 1611.

Designated "General Baptists," because of their belief in free will, they opposed the rigid predestination of John Calvin but also criticized the Mennonites for being too radical in their emphasis on self-determination. Helwys wrote four volumes delineating his group's beliefs, placing major emphasis on the doctrine of religious freedom. His assertion that the English king did not have authority over the souls of his subjects resulted in imprisonment, where Helwys remained until his death in 1616.[2]

British soil produced another variation of this sect in 1638 known as "Particular Baptists." Having separated from the Puritans over the issue of who should receive the ordinance of baptism while retaining much of their Calvinism, this body formulated the first Baptist confession in 1644. Stressing baptism by immersion and religious liberty, General Baptists found this statement sufficiently inclusive of their own views to adopt it.[3]

Religious and civil authorities in England perceived the Baptists as a radical sect and viewed them with suspicion. Considered "anarchists," incarceration in English jails became commonplace for the faithful. Court records and prison rolls form the primary documents for the student of Baptist history during this period.[4] Thus, it is not surprising that independent congregations sought affiliation with others who thought as they did.

Although each church functioned as an autonomous body, regional congregations began coming together for comradeship and protection. The emergence of this "associational" method of cooperation would later develop into a major element of Baptist polity. While the association exercised no specific control over the individual churches, it provided a forum to discuss doctrine and discipline pastors who had moved beyond accepted beliefs.

Despite persecution, the Baptists grew from a handful of believers in 1611 to between twenty thousand and thirty thousand at the time of the Glorious Revolution in 1688. Under the rule of Charles II, however, Baptist suffering increased. The Restoration Parliament passed several acts that singled out nonconformists for attack. Under this new legislation such groups could not absent themselves from the Church of England, teach school, or conduct services within five miles of any town.[5] These restrictions stimulated an exodus of Baptists to America during the 1690s.

Baptists Come to America

Roger Williams originated the first Baptist work in the New World when he challenged the Puritan establishment in Massachusetts by advocating the separation of church and state. Expelled from Massachusetts, Williams fled to Rhode Island where he helped establish the first Baptist church in the colonies at Providence in 1639.[6] Ill-treatment in New England, however, paralleled their difficulties in the mother country. Baptist emphasis on religious liberty threatened the "theocracy" of the Puritan clergy. Members of a Baptist church could not vote or hold office, and their children could not marry the Puritan orthodox.[7]

Baptists migrating from England in the 1690s encountered similar treatment in the southern colonies. Although a church existed in Charleston by 1696, settlement in the region prior to the 1740s remained marginal. Civil authorities tied to the Church of England dominated the South, and they routinely harassed dissenters, arrested them for disturbing the peace, and thereby inhibited growth.

Persecution in the North and South redirected Baptist settlement toward the middle colonies. Beginning in 1698, Baptists established a church in Philadelphia that exerted tremendous influence over their development for the next 140 years. Its leadership in forming the Philadelphia Association in 1707 extended the associational method of organization throughout America. Composed of five churches, this body acted as an ordination council, settled disputes, and adjudicated doctrinal matters. The first faith statement in America, the "Philadelphia Confession," also came from this group during the 1740s. It established Calvinism as the primary form of Baptist theology for the colonies.[8]

Baptists might have remained on the periphery of the nation's religious life had it not been for two events in American history: the Great Awakening of the 1740s and the American Revolution of 1776. At the beginning of the Awakening, there were 60 Baptist churches on record; by 1776, the number had increased to 472.[9] The revival generated a climate of dissent that contributed to rapid growth by stimulating interest in the ideas of free grace and religious freedom. As individuals exercised their newfound liberty, Baptist beliefs became more appealing, especially the emphasis on separation of church and state. Dissension produced by the revival caused many churches to break away from their former affiliations, and some entered the Baptist fold. For subsequent denominational development, the most noteworthy separationist was a former Congregational minister, Shubael Stearns.

Stearns moved to Sandy Creek, North Carolina, in 1755. During the next seventeen years he established forty-two churches. These congregations produced 125 ministers for pulpits in the colonies of Virginia, North Carolina, South Carolina, and Georgia.[10] Out of this evangelistic explosion came the Sandy Creek Association whose revivalist orientation helped shape Baptist practices in the South. The association emphasized an emotional conversion experience, augmented through camp meetings. This practice gave rise to a divergent "Southern" Baptist identity, in contrast to their more cerebral and Calvinistic relations in the "North."

The American Revolution also accelerated growth by merging traditional Baptist ideas with contemporary politics. Baptists were conscious of themselves as a "persecuted people." Even as late as the 1770s, beatings, imprisonment, and banishment in New England and the South were commonplace. Thus, many Baptists perceived in America's rebellion a battle not only for civil liberty but religious liberty as well. Isaac Backus, a Baptist leader in colonial Massachusetts, argued that the government had no right to prescribe religious beliefs and practices. He further maintained that the fight for religious liberty was also a fight for equality and acceptance, an opportunity for all Christian religious groups to function in society as equal partners.[11]

Participation in the Revolutionary War gave Baptists the opportunity to earn the respect and acceptance they craved. Their patriotism and beliefs also contributed to finding that place in society. Doctrines such as the priesthood of the believer and local church autonomy, along with Baptist associational structure, coincided with the growing democratic and egalitarian ethos that the rebellion fostered. After the Revolution, Baptists were no longer religious outsiders. From 60 churches in 1740 and 472 in 1776, Baptist congregations expanded to 1,152 in sixteen states and territories by 1795.[12]

An Overview of Baptist History

An Emerging Denomination: 1800 to 1845

Now a part of the national mainstream, Baptists embarked on an era of expansion. Their beliefs paralleled a nationwide trend toward a more democratic and egalitarian society. Denominational practice and national development were moving toward convergence. These nonconformists had finally found a home.

As in the preceding century, historical factors during the next fifty years augmented this dramatic growth. Baptist polity and beliefs intersected with the "age of the common man." Jeffersonian/Jacksonian democracy, in its elevation of the individual, fostered a spirit of revolt against elites, social distinctions, traditions, and hierarchy.[13] At the same time, Baptist positions on religious liberty, separation of church and state, freedom from ecclesiastical control, the congregational structure of the church, and the concept of "soul competency" lent theological substance to the undermining of established authority. Antebellum thinking exalted the ability of the masses, whether in business, education, or government; and this attitude also extended to religion. Baptist theology and practice mirrored this "democratization," placing them in step with the convictions of the nation.

Another catalyst contributing to the emergence of a more individualistic religious expression was the outbreak of the Second Great Awakening, 1800 to 1830. In some respects this revival was a continuation of the earlier manifestation that the Revolution had interrupted. Baptists certainly perceived the new movement in this light. Having honed their revival skills during the Great Awakening, they were ready when this second opportunity appeared.

The Second Great Awakening stimulated the promotion of evangelism and missions by "Protestantizing" the West. The expansion of the United States into the Ohio and Mississippi River Valleys opened up new areas of settlement. Frontier conditions fostered an intense individualism because of the self-sufficiency required to live in such a demanding environment. Baptist emphasis on local church autonomy and personal salvation, as opposed to the more corporate experience of Puritan New England, adapted well to these living conditions.

The combined effect of a "common man" ideology, revival, and westward expansion contributed to one of the greatest growth periods in Baptist history. Between 1804 and 1844, the denomination grew 360 percent, at a time when the national population only increased by 140 percent. At the end of this era, membership totaled 220,046, in 9,385 churches.[14]

Growth stimulated Baptists to expand their horizons, leading to new developments in their organizational structure. William Carey, an English Baptist, sailed for India in 1792, thus inaugurating the modern period of

Protestant overseas expansion. Baptists in New England organized to support him, beginning the development of mission societies in America. Women took the initiative in forming these bodies for both home and foreign activity. Growth was so rapid that by the second decade of the century more than two hundred such organizations existed. These societies extended the associational method to Baptist polity, bringing them together around a special project. In 1814, missionary groups convened to form what later became the "Triennial Convention," which met every three years. In agreeing to support Luther Rice and Adoniram and Ann Judson in their missionary efforts in India and Burma, Baptists laid the base for a national organization.

This commitment to share the gospel message overseas extended to Blacks at home. While the first awakening bypassed most African Americans, the slave community felt the impact of the second revival's "brush arbor" meetings. Independent Black churches began to appear in both the North and South, although in the southern states most were under White supervision.[15] The Triennial Convention worked with the African American, Richmond Baptist Missionary Society, which in 1821 had sent ex-slave Lott Cary to Liberia to become the first Black Baptist missionary on a foreign field.[16]

During the 1820s, denominational development suffered a severe setback. An "anti-mission movement" flared up along southern and western frontiers. Initially, the call for missions received a good response. But opposition soon arose among hyper-Calvinist branches, such as the Two-Seed-in-the-Spirit Predestinarian Baptists and Primitive Baptists. These groups argued that since people were predestined by God to be saved, human efforts to evangelize them were fruitless. Using this theology as a base, they not only opposed missions but also Bible societies, Sunday schools, temperance unions, and virtually any activity beyond the local church.[17] Division quickly set in, especially in the South. Alexander Campbell, who had left the Presbyterians and joined the Baptists, was adamant. He argued that mission societies were contrary to the Bible because they violated predestination. A forceful personality, he eventually left the Baptists, taking many with him, and later formed the Disciples of Christ.

Other issues besides theological ones contributed to this revolt, underscoring the growing sectionalism developing in the nation. Many Southerners and Westerners felt that Easterners were attempting to "control" them through the missionary societies. The leaders, headquarters, and most of the speakers on the mission circuit were from the East. Many ministers west of the Appalachians felt that the well-educated, polished Easterners who came to raise money for the societies were usurping their position. Fueling this jealousy was the concern that such national groups would undermine the local church. Pastors feared that the mission societies would lead to the formation of a hierarchy, bringing the congregations under their control, thus undermining local autonomy.

While the anti-missions controversy severely thinned the denomination's ranks, the impact on Baptists was not all negative. The battle sharpened their focus and refined their theology. Even though many members left as a result the debate, those who remained intensified their commitment to missions. In the South, Baptists emerged from the battle far less Calvinistic and more favorably inclined to support a centralized operation to conduct evangelism. They affirmed God's sovereignty in human affairs, but this acceptance did not rule out free will or personal responsibility. Humanity was not a puppet manipulated by outside forces but an active participant in God's plan.[18]

Formation of the Southern Baptist Convention: 1845 to 1900

Sectionalism and the anti-missions controversy put a severe strain on Baptists, but slavery eventually divided the denomination.[19] The event that precipitated the split was the refusal of Baptists in the North to agree to the appointment of a slave owner as a missionary. Southern messengers (representatives of Southern churches) met in May 1845 in Augusta, Georgia, and formed the Southern Baptist Convention (SBC). Prior to 1800, most Baptists in the South had opposed slavery. Several economic and social factors, however, altered this stance, including the profitability of the practice that came with the cotton gin, Baptists' gradual rise up the social scale, and ministers who owned slaves (in some states as many as a third). The new convention sought to avoid the issue by disengaging it from theology. Convention participants deemed slavery a "civil" institution, governed solely by politics, and beyond the scope of the church.[20]

Records for 1845 show that the new organization started with a membership of 351,951 in 4,126 churches.[21] From the beginning, several differences set Southern Baptists apart from their Northern brethren. For one, they created a more centralized denominational structure that functioned around an annual convention with "messengers" sent from the churches and associations. In addition, Southerners established denominational boards that governed foreign and home missions. The new convention immediately set plans in motion to evangelize Blacks, Indians, and immigrants.

Blacks comprised a significant minority of the SBC, numbering approximately one hundred thousand members. Efforts to evangelize this part of the Southern constituency, however, were often "presented as a means of upholding the existing racial system," and had marginal results.[22] After the Civil War, Blacks exited the denomination in droves and in 1866 established their first state convention in South Carolina. Additional state organizations developed until there was enough strength to form their own body, the National Baptist Convention.

Cooperation between Blacks and Whites did not come to a close in the post-Civil War period. African-American missionaries served under the Foreign Mission Board until they formed their own organization in 1880. The Home Mission Board also sponsored short-term institutes for Black pastors. In 1895, the SBC, in cooperation with the National Baptist Convention, provided missionaries to work in Black churches, associations, and in African-American schools as teachers.[23]

Mission work began among the Cherokee and Creek tribes in the South even before the formation of the convention. When the federal government removed these groups to the Indian Territory after 1830, Native American ministers carried Christianity with them to the new land. In 1842, their churches formed the American Indian Association in Kentucky and affiliated with the SBC in 1855. Shortly afterward, the Home Mission Board appointed a missionary and ten Native American assistants to work among the Creek people. A Cherokee Baptist, Alford Corn, preached throughout the Smoky Mountains to those of his nation who had escaped removal. The Home Mission Board appointed him as a missionary to those he was already serving in 1858.

The Civil War interrupted the convention's mission activities, leaving these tribes to continue the work on their own. Renewed activity among the Indian nations in Oklahoma began in 1874. Two years later, the Southern Baptists held a conference to discuss extending missions to the Plains Indians. This decision resulted in the establishment of work among the Cheyenne and Arapaho later in the century.[24]

Ethnic missions comprised a third area of Home Mission Board activity. In 1854, Southern Baptists opened a mission to the Chinese in San Francisco. A year earlier they began work among Germans in Baltimore, with subsequent expansion to New Orleans, Louisiana; Louisville, Kentucky; and St. Genevieve, Missouri. After the Civil War, the denomination initiated missions among the French, Italian, Mexican, and Cuban populations in the United States.[25]

The main emphasis of the Home Mission Board during the mid-nineteenth century, however, was to carry the gospel to the destitute areas of the South. Large areas of the region were still untouched, because anti-mission forces hindered evangelism. Between 1845 and the beginning of the Civil War, nine hundred missionaries traveled more than nine hundred thousand miles, mostly on foot, preaching the gospel to the backwoods peoples of the region.[26]

Membership records attest to the success of the effort. By 1860, the SBC had grown to 649,518 with 7,701 churches.[27]

The Civil War proved to be a major catastrophe for the newly formed Southern Baptist denomination. Not only were Southerners a defeated and occupied people, the conflict also stripped the convention of its financial resources, interrupting all evangelistic efforts. In addition to causing financial turmoil, the war had a profound religious and moral impact as well. Southern Baptists interpreted the loss as an "apostasy" perpetrated by the rest of the nation. They reasoned that the North had turned away from the truth by adopting abolitionism, feminism, and other disruptive causes. Baptist theologians argued that the South alone had remained true to the biblical faith.[28] Evangelizing the world for Christ thus fell upon their shoulders as the last hope of righteousness. Further, Southern Baptists attributed defeat to personal moral inadequacies. This conclusion produced an evangelism aimed at driving out sin in the form of personal excess and wickedness. Purging this evil from the land became a major goal, leading to the development of a social conscience centering on the issue of prohibition.[29] Leaders viewed liquor as a primary contributor of moral delinquency and believed that its expulsion from the South would lead to a more godly society. Both of these factors contributed to a zeal for missions that, in part, accounts for Southern Baptist expansion in the face of numerous obstacles.

Defeat, military occupation, and limited resources were not all that Baptists in the South had to overcome in their quest to evangelize. Immediately after the Civil War they faced a "religious occupation" as well. Northern Baptists reentered the region with their missionaries, teachers, church literature, and Sunday schools. Many churches and associations had continued to work with Northern Baptists after 1845, depending on them for Sunday school literature that the SBC was unable to supply. In 1868, there was talk of realignment, but a separate Southern identity along with organizational differences prevented any such merger. Northern Baptist presence continued in the South, however, until 1894.

Facing Northern Baptist inroads, Southern Baptist leaders fought to build a denominational consciousness among their people. They moved the headquarters of the Home Mission Board to Atlanta, the heart of Northern Baptist activity in the South. Dr. I. T. Tichenor took over the leadership of the board in 1882. During the next five years, he sought to remedy the problem by traveling to churches and associations in an effort to win their loyalty to the SBC. His efforts were successful. By 1887, all missionaries to Whites in the South came under Home Mission Board appointment. With the assistance of

Annie Armstrong and the Women's Missionary Union, evangelism resumed to Blacks, Indians, and immigrants. The establishment of a Sunday School Board in 1891 weaned Southern churches away from reliance on Northern literature. As the new century dawned, a distinct denominational identity existed.

This new consciousness did not come without a battle. Not only did Southern Baptists have to struggle with Northern "encroachment," they also found themselves embroiled in a major internal controversy of their own known as "Landmarkism." Led by J. R. Graves, the turmoil began in the early 1850s. Landmark ideas were not new to Baptist thinking, but rather formed an intensification of established beliefs. They occurred at a time of increasing denominational rivalry. Graves maintained that Baptists could trace their lineage back to John the Baptist and thus were not Protestants, giving them hegemony over other ecclesiastical bodies.

In practice, such views meant that Baptists constituted "the only true church" and should not recognize clergy from other denominations. Graves and his followers believed that through the right of unbroken succession, only Baptists could ordain ministers. Thus, pastors from other religious groups should not be allowed to preach in a Baptist church. Baptism, if administered by another denomination, was considered "alien immersion" and unacceptable. This meant that a new member coming from a non-Baptist church would have to be re-baptized. Since Baptists made up the "true" church, communion was for their members only. Visiting Christians from other churches could not partake.

Landmarkists opposed the activity of the Foreign and Home Mission Boards, maintaining that only individual congregations had the right to conduct evangelistic efforts. Graves's legacy continued to plague Southern Baptists until 1908, when his followers left the convention to form their own denomination. A residue of Landmark doctrine, however, continues, most notably among Southern Baptist churches outside the traditional boundaries of the South.[30] Like earlier disputes, the Landmark controversy ultimately strengthened Southern Baptist commitment to evangelism and missions. Refusal to capitulate to such extreme exclusivity prevented them from a descent into theological dogmatism that might have restricted growth. By 1900, membership had grown to 1,657,996 in 19,558 churches.[31]

The denomination overcame the ravages of the Civil War, met the Northern Baptist challenge, ensured Southern territorial integrity, and overcame another internal controversy. As the twentieth century opened, Southern Baptists found themselves in a situation similar to the one that Baptists had encountered in 1800: They were ready to expand to new frontiers.

Southern Baptists in the Twentieth Century

Although aggressive evangelism and missionary activity were important factors, the primary cause of the denomination's geographical expansion in this century lay with migration out of the South. During the final quarter of the nineteenth century, Southerners spilled over into adjacent territories in the West. Then, as a result of the Great Depression and World War II, Southern Baptists extended their presence throughout the rest of the country.

As early as 1849, a report before the convention called for more activity in New Mexico and Texas. It served as a clarion call for an increased home mission effort. Since people were moving into new areas, missionaries should be there ahead of them.

> Our missionary should not wait to ride on the cow catcher of the first engine of the new railroad, but should already be on the ground ready to welcome the engineer and his passengers, preaching the gospel to them, and baptizing them as fast as they believe.[32]

A new era began for Southern Baptists in 1894 when both branches of Baptists met at Fortress Monroe, Virginia, to discuss mission activity. Two important decisions emerged. In new areas, where each body had previously worked (such as New Mexico), they would cooperate. In regions where only one had a presence, the other would not infringe. These understandings became known as the "comity agreements" and functioned imperfectly until World War II.[33]

In the intervening years, Southern Baptists advanced into the adjacent areas of New Mexico, Arizona, Oklahoma, and California. The era of relative cooperation between the two bodies ended in 1942 with California's admission into the SBC. The Great Depression had scattered Southerners westward as they searched for jobs in the ranching, lumber, and oil industries. Military service and defense plant employment intensified this migration out of the South during World War II. Wherever Southerner Baptists moved, they started churches.[34] Based on the Fortress Monroe Conference, California was Northern Baptist territory, but changing demographic conditions along the Pacific Coast led to the development of a Southern Baptist presence. In 1945, the convention disavowed any geographical limitation on their churches in the United States or its territories. The years from 1894 to 1942 were good ones for the denomination. At the end of the period, their membership had grown to 5,367,120 in 25,737 churches.[35]

Even though war and the depression propelled Baptists out of the South, the prosperity that the war generated helped fuel a continuation of Southern Baptist expansion. As individual church members prospered, they shared their wealth with the church. Between 1939 and 1945, per capita giving among Southern Baptists doubled. This increase in giving grew at four times the rate of the consumer price index. Bountiful contributions continued after the war. The average individual gift to the church in 1945 was $16.79; by 1975, it had grown to $108.93.[36] Financial strength contributed to denominational growth. In 1942, Southern Baptists counted eighteen state conventions; by 1980, that number had increased to thirty-four, with churches in all fifty states. These new conventions added 3,198 churches with a total membership of 918,432.[37] Baptists outside the South were more numerous than many smaller Protestant denominations.

To support evangelization of the nation, Southern Baptists in the new areas could count on the support of the Home Mission Board. With the recognition of California, the board accelerated its activities, which altered traditional thinking. Their ministry had to expand beyond the confines of a homogenous people who shared a common culture, language, and tradition. The Home Mission Board began designing programs to cross barriers: cultural, religious, geographical, and socioeconomic.

After the war, ethnic missions accelerated so that by 1980 Southern Baptists were conducting evangelism among seventy-nine groups in seventy languages, becoming the single largest area of Home Mission Board work.[38] At a forum held by the National Council of Churches in Washington, D.C., in that same year, James Reese reported on a yearlong study of minority ministries among denominations that were primarily Anglo in membership. He stated that "Southern Baptists are further ahead than most of them realize, and than others are willing to give them credit."[39]

Denominational support for this expansion fell most heavily on the Home Mission Board, although all departments participated. In 1980, the board employed 2,921 missionaries, of whom 1,549 were working in areas entered after 1942.[40] Through the cooperative Missions Department, state conventions received help in the form of financial aid to pastors and churches via salaries, operational expenses, and construction loans. The Sunday School Board assisted with administrative and programmatic aid, and Southern Baptists built three new seminaries to train leaders. These schools included Golden Gate Seminary in San Francisco, 1950; Southeastern Seminary in Wake Forest, North Carolina, 1950; and Midwestern Seminary in Kansas City, 1957.[41]

Numerical and territorial expansion also brought internal change to the Southern Baptists. In 1900, the convention had only three governing bodies:

the Foreign and Home Missions Boards, and the Sunday School Board. In order to consolidate the various ad hoc committees that had come into existence they adopted a corporate model of administration. In 1917, the convention established an Executive Board. It worked in an advisory capacity, making recommendations to the national body at the annual gathering. Executive Board responsibilities expanded in 1927 to include the development of a budget, recommendations for the allocation of undesignated funds, provision for the needs of convention institutions, and establishment of a base for meeting future financial obligations. To ensure a more business-like handling of moneys, the SBC also created the Cooperative Program in 1928, which centralized the disbursement of funds. As the number of agencies and commissions increased, the need for an inter-agency council to improve communication became apparent. Under the label of program planning each department now delineates its operational procedures to avoid over-lapping jurisdiction.[42]

Changes in bureaucratic structure reflected the changing composition of the denomination. Baptists, traditionally, were from rural areas and came from the lower socioeconomic classes. In the twentieth century, however, this classification underwent substantial revision. Post-World War II surveys revealed that the membership shifted from rural to urban and from lower to middle-class status.[43]

Depression and war created this demographic shift, as many Southern Baptists left their farms in search of employment. Rural churches declined as urban congregations grew.[44] The "mixed congregations" of an earlier era vanished as the new middle class felt uncomfortable around their poorer brethren. In 1922, 70 percent of Southern Baptists churches were rural; by 1978, that number had declined to 30 percent.[45]

This rural-to-urban migration also led to a subtle transition in Southern Baptist worship forms and values. Steady jobs, with consistent weekly or monthly paychecks, enabled members to contribute on a systematic basis throughout the year. Increased giving supported more church programs, thus leading to the employment of full-time staffs. The urban church became an institution designed to meet the diverse needs of its members. The shift from rural to urban living also moved Southern Baptists toward the development of a corporate social consciousness. During the Progressive era, Baptists became involved in such institutional ministries as literacy programs and health clinics and in such reform movements as child labor, suffrage, and prohibition.[46]

Prior to World War I, Southern Baptists exhibited a traditional regional attitude toward African Americans. They accepted White superiority and approved of segregation, believing in the corrupting influence of the Black race on Whites. During the period between world wars, however, this position gradually moderated. In the decade after the Great War, Southern Baptists viewed African Americans as a race rather than as individuals and exploited them politically and economically. Paternalism and jokes about Blacks were common. But by World War II, this attitude had begun to diminish, although Southern Baptists accepted and defended existing conditions in race relations. News items favorable to African Americans began appearing in Southern Baptist periodicals, along with an occasional article by a Black author.[47]

Even with this partial thaw in racial attitudes, there were only two African-American congregations in the SBC in 1942, and both were in states outside the SBC stronghold ("expansion" states). Some agency leaders and state Baptist newspaper editors began challenging this institutional racism in the 1940s and 1950s. It was not until the 1970s, however, that African Americans moved into denominational leadership positions. During that decade, conventions in Alaska, California, and Michigan elected Blacks to the offices of president and vice president; positions on denominational boards were also opened to them. In 1974, Charles M. King became the first Black elected second vice president of the SBC. By 1981, the number of African-American churches had grown to six hundred, with a total membership of 160,000. The largest concentrations of these congregations were in the expansion states.[48]

Attitudes toward the place of women in Baptist life also underwent a restructuring in the post-World War II era. Women had always played a strategic role in denominational affairs, particularly in the area of missions, but leadership roles in the convention's business always eluded them. Beginning in 1918, women resumed their place as messengers, but not until 1963 did they begin assuming management positions.[49] Today women serve on all agency and commission boards, including the Executive Committee. Expanding administrative roles, however, have not translated to positions in the pulpit. A majority of the denomination's leaders and pastors still oppose female ordination.[50]

Not only have attitudes toward African Americans and women changed, so have Southern Baptists' relationships with other religious groups. Territorial expansion forced them to reconsider their position. Prior to World War II, Baptists in the South preferred to remain aloof from all ecclesiastical involvement. One might say that they took George Washington's farewell address that warned against entangling relationships with foreign nations and applied it to ecumenical relations. Yet in the postwar period there has been a guarded, but consistent, movement toward more cooperative relations with other Christian denominations.

Changing attitudes first appeared in renewed participation with American and Canadian Baptists in the Baptist World Alliance, Baptist Jubilee Advance, and the North American Baptist Fellowship. The decades of the 1960s and 1970s stimulated increased cooperation as Southerners discovered the wider world of evangelicalism. Denominational support for revivalist Billy Graham and for the conservative theological works of Carl F. H. Henry has also increased exposure to interdenominational activity.[51]

Undoubtedly, the greatest thaw in Southern Baptist thinking lies in the denomination's new dialogue with Roman Catholics. The impact of Vatican II (1962–1965) initiated the change, and the emergence of Catholic charismatics further opened areas of common ground. Similar beliefs on social issues, such as abortion, have drawn both sides closer together. The Home Mission Board now has an Interfaith Witness Department, and Southern Baptists no longer define themselves in opposition to Catholics.[52]

Despite the changes that have occurred among Southern Baptists, one constant remains: controversy. Disputes have raged throughout Baptist history, and the twentieth century is no exception. The conflicts have changed, however, from quarrels about doctrine to battles over threats to Christianity, from disputes concerning missions and denominational exclusivity, to issues of biblical authority. The roots of this modern challenge to the faith began in the late nineteenth century, emerging as the fundamentalist/modernist controversy.

Theological liberals questioned the inspiration of the scriptures and the deity of Christ. They viewed God as immanent within human nature and history rather than a transcendent being. Activity turned toward the salvation of society through social and political reform. Fundamentalists, conversely, championed the inerrancy of the Bible and the lordship of Christ as the mediator between God and humanity. They placed emphasis on a personal conversion experience with social change coming through a transformed heart and individual piety.

In part, this rift among Christians was also a response to the dramatic alterations occurring in American society brought about by urbanization, industrialization, and immigration. These forces largely bypassed the South. Nevertheless, a small core of fundamentalists sought to purge the SBC of any taint of so-called modernism. A. C. Dixon, a fundamentalist crusader, and J. Frank Norris of the First Baptist Church in Fort Worth, Texas, and their followers insisted that the issues were clearly defined and that church members had to take sides. There could be no middle ground. It was good versus evil, God versus Satan. The SBC had to be purged of liberals in the denomination's colleges and seminaries. These efforts were only moderately successful, as there simply were not that many liberals in the denomination. Most professors who used scientific methods to study the Bible rejected higher criticism and Darwinism.[53]

The battle climaxed in 1925 at the annual meeting. E. Y. Mullins, a professor and theologian at Southern Seminary in Louisville, Kentucky, and president of the SBC that year, led moderate creationists against the attacks of the fundamentalists. He cautioned the convention about the danger of basing biblical truth on a literal reading of Genesis. Fundamentalists were pushing for a clear statement of beliefs that led to the adoption of the "Baptist faith and message" in 1925. For the first time in its history, the SBC issued a confession. Prior to this time the New Hampshire confession of 1830–1833 had served this need. A critical clause in this earlier document stated that the Bible was the "supreme standard by which all human conduct, creeds, and opinions should be tried." Mullins was able to have the word "religious" inserted before opinions.[54] Southern Baptists had refused to make any doctrinal statement based on scripture as the test of opinions in nonreligious areas.

Depression and war forestalled further confrontation until the issue broke out again in 1962. This time the fight centered on the publication of a book by Ralph Elliott, a professor at Midwestern Seminary, entitled *The Message of Genesis*. In his book, Elliott suggested that the first eleven chapters of Genesis were theological fact but not day-by-day physical history. Reaction was swift: Messengers at the convention saw this view as "liberalism." A symbolic interpretation, they thought, reduced the trustworthiness of the Bible, casting doubt on its historical accuracy.[55] Elliott lost his job, and Southern Baptists adopted a new confession of faith in 1963, based on the 1925 document. This confession added to its preface the caveat that Baptist emphasis on soul competency, religious freedom, and the priesthood of the believer should not be taken to mean that there were no definite Baptist doctrines.[56]

Less than a decade later, this same issue reappeared in an essay in the first volume of the *Broadman Bible Commentary*. Here debate centered on Abraham's sacrifice of Isaac. The article's author, G. Henton Davies, said that Abraham must have misunderstood God. Such a command was inhumane and had to be the result of Abraham's psychological characteristics.[57] This time the repercussions were more dramatic and severe. The convention voted to withdraw the volume and have it rewritten. Fundamentalists charged that liberals had taken over the denomination's bureaucracy, especially the Sunday School Board and the Christian Life Commission, staffing those agencies with a clique of "seminary insiders."

The impact of the Elliott and Broadman Commentary issues led to a conservative resurgence in the SBC. The 1963 confession began to take on a larger role in convention life, moving in the direction of a creed to test members' beliefs. Moderates were quick to react. They reasoned that such a policy would lead to the loss of cherished Baptist principles, such as soul competency, religious liberty, and church autonomy. For the conservatives, the Bible was under attack. For the moderates, being Baptist meant "freedom": freedom from civil government, ecclesiastical authority, and any form of mind or soul control.[58] Both sides drew swords to do battle over biblical authority and religious liberty.

Conservatives tied Christianity and the rise or fall of the SBC to the issue of biblical authority. Unable to achieve their goals through argument, they sought to change the power structure of the denomination. The beginnings of institutional conflict occurred in the late 1960s when a North Carolina pastor, Mo Owens, initiated a movement to stop liberalism in the convention. During the 1970s, educator Paige Patterson and Judge Paul Pressler took over operational control of this fledgling movement and solidified its organizational structure. They mustered financial support and forged a coalition between rural and big city churches. Prepared for battle, the political dimension of the controversy began in 1979 over gifts to the Cooperative Program. Conservatives sought to cut off funds to Southern Baptist agencies they considered liberal.[59]

In order to withdraw financial support for offensive departments, conservatives needed control of the convention. A 1937 revision of the denomination's constitution provided for representatives from the various states to serve as trustees on boards, agencies, and committees. The effect of this change was to place control of the denomination in the hands of the trustees. Ultimate sovereignty still lay with the messengers at the annual convention, but to maintain such power required the replacing of all trustees, which would take several years. This sweeping change necessitated gaining command of the presidency, a long and involved process. The president, in consultation with the two vice presidents, appoints the Committee on Committees. This body selects members to serve on the Committee on Boards, Commissions, and Standing Committees, and these members, in turn, nominate trustees.[60]

Herein lay the root of the political problem in the current crisis. Conservatives charged that moderates had packed the various denominational posts with more than one thousand trustees of their own people. Those of a more conservative persuasion found themselves excluded. Over time this "clique" began to function as a hierarchy, removed from and not sensitive to the beliefs and wishes of their constituents. Bill Powell, editor of the conservative publication the *Southern Baptist Journal,* therefore developed a strategy that Patterson and Pressler administered over the next ten years. By orchestrating the selection of successive presidents, conservatives were able to replace trustees with like-minded people. By the 1990 convention in New Orleans, they had achieved their political takeover of the SBC.[61]

Where Do Southern Baptists Go from Here?

Today, Southern Baptists are, by far, the largest Protestant denomination in the country. Statistics for 1994 place their total membership at 15,619,912 with 39,910 churches.[62] They are not the same Baptists they were a century ago, however. Having expanded throughout the nation, they have encountered new turmoil. Increased diversity has made them less cohesive, and greater numbers have produced less tranquility.[63] No longer a geographically defined, homogeneous culture, Southern Baptists have become almost as diverse as the nation they have sought to convert. (The years 1994 and 1995 marked a turning point in the convention's history. In this period, ethnics and African Americans started more churches than did their Anglo brethren.[64])

Baptist numbers grew in America primarily because their values fit the emerging American consciousness. As America has expanded and become less cohesive, however, that consciousness has declined. Will Baptists be successful in maintaining unity of belief among an ever-increasing and diverse membership?[65]

An examination of Southern Baptist presence in one western state may provide some answers. Beginning in 1849, Baptists in New Mexico encountered social conditions that the national convention has only recently faced. Religious diversity, cultural pluralism, and racial heterogeneity are, and have been, the norm. Yet, in spite of conditions foreign to their place of origin, by 1960 Southern Baptists became the largest Protestant body within the state and second in size only to the Roman Catholic Church. How they were able to achieve this position and the impact such growth has made on their beliefs, structure, and fellowship form the basis of this study.

CHAPTER 2

The Formative Years in New Mexico: 1849 to 1937

Baptist entry into New Mexico Territory was accidental. The Northern Baptist Home Mission Society had intended to start working among the "forty-niners" in California. To that end, they sent Hiram Walter Read to the gold fields. Unforeseen events, however, prevented him from reaching that destination. Upon learning that a minister and his wife were coming down the Santa Fe Trail, Colonel John M. Washington, commander at Fort Marcy in Santa Fe, determined to have them stay. Read's purpose in going to the West Coast was to bring the light of the gospel to that "destitute place." Seeking to detain him by offering a post chaplaincy, the colonel sought to convince Read that he could travel the world over and not find a land more indigent than New Mexico. A few days' observances convinced the missionary of that statement's accuracy. Read notified the Home Mission Society of his decision to stay in New Mexico Territory and began work in July 1849.[1]

Entrada

In addition to assuming duties as chaplain, Read also set up a place of worship and a school in Santa Fe.[2] His enthusiasm for the work soon influenced three other couples to make the journey west. Lewis Smith became the first missionary appointed by the society to assist Read, joining him at Santa Fe in 1851. Samuel Gorman arrived in 1852 and shortly thereafter was honored with adoption by the Laguna Pueblo, an important event since it enabled Gorman to obtain the land necessary for a mission. He became the first "all-Indian" Baptist missionary as his work eventually extended to Acoma and among the Navajo. John M. Shaw was the third to arrive and like Read before him received military assistance. He accepted a position as post chaplain at Fort Defiance, Arizona, enabling him to begin a mission to the Navajo. Shaw later established a church in Socorro, New Mexico.[3]

From the beginning, these Northern Baptists approached their work in New Mexico as a foreign mission field, concentrating their efforts among Hispanics and Native Americans. To aid in disseminating the news of the gospel, the Home Mission Society employed colporteurs to distribute literature and also appointed indigenous converts to preach.[4] Jose Sannon, the first Indian convert, eventually took over the mission at Laguna. Blas Chavez became the first Hispanic missionary minister, ultimately rendering more than fifty years of service in the Las Vegas, New Mexico, area.

The lack of an educational system in New Mexico provided an opportunity for the Baptists to extend their evangelistic activity through the establishment of schools at Santa Fe, Bosque de Los Pinos, Albuquerque, Laguna, Peralta, and Fort Defiance, Arizona. It was over this issue of education that Baptists and Catholics would have their first clash.

Initially, relations between Protestants and Catholics, although not cordial, were also not hostile. Priests occasionally invited Baptist missionaries to preach in their churches.[5] The arrival of Archbishop Jean Baptiste Lamy in 1851 brought this early era of accommodation to an end. The archbishop viewed Baptist schools as a threat that he attempted to counter by establishing a Catholic educational system. To this end he brought in the Sisters of Loretto and the Christian Brothers. Lamy instructed the priests to forbid their parishioners to attend Protestant schools. Faced with such a direct challenge, the Baptists chose to deal with the problem in an oblique fashion. They turned their efforts toward assisting the territorial governor in establishing the first public school in New Mexico so that children could obtain an education without having to attend a Catholic facility.[6] Although direct conflict was avoided, the issue lay dormant, but it reemerged in the twentieth century.

With the coming of the Civil War, the Home Mission Society ceased providing aid, and Baptist work came to an end in 1866.[7] Without support, converts among Hispanics and Native Americans were unable to sustain a distinct denominational presence, leading to the selling of Baptist property to the Presbyterians. Seventeen years of Baptist labor had produced 112 conversions, but their evangelism influenced many others, who joined other Protestant denominations.[8]

Railroads and Homesteads

A thirteen-year period, often referred to as the "silent years," descended on Baptist activity in New Mexico. When Baptists returned in 1879, the nature and direction of the denomination's work changed radically. During the first period, society-sponsored, well-educated clergy concentrated their work among the indigenous population. The society focused its evangelistic efforts through schools and in the training of Indian and Hispanic leaders. In the subsequent era, itinerant pastors accomplished the work by laboring largely on their own among the now burgeoning Anglo population.

Reentry occurred with the coming of the railroad. Tracks laid across New Mexico opened up new lands, and settlers poured in to take advantage of them. Many of these immigrants were Baptists from adjacent states desiring a church home. The first work was typical of the new era. Homer Newberry, a Baptist layperson who worked for the Santa Fe Railroad, arrived in Las Vegas in 1879 and immediately began canvassing the town for Baptists. The Home Mission Society responded to the resumption of activity by sending H. N. Wingate to Las Vegas in 1880, where he established a church based on Newberry's labor.[9] Soon additional churches appeared in Raton, Silver City, and Cerrillos. Baptists also reactivated former congregations in Albuquerque and Socorro. Initially, storefronts served as meeting places since financial limitations prevented the erection of buildings.

Despite their precarious position, Baptists were quick to organize beyond the bounds of the local churches. The Rocky Mountain Baptist Association, formed in 1883, consisted of churches in Colorado, Wyoming, Utah, and New Mexico. For ease of administration, the association was divided into two parts, with New Mexico and Colorado comprising the southern division. Eventually, the geographical expanse of the area proved unwieldy. Traveling as a colporteur through New Mexico via the railroad, Homer Newberry organized the New Mexico Missionary Baptist Association on October 3, 1888, at the Presbyterian church in Socorro. (This was the same church that John Shaw organized in 1857.[10]) Unfortunately, Newberry's association did not survive; no records exist after 1889.[11]

Although churches in the central and western sections of New Mexico organized with help from missionaries sent out by the Home Mission Society to the Santa Fe Association, Baptist work in the southeast developed independently. As in the case with Las Vegas, a layperson began initial activity. An emigrant from Texas, Ananias Green, began a letter-writing campaign to his home state to look for pastors. Two responded and soon started congregations, leading in 1888 to the formation of the Lincoln Association.[12]

Since most of those migrating into the southeastern part of New Mexico were from the South, they naturally sought affiliation with the Southern Baptist Convention (SBC). Financial difficulties prevented that denomination from honoring requests for affiliation, forcing churches to turn to the Northern Baptists. The result was an association Southern in membership but Northern in subsidy. Such a state of affairs foreshadowed trouble.[13] Northern Baptists responded by sending associational and Sunday school missionaries, J. Midd Hill and S. Y. Jackson. Meanwhile, Mina Everett, sent by the Women's Baptist

Home Mission Society, became the first female Baptist missionary to the state.

By 1900, Baptist work had advanced sufficiently for the formation of a territorial convention that included twenty-nine churches with a combined membership of 1,108 persons.[14] On November 16, messengers from the churches met in Las Cruces to form the New Mexico Baptist Convention, affiliating with the Northern Baptists because of financial support. Typical of Western development, women actively participated. At this first convention, four of the fifteen messengers from the Lincoln Association were women, as were three of the ten from the Santa Fe Association. Women also served on four of the six standing committees. Even though the SBC did not resume seating women as messengers until 1918, in New Mexico women comprised 25 percent to 30 percent of the delegates to the state convention.[15]

Formation of the new convention coincided with accelerating migration into New Mexico. Homesteading burgeoned after 1900. People poured into the northeastern, southeastern, and southwestern areas of the state. For example, in 1906, 3,701 new homesteads opened near Clayton, which brought in more than 16,000 people. The federal Land Office in 1909 reported 4,095 new homesteads for the southeast, including portions of Eddy, Roosevelt, and Chavez counties.[16] The Deming-Lordsburg area recorded over 2,500 homesteads. This influx of settlers had a dramatic impact on church growth. The Baptist church in Clovis had only 4 members in 1908; a year later, the congregation numbered 123. Tucumcari experienced similar growth, with church members increasing from 76 to 121 during the same period.[17] By 1910 the Baptist presence, especially in southeastern New Mexico, had expanded considerably. There were now 113 churches with 3,932 members. Baptist church associations in the state grew from 2 to 6, while the number of pastors increased from 13 to 56.[18]

Burgeoning numbers stimulated many members to do more than start new churches. Since 1899, the Lincoln Association had desired to establish an institution of higher education. In 1900, they approached C. C. Waller, who had founded a Baptist college in Texas, to do the same in New Mexico. Waller began by developing one hundred acres of land in Alamogordo. He kept twenty for the college and used the proceeds from the sale of the rest to finance construction.

The school opened in 1900 as New Mexico Baptist College. In 1905, the Home Mission Society began using part of the facility as a Bible training center for Hispanics, providing much needed additional funds. That same year, the New Mexico Baptist Convention took over operation from the Lincoln Association. Unfortunately, fiscal difficulties plagued the school from the beginning. In some cases teachers' salaries came from personal loans secured by board members' assets. Unable to maintain financial support, the convention returned the college to the Lincoln Association, which closed the college's doors in 1911.[19]

Another attempt to develop a denomination-wide entity came with efforts to establish a territorial newspaper. Initially, papers were individual affairs, such as *The Southwestern Baptist,* which emanated from the college, or *The Baptist Workman,* produced by the church in Roswell. Circulation faltered since the newspaper offices were too far from the centers of Baptist activity to be effective. When division arose over the issue of national affiliation, other papers emerged. E. P. Aldredge, pastor at the church in Portales, and well known for his Southern sympathies, organized *The New Mexico Baptist* in 1909. Those favoring Northern allegiance authorized *The Baptist Bulletin* in 1911 to represent their perspective. Despite these endeavors to develop a denominational identity through an official publication, all undertakings fell victim to regional hostilities.[20]

Ethnic work (targeting non-Whites), although not the main emphasis of Baptist evangelism, began to receive attention. In addition to the Bible training center associated with the college, Northern Baptists had previously opened a school for Hispanics at Rinconada in 1894. Later moving to Velarde, the Echo Valley Mission provided education for up to 167 students. This educational facility continued until 1912 when Southern Baptists assumed leadership. Unable to continue the school for financial reasons, the denomination turned it over to the United Brethren.

Baptists also maintained a mission to the Navajo at Two Grey Hills, Arizona, during the early years of the century. The Women's National Indian Association had initiated this work, with only mediocre success. Upon hearing of Baptist interest, the association conveyed their facility to the Baptists, stipulating only that the work continue. With the transfer completed in 1901, missionaries maintained the work until 1912. Here, too, Southern Baptists were unable to carry through, surrendering the ministry to the Christian Reformed Church.[21]

Despite the increased numbers and attempts to establish denominational structures, the New Mexico Baptist Convention found itself operating under serious handicaps. For one, short-term clergy plagued Baptist churches well into the twentieth century. The average minister served for only two to three months before moving on. In 1907, several of the larger churches that the convention depended on for most of its income were without pastors. In 1912, fifty congregations needed preachers. Ministerial interest lay in "planting" churches rather than remaining to nurture a congregation.

Migratory settlement patterns in New Mexico hindered the development of stable communities, making it difficult to maintain churches.[22] Itinerant, bivocational pastors compounded the problem. During the period 1900 to 1916, only one pastor in New Mexico served the same church for four years. The 1916 annual report noted that there were no permanent pastors in the state west of the Rio Grande.[23] This problem continued into the 1920s, subsided for a time, but reappeared with the depression.

During these difficult times Baptist churches functioned through the use of laypersons, colporteurs, and traveling missionaries to fill the pulpits. Pastors who did accept a position often found it taxing. They had to fill several roles, including preacher, teacher, evangelist, janitor, collector, and, oftentimes, chief contributor. Their remuneration was meager. A reference in a 1919 convention annual suggested that married pastors be paid a base salary of $1,500 per year and a single pastor $1,000.[24] During the depression, it was not at all uncommon for a church to call a pastor with the stipulation that he support himself.

Since many Baptists were farmers, the unpredictable weather on New Mexico's eastern plains became an important factor in church prosperity. When drought or too much rain plagued the state's agriculturists, contributions declined. Many homesteaders found that they could not survive on 160 acres. Not until New Mexico's economy became more stable and diversified did Baptists become self-supporting.

Disruptive as these issues were, division within the convention proved to be an even greater problem. A large portion of the newly arrived emigrants were Southern Baptists, and they were not silent about their desire to affiliate with that convention. In fact, as early as 1894, Southern Baptists passed a resolution calling for expansion into New Mexico.[25] The Home Mission Board, however, delayed entry until 1910 because there was no money to support such work.

The issue began to intensify in 1907. J. F. Love, assistant corresponding secretary of the Home Mission Board, began appearing at associational meetings. Love authored *The Mission of Our Nation,* in which he delineated his plan to expand Southern Baptist work to the Pacific. Meeting with the Board of Managers, he announced that the Home Mission Board was going to initiate work in New Mexico, and he wanted them to realign. The managers declined, refusing to turn their backs on fifty-nine years of Northern Baptist support.[26]

Northern Baptists interpreted the Southern Baptists' intentions as a violation of the Fortress Monroe Agreement. New Mexico was clearly a territory that the Northern body had established. Conflict led to further comity talks in 1910 between the two national organizations. Since New Mexico was geographically aligned with the South, Northern Baptists agreed to withdraw.[27] Unfortunately, resolving the issue at the state level still proved troublesome. The New Mexico territorial convention disregarded the agreement and voted to stay with the Home Mission Society. E. P. Aldredge, leader of the Southern sympathizers, charged that the vote did not represent the true sentiment of the churches. He attempted to turn the debate into a doctrinal issue by claiming that the battle was not territorial, but over the autonomy of the local church, a cherished Baptist principle.

The SBC pressed the issue in 1910, instructing the Home Mission Board to render assistance to any church that requested it. They argued that since each church was autonomous, the congregation could align with whomever they wished.[28] In November, the annual convention met at Tucumcari. Aldredge offered a resolution giving each church the right to align with whomever it chose. Messengers voted down the measure. On November 12, Aldredge and his followers staged a walkout and reassembled at the nearby Presbyterian church where they formed the Baptist General Convention of New Mexico.[29] For the next two years, New Mexico had two separate Baptist conventions.

Such conditions could not continue. Leaders devised two plans to bring the impasse to an end: let the individual churches decide, or submit the matter for arbitration before the two national bodies. Pastors accepted the latter plan. A joint committee of Northern and Southern Baptists met in 1911 and came to the same decision as before. Southern Baptists were to take over sponsorship. On June 19, 1912, both New Mexico Baptist conventions met in Clovis for the "Great Get Together Meeting" and adopted a transfer agreement. The Home Mission Society ceased operations on July 1, 1912. Exactly one month later the Baptist Convention of New Mexico (BCNM) officially became an affiliate of the SBC.[30] Ironically, despite the fight over the right of the local church to align with whomever it pleased, ecclesiastical bodies at the national level made the final decision.

Striving to Stay Alive, 1912–1937

After the decision, healing of wounds proved to be the first major hurdle to overcome. Corresponding Secretary E. B. Atwood traveled the state seeking to bring unity by mending the dissension, a task he likened to "trying to press together a handful of dry sand."[31] To facilitate cooperation, the new leadership launched a denominational newspaper, the *Baptist New Mexican,* which remains to the present day the official publication of the BCNM.

Atwood was able to make the sand stick. Nearly all churches sent messengers to the first statewide meeting in 1912 at Alamogordo. The new convention began with a total of 146 churches, 103 ministers, and a membership of 5,321.[32]

In their first eight years under Southern sponsorship, New Mexico Baptists experienced slow, steady growth. It was primarily a period of consolidation. The waves of homesteaders pouring into the state had begun to subside. By 1920, the number of churches increased by only two, but membership rose by 1,717 or 32 percent.[33] During this decade there were no major problems to confront or battles to fight. The Prohibition crusade received only meager attention. The suffrage question aroused even less interest. As a result, the convention had time to catch its breath before the tumultuous 1920s descended upon them with full force.

After World War I, financial difficulties once again plagued New Mexico Baptists. Drought forced many small churches to close. Other Protestant groups attempted to deal with this statewide problem through the Church Union Movement, which sought to consolidate rural congregations into nondenominational churches. Baptists, however, refused to participate. They were glad to see other denominations progress, but, as they put it:

> Baptists are a peculiar people and cannot be guided by rules of conduct that seem perfectly acceptable to others. We feel that we have the whole truth for the whole world, and we are unwilling to surrender either a part of the truth or a part of the world as a field in which to preach.[34]

Since Baptists felt that they had the "whole truth" for the "whole world," union with other denominations would compromise their principles. Submitting to an ecclesiastical authority also violated their belief in local church autonomy. Landmark tendencies remained strong among Baptist churches in New Mexico. Union meant acceptance of open communion and alien immersion, and non-Baptist preachers might fill their pulpits. Such practices were unacceptable to Southern Baptists.

The postwar depression created financial difficulties for New Mexico Baptists and for the rest of the denomination as well. In 1921, the Home Mission Board had to reduce appropriations for New Mexico from $36,000 to $25,000. Loss of income caused the state mission board to abandon new work and to curtail existing programs.[35] Conditions worsened as the decade progressed. In 1921, only thirteen churches in the state remained self-supporting. Reporting to the convention that same year Corresponding Secretary Dr. J. W. Brunner noted that, "Taking care of churches already established, living within available funds, holding ground already won, has, within itself, been progress for us."[36]

The state mission board refused appropriations to churches showing no signs of development or denominational loyalty. Many church financial requests were increasing instead of diminishing, but the board made clear that they were unwilling to continue to underwrite these congregations.[37] Pastoral reliance on the Home Mission Board to supplement salaries further exacerbated the problem, making it difficult for some ministers to remain in the field. After the initial reduction from $36,000 to $25,000, additional cuts became necessary. In 1924, the board told the churches to reduce their requests by 20 percent.

Appropriations continued to decline. In 1925, the Home Mission Board allocated only $23,000 for New Mexico. The following year, another $3,000 reduction occurred. Economic hardship, however, did stimulate resourcefulness. Convention records show in 1924 that the income churches provided for pastors exceeded the amount of aid.[38] In other words, reduced subsidies forced many congregations to increase their giving.

Fiscal curtailment not only affected pastors. Convention staff experienced a tremendous turnover, especially during the first half of the decade. During this period the convention had to replace two Sunday School secretaries, three Women's Missionary Union secretaries, two state evangelists, and two editors.[39] These financial difficulties occurred at a most inconvenient time, as the state convention had just entered a period of institutional expansion.

Prosperity and growth before and during World War I motivated New Mexico Baptists to undertake several capital projects. Having already committed, they resolutely pushed forward despite the onset of hard times. First Baptist Church in Portales sponsored the initial undertaking. The church offered the convention 40 acres and $6,500 for an orphanage if the convention would assume responsibility for the facility. Officially named the New Mexico Baptist Orphan's Home, it opened on May 1, 1919. Four years later the BCNM sold the land and moved the home to a 160-acre parcel south of town. Beulah Fonville, the first matron, managed a small farm on the property. She saw in the operation an opportunity for teaching the children horticultural skills as well as providing a food supply.[40] Fund-raisers and food drives kept the facility operating.

At the end of World War I, Baptists in Clovis launched a campaign to build a hospital for eastern New Mexico since no such facility existed in the entire region. The hospital opened on October 27, 1920, a twenty-three-bed facility costing $35,000. Of all New Mexico Baptist projects, the hospital was the only one that was able to fund its own operating expenses, enabling it to keep functioning during the Great Depression. The hospital closed in 1939, but only after the county built a new facility.[41]

The desire for higher education had not vanished with the closing of the Alamogordo campus in 1911. For New Mexico Baptists, such an institution meant far more than having a school to train pastors and provide an education for their youth. State conventions had a duty to establish a college; they were part of the overall evangelistic program to proclaim the truth of Christianity by providing intellectual as well as spiritual leadership.

In 1919, New Mexico Baptists voted to establish a college and appointed a committee to solicit bids from New Mexico communities. They accepted a proposal from the Commercial Club in Las Vegas, to take over the Montezuma Hotel, which had once been Santa Fe Railroad property with a value of $350,000. Enthusiastic response to the idea swept throughout the state. Popular sentiment was optimistic. Even though the old hotel required a great deal of renovating, Baptists in the state believed in their ability to raise funds, augmented by the promise of $100,000 from the denomination's Educational Commission.

Despite the outpouring of support, the board of directors twice postponed the opening date because a shortage of capital prevented completion of repairs. Montezuma College finally opened in September 1922, with 231 students. Schooling was available for elementary and secondary students, along with the first year of college. The school added additional levels of instruction during the next three years.

At the end of the first year of operation, it became apparent that New Mexico's leadership was working under a misconception: They had understood that money was immediately available for equipment and improvements. The national body's educational commission had intended these resources for an endowment. The SBC waived that concept, agreeing to grant Montezuma College $20,000 per year for five years. BCNM leaders accepted this solution. At the time of the first annual report, however, the college had received only $5,000 from the commission.[42] Once started, this pattern became constant: Approved expenditures often failed to materialize because of lack of funds.

In spite of enthusiastic support, Montezuma's problems continued. To keep the college operating, board members and administrators pursued opportunities for additional financing outside the state. The school struggled on until 1930. In that year, with the depression gripping the nation, the college closed its doors. In 1937, the convention sold the Montezuma facility to the Roman Catholic Church for $19,537.[43]

In addition to institutional projects, the BCNM sought to extend its work among the non-White population during the 1920s. Baptist work among ethnics followed much the same course as Anglo development. Individuals initiated evangelistic activities and then the denomination extended support. Hence, church planting became largely the province of ethnic pastors. When Susano P. Becerra came from San Antonio, Texas, to Roswell in 1892, he established the first Spanish Baptist church. Candelario Castillo organized another congregation in Carlsbad after Mina Everett persuaded him to leave California.[44] In 1923, five Hispanic Baptist churches formed their own convention, with the encouragement and support of Anglo Baptist leaders. In the years to follow, the State and Home Mission Boards jointly supported this work. The state provided two full-time workers and a part-time student, while the national body supported up to three full-time ministers.[45]

The first record of Black Baptist activity appeared in the 1903 state convention annual report with recognition of J. B. Bell as the organizer of a church in Albuquerque. The 1905 annual listed Bell as a worker among Blacks in Arizona and New Mexico, receiving a small supplement from the convention. Later, he received full-time support, limiting his service to New Mexico exclusively. Black Baptist congregations continued to grow, leading to the formation of their own association in 1913 with seven churches and 210 members.[46] During the 1920s, state aid increased to include salary support for five Black pastors, and by 1927 the number of churches had increased to fourteen.[47]

Work among Native Americans received more denominational support than among Hispanics and Blacks. Home Mission Board activity began among the Navajo in July 1922. The first Indian church originated in Gallup during the early 1920s when members petitioned the denomination for funds.[48] Beginning in 1925, First Baptist Church in Albuquerque sponsored a mission to Native American students at the Indian School. This work grew, and as many as one hundred students attended Sunday services by 1928.[49] The Home Mission Board assigned George Wilson, a Sioux, along with his Navajo wife, and C. W. Burnett to work among the Isleta, Zia, San Felipe, Santa Ana, Cochiti, and Sandia Pueblos in 1929. Two years later, the board added ministry to the Navajos at Alamo and Cañoncito through the encouragement of Seferino Jojola of Isleta Pueblo.[50]

Expansion continued despite problems and monetary setbacks. By 1922, Baptists had established a hospital, children's home, and college in the state. Ethnic work, although limited, moved forward under a cooperative arrangement between the State and Home Mission Boards. Numerically, Baptists continued to grow. In 1925, the number of churches had risen to 168, and membership totaled 10,925. More churches supported themselves than ever before. It appeared that the worst times had passed. A report on Baptist activities in 1927 by Corresponding Secretary C. W. Stumph was hopeful. He noted with pride that Baptists were the only denomination in the state attempting to run both an orphanage and a college.[51] Then came 1929.

During the Great Depression, austerity dictated Baptist operations. Curtailed programs and reduced expenses became a necessity. Payroll cuts thinned state convention workers' ranks. Next on the list was the reduction in the number of editions and pages of the state's Baptist newspaper. Churches canceled many activities. Sunday School and an occasional preaching service were all that many congregations could afford.[52] The annual reports for 1930–1933 consisted of only mimeographed convention minutes, with no statistics or associational reports. From 1932 until 1938 a layperson filled the corresponding secretary's office at a dollar per year salary in order to meet convention charter and legal requirements.[53] Aid to ministerial students also came to an end. As difficult as these problems were to bear, the greater blow came with the loss of Montezuma College. Debt left over from the school became an overwhelming burden, and retirement of this debt became the major issue shaping Baptist activities in the 1930s.

In addition, mission activity virtually ceased. State support of Hispanic and Black associations ended. Ethnic work became the sole province of the Home Mission Board, thus ending the policy of shared responsibility.[54] Churches either became self-supporting or they disbanded. With evangelism curtailed, Sunday Schools became the primary vehicle for that work.

On the basis of contributions and membership, the years 1933–1934 were the low point of the depression for New Mexico Baptists. Gifts to the state mission offering totaled less than $1,000, the lowest in twenty-two years.[55] Numerical growth slowed significantly. Records show total membership in 1929 at 11,597. Five years later the number had grown to only 11,983, an increase of fewer than a hundred members per year.[56]

In the mid-1930s, signs of life began creeping back into the convention. Denominational giving rebounded slightly in 1934. Membership picked up in 1935 and by 1937 totaled 13,522. The number of churches, however, remained constant at 126.[57] The State Mission Board in 1936 was able to support five missionaries. Also in 1936, the convention entertained a recommendation that a Bible chair be established at Eastern New Mexico Junior College in Portales.[58] As World War II approached, Baptists had large debts and morale was low, but prospects at least allowed discussion of hiring a corresponding secretary.

CHAPTER 3

Harry Stagg and the Rise of New Mexico Baptists: 1938 to 1960

Since its inception, the Baptist Convention of New Mexico (BCNM) had experienced numerous hardships. The strain caused by the financial collapse of the 1930s further damaged the organization. Bickering and infighting became commonplace. A "grouchiness" epidemic pervaded the convention manifesting itself in an arbitrary and uncooperative spirit. Commenting on this phenomenon, Sunday School Secretary E. A. Herron declared that faultfinding had become so intense that it led many women to speaking out against the poor behavior of the men.[1]

Dissension permeated Baptist ranks. Convention debt, brought on in large part by the failure of Montezuma College, weighed heavily. The closure of the college damaged the convention psyche as much as the financial difficulties it caused. Montezuma had represented the epitome of their denominational achievement, and now all the years of sacrifice seemed to be for nothing. The failure of Montezuma pitted those who wished to try again against those who feared another financial disaster.[2] In addition, cutbacks in programs further alienated churches and their pastors from the state organization.

The convention desperately needed pulling together. Reestablishing leadership seemed the only viable solution. In searching for someone to fill the position, attention centered on one man who had served both as president of the State Mission Board and president of the convention. His ability to work with people made him the most likely candidate. Meeting in October 1937, the nominating committee asked the Reverend Harry P. Stagg to assume leadership. Convinced that he could not withstand the pressures of office because of injuries sustained in World War I, Stagg suggested Dr. Julian Atwood, a pastor from Roswell. After initially accepting the nomination, Atwood reconsidered and tendered his resignation.[3] Following further deliberation, the nominating committee once again put Stagg's name forward. This time he accepted, taking office in January 1938.

Harry Stagg came to New Mexico from Louisiana in 1925 at the insistence of a friend making a cross-country journey in the hopes that a new environment might improve his health. Arriving in Albuquerque, Stagg called upon C. W. Stumph at the BCNM headquarters. The corresponding secretary prevailed upon him to fill the pulpit at the Baptist church in Gallup, which was without a pastor. After hearing him speak, the congregation extended a call. Given his health problems, this service appeared to be an impossibility, but Stagg agreed to stay two months to give the church an opportunity to find someone else. The two months extended to thirteen years. When he finally left Gallup, it was to assume the leadership of the convention.[4]

Pulling the Convention Together

Upon assuming the position of executive secretary, Stagg faced two seemingly insurmountable problems: a disjointed convention and crushing debt. Nevertheless, he moved rapidly to reinvigorate the denomination. Stagg began writing articles in the *Baptist New Mexican* under the column title, "We Are Well Able—Let Us Go Up!"[5] In these essays, Stagg announced goals, encouraged evangelistic outreach, related stories of church visits, reported on the numerous activities of the Southern Baptist Convention (SBC), and introduced new staff members and pastors to the state.

To unite the churches and demonstrate that the convention was concerned about them and had a worthy program, he obtained a "clergy pass" from the Santa Fe and Southern Pacific railroads. With this pass, Stagg visited numerous churches and attended district meetings, staying in homes to be closer to his people. Taking personal interest in each individual was the cornerstone of his management philosophy. The case of Roy Sutton, who later became the executive secretary of the Arizona Baptist Convention, illustrates this point. Between the time that Sutton accepted employment and the formal assumption of his duties, Southern Baptists held their 1952 convention. Stagg thought that it would be beneficial for Sutton to attend the meeting, but while traveling to New Orleans, he became involved in an auto accident. Notified that he lay in critical condition, Stagg had convention stationery printed with his new employee's name on it. Arriving at the hospital, he presented Sutton with the letterhead, and described how they were already preparing his office in anticipation of recovery. Sutton later credited that visit with saving his life. Thirty minutes before Stagg's arrival, he had overheard two doctors say that it was unlikely he would live.[6]

At the same time that Stagg was pulling the BCNM together, he was also tackling the debt problem. To maintain the credibility of Baptists in the state, Stagg contacted all Montezuma creditors, either in person or by phone. He assured them of the convention's willingness to stand by its obligations and his desire to work out a suitable payment plan. In many instances, Stagg's action resulted in the reduction or waiving of the liability.

Stagg's efforts to pull the convention together and reduce its debt produced rapid results. In 1937, the denomination included 120 Baptist churches in New Mexico with 14,500 members. Within two years rolls increased by 28 percent, and the number of churches rebounded to 133.[7] This rejuvenation occurred at a most propitious time. War was about to send a new round of immigrants pouring into the state, and New Mexico Baptists were ready for them.

Expansion

World War II brought large numbers of people westward. In 1940, New Mexico's population numbered 531,818; ten years later that figure had increased by 28 percent or 146,369. Cold war tensions and an oil and gas boom continued to fuel population growth. By 1960, state residents had increased to 951,023, up 79 percent in twenty years.[8]

The population boom altered the convention in two ways: monetarily and demographically. Many people who arrived at the military bases, national laboratories, and support industries were of Baptist backgrounds. Immigrants from a half-century before had often tried to eke out an existence as home-steaders on questionable land with incomes about as consistent as New Mexico's rains. The new arrivals were different. Many came with well-paying jobs as befitted skilled laborers and professionals. More importantly, they shared their prosperity with the church.[9]

Financially, the convention exploded. Beginning in 1942 under the heading "Gifts to all Causes," the state body began reporting church contributions to all Baptist work, in the state and to the SBC. The first year's donations totaled $37,201.45. By 1948, that amount had mushroomed to $482,062.37. Two years later, offerings more than tripled to $1,735,376. In 1958, the last year of this lump sum reporting, yearly gifts had more than doubled from the 1950 figure to $3,600,890.[10] Budget increases paralleled this growth in giving. The amount allocated for convention work in 1940 totaled $48,611.95. By 1950, it had increased to $287,815 and to $735,824.24 in 1959.[11]

Although newcomers to New Mexico helped to fill church coffers, they also accelerated the change from a rural to an urban denomination. Unlike the homesteaders who followed the railroad to new lands, the new immigrants followed national defense jobs to the cities. In the process, New Mexico's demographics reversed themselves. Statistics for the state in 1940 revealed that 67 percent of its residents lived in the country. By 1960, nearly two-thirds of the population, 62 percent, lived in urban areas. For Baptists, the change was even more dramatic.[12]

An editorial in the *Baptist New Mexican* in 1940 acknowledged that many rural churches were losing influence and often closing their doors.[13] To stem this downturn, B. I. Carpenter, in cooperation with the Home Mission Board, came to New Mexico in 1944 to direct rural missions work. In 1946, his report on the situation revealed that 81 percent of the denomination's churches were in the country.[14] Four years later a convention report showed that nearly 50 percent of New Mexico's population resided in the fifteen largest cities and towns.[15] Rapid urbanization produced a dichotomy among the denomination's churches and its membership. It also set the convention at variance with the state's demographics. The BCNM found itself to be an organization composed of rural churches but with an urban membership.

Statistical data extrapolated from the convention's 1940 annual reveals that although 75 percent of the churches were in the country, 65 percent of the membership attended metropolitan congregations.[16] At the same time, a declining rural population placed strains on the organization's ability to service the majority of their churches, which averaged 78 in attendance, compared to city pastorates averaging 369. Such low figures in the countryside clarified why keeping ministers remained a continuing concern. Secretary Stagg reported in 1940 that nearly a third of the "houses of worship" lacked a shepherd.[17]

Throughout the 1940s Baptists continued moving into metropolitan areas along with the rest of the state's population. In 1950, membership in city churches climbed to 74 percent and by 1960 it had escalated to 87 percent. As membership flocked to the cities, the percentage of rural churches necessarily declined, from 63 percent in 1950 to 42 percent in 1960. Conversely, the SBC reported in 1960 that 75 percent of its churches were still located in the country.[18] With the majority of churches in New Mexico now urban, pastorless congregations ceased to be the burden that they had been for over half a century.

In an earlier period of Anglo migration into New Mexico, Baptist homesteaders followed the railroad to new lands opened in the eastern and southern portions of the state. A map from a Works Progress Administration report on "Religion in New Mexico" compiled in 1939 shows the Baptist churches situated along the eastern border. Data from the 1940 BCNM annual report supports this picture: 72 percent of the membership and 75 percent of the churches were in the eastern part of the state. More significantly, the five counties that bordered Oklahoma and Texas—Union, Quay, Curry, Roosevelt, and Lea—accounted for 47 percent of the members and 39 percent of the congregations. With war on the horizon, Southern Baptists clung to a beachhead in a "foreign land."

Changing demographics altered Baptist distribution over the next twenty years, with the greatest shift in concentration occurring in the northwest part of the state. From 19 percent in 1940 and 21 percent in 1950, this section continued to gain on the southeast, eventually reaching 31 percent of Baptist membership by 1960. The eastern half of the state still accounted for the majority of members in New Mexico, but its dominance had slipped. In 1960, 59 percent of the membership and 61 percent of the churches remained in this region, down 13 percent and 14 percent, respectively, from the 1940 figures. The denomination no longer consisted of recently arrived Anglos living on the eastern plains. By 1960, a Baptist presence pervaded the entire state.

When Stagg took over the reins of leadership, Baptists numbered 14,500. Twenty-two years later those numbers had swelled to 77,742, an increase of 536 percent. The western half of the state now contained 41 percent of the membership. Even though Bernalillo County accounted for nearly half of the state's western membership roll, nevertheless, in 1960 there were 32,118 individuals in a region that two decades before had been virtually a foreign territory. In 1938 Baptists could be geographically compartmentalized; by 1960 that was no longer possible.

Conventional wisdom attributes Baptist growth during this era to immigration. Certainly this factor is the most important. But, it falls short of adequately explaining the phenomenon. Other Protestant denominations also benefited from the same influx into the state. Why did they not post similar gains? The role of Harry Stagg provides one explanation, and assistance from the Sunday School and Home Mission Boards another. By themselves these factors are inadequate, however. New Mexico Baptists were successful from 1940 to 1960 because they were able to internally generate much of the convention's expansion. Leaders and church members alike turned their organization into a model of evangelistic efficiency.

Evangelism

Clearly, Stagg's leadership revitalized the denomination and produced accelerated evangelistic endeavors. Both the state convention and the district associations, with the help of the Home Mission Board, employed evangelists to spread the gospel. To support this outreach, the core church programs of Sunday School, Vacation Bible School (VBS, Bible school for youth during summer vacation), and Training Union (Sunday-evening program that trained youth and adults in church organization, beliefs, and evangelism) provided the infrastructure to penetrate communities without a Southern Baptist presence. Regular campaigns involving the churches brought leaders and laity together in a cooperative mission effort.

Baptists organized campaigns to reach two separate groups—those who had been church members but had not joined since their move to the West and those without a spiritual home. The "Ten Weeks" campaign, running from February 9 to April 13, 1941, provides an example of a specific effort to reach former Baptists. The idea was to strengthen individual fellowships by involving all congregations in finding Baptists who had not yet affiliated with a local body.[19]

For those outside the church, New Mexico Baptists used a technique known as the "Enlargement Campaign." Denominational officials designed this program to reach individuals and geographical regions previously neglected. The heart of this program was the census. Congregations received training in how to canvass a specific community or section of a city by going door-to-door and conducting religious affiliation surveys. Such fieldwork became the primary tool to discover prospects for the nearby church. It was also helpful in identifying new areas that might be open to holding a VBS or a Sunday School.

In tandem with this campaign, New Mexico's Southern Baptists also made use of electrical connections to keep abreast of newcomers in the local community. Churches obtained a list of recent residential hook-ups from the utility company. Then, a visitation team would call upon the new arrivals, and invite them to attend services. In many instances this approach found Baptists who had not reaffiliated when they moved west.

The Evangelism Department used the results from these censuses to put together its Simultaneous Revivals program. These meetings were part of a denomination-wide effort to saturate a state by dividing it into zones, with revivals held at the same time throughout the area. The dividing line in New Mexico ran along Highway 60 from Clovis through Vaughn to Mountainair and Socorro.[20] Services occurred in the spring, one region following the next so that pastors could assist each other. The Home Mission Board helped with this effort by providing evangelistic and music ministry teams.

A Simultaneous Revival was a carefully planned and orchestrated event. Meetings usually lasted two weeks. Preparation began months before with a census, associational rallies, and a program of prayer. The church promoted the revival in all its departments, with soul winners (individuals trained to tell non-Christians about Jesus Christ) organized to encourage people to attend the meetings. The local congregation advertised the upcoming event by placing ads in the newspaper, combined with the liberal use of screen-door cards.[21]

Revivals remained popular throughout the 1940s and into the 1950s. In addition to their spiritual significance, these gatherings also served rural areas as a form of entertainment. Residents often had only the local bar for recreation, but religious meetings provided a welcome alternative. New Mexico Baptists were quick to capitalize on this social aspect of evangelism. It was not uncommon for services to continue for several weeks.[22]

The core church programs—Sunday School, VBS, and Training Union—supported these evangelistic drives. Sunday Schools lay at the heart of this effort. As the depression drew to a close, the BCNM's Sunday School Department secretary, E. A. Herron, began a vigorous promotion program throughout the state. Utilizing the demographic data gathered from the Enlargement Campaign, he assisted churches in using their educational programs as a tool for evangelism.

Congregations contemplating expansion into adjacent neighborhoods and communities consulted the census data to determine if there was sufficient interest in establishing a Sunday School. If successful, this effort often led to a mission, and eventually, a church. The parent body assisted the new work until it became self-supporting. First Baptist Church in Albuquerque, for example, excelled at this type of activity. Over the years, it started thirty-five missions and churches, including Hoffmantown, which later became the largest Southern Baptist church in the state. Increase in enrollment underscores the impact that an aggressive Sunday School Department had on evangelism. From 17,652 in 1938, the numbers soared to 62,469 by 1960, involving 80 percent of the membership.[23]

The Sunday School Department also used VBSs for outreach. W. J. Lites, who succeeded Herron as Sunday School secretary in 1943, credited its VBS expansion to Ed Storm, who joined his staff in 1953. As a summertime educational program for youth, these schools also served an evangelistic purpose by providing contact with nonaffiliated families. Nearly 10 percent of the children enrolled in any given year did not attend a church. Vacation Bible schools also became an instrument for outreach to various ethnic communities. These mission efforts carried the work into Native American, Hispanic, and Black neighborhoods and prepared the way for revival meetings in communities without Baptist churches. In some cases, these activities led to the establishment of year-round preaching stations. As VBS enrollment rose from 5,538 in 1938 to 29,994 in 1960, its impact as an evangelistic tool increased.[24]

The Training Union served as the last in this triumvirate of core church programs. Like VBS, it too was a part of the Sunday School Department until 1948, when Charles Polston became secretary of this newly created department. Unlike the other two, however, the Training Union concentrated on developing leaders. Instruction centered on a fivefold program designed to produce more effective church members. This program included teaching in (1) systematic Bible study, (2) discipleship, (3) church service, (4) Baptist heritage, and (5) missions.[25]

Although not directly involved in evangelism, the Training Union assumed an important role in preparing Baptists for effective service by supporting that outreach. Members received training that enabled them to assume leadership roles in church programs and administration. Such instruction produced a cadre of personnel from which to promote expansion.[26] During this era, Training Union enrollment increased dramatically, as sessions for adults augmented what had primarily been a youth program. Yearly attendance increased from 3,942 in 1938 to 26,009 in 1960.[27]

New Mexico Baptists had always supported evangelism, but during the period from 1938 to 1960 these efforts reached new highs. The large numbers of individuals enrolled in church educational programs all receiving the same education and instruction produced a Southern Baptist identity in a "foreign" environment. A unity of purpose pervaded the membership that enabled them to "spread the gospel" at previously unprecedented levels. Numerous baptisms were their reward.

Evangelism swelled the ranks of New Mexico Baptists. During the early years of Secretary Stagg's tenure, from 1938 through 1945, baptisms averaged 1,575 per year. In the half decade after the war, that annual number increased to 2,740. Then, beginning in 1951, baptisms accelerated, averaging 4,120 each year through 1960. Additions by transfer of letter[28] and statement of faith also posted similar advances. For the entire twenty-two-year period, the BCNM listed 172,855 additions, of which 67,506 came by profession of faith and 105,349 by letter or statement.[29] For every five additions, three were new arrivals and two came from "soul winning." A strong program of evangelism designed to capitalize on this new round of immigration enabled the BCNM to become the largest Protestant denomination in the state by 1960.

Departmental Expansion

Rapid expansion necessitated reorganization. To provide a support base for growth, the convention adapted to the changing conditions by adding new departments and expanding existing ones. The financial, material, and personnel support of the Home Mission and Sunday School Boards of the SBC underwrote this restructuring. In the post-comity era, the denomination committed itself to Western expansion, with New Mexico Baptists eager recipients of their convention's benevolence.[30]

Prior to 1944, the executive secretary carried the torch of evangelism. By that year, however, the convention realized the need for a separate rural missions and evangelism program. Under the administration of B. I. Carpenter, the work became a cooperative effort between the State Mission and Home Mission Boards. Four years later, Eual Lawson became the first secretary of a newly reinstated Department of Evangelism.[31] This separate status enabled the "business" of outreach to proceed in a more orderly fashion. Now able to concentrate on the three elements of enlistment, education, and mass revival, the outreach program became more professionally coordinated.[32]

Expansion also facilitated the need for a separate men's organization, known as the Brotherhood. This group acquired its first full-time secretary in 1947 when Charles Ashcroft took over as director. Its purpose was to support overburdened pastors, a common occurrence during this period of rapid growth. Activities included sponsoring Royal Ambassadors[33] for boys, assisting with revivals, and aiding in fund-raising. In addition to involving men in promoting denominational work, the Brotherhood became active in the community. Civic projects, such as establishing blood banks, providing legal counsel, and setting up veterans committees to aid returning armed services personnel, extended the New Mexico Southern Baptist influence beyond the doors of its churches.[34]

Further departmental expansion also extended that presence into higher education. With the loss of Montezuma College, the convention sought to provide spiritual guidance for Baptist students at the various state universities. By 1945, a Baptist student union (BSU) had been established on all six campuses in the state. Even though the director at each college attempted to involve students with a local church, the BSU actually functioned in a surrogate capacity as a Christian support group. Students received counseling regarding marriage, personal problems, and spiritual growth. Daily devotionals and weekly social activities, usually with student planning, also became an important part of the program. To coordinate this work more effectively, the convention likewise established the Student Union Department in 1947, with C. R. Barrick as its first secretary.

Financial underpinning proved critical to facilitate expansion and necessitated the establishment of a Missions and Stewardship Department in 1952. Before this time money-raising efforts had been ad hoc. Pastors participated in statewide tithing campaigns and preached sermons on the duties and benefits thereof. Members participated in programs such as "Baptist Dollar Days," which encouraged people to give $1 over and above other pledges. This and other efforts clearly raised revenue. When Jeff Rutherford took over the department, however, he introduced an overall program that consisted of educational training, steward-ship revivals, and enlistment of churches to increase giving on all fronts.[35]

To augment church growth, the convention established the New Mexico Baptist Foundation in 1947. Charles Ashcroft divided his time between the foundation and Brotherhood work, serving as secretary for both organizations. In 1959, W. C. Ribble became the foundation's first full-time secretary. The agency received money, gifts, property, and bequests to help finance denominational work. Establishment of a revolving church-loan building fund that advanced funds to congregations at 4 percent interest occupied the majority of the department's efforts. Ability to generate money internally for construction projects moved the state organization toward less dependence on the national body.[36]

Increasing convention activity necessitated a place to house an expanding staff. When Stagg became executive secretary in 1938, the headquarters in Albuquerque consisted of a shotgun series of rooms, one telephone, a bookstore, and four staff members. A year later, the Baptists purchased an apartment building on Gold Avenue. Continued growth made even these facilities obsolete. Again Baptists bought property, this time two lots on Central Avenue, the site of the present convention headquarters. Begun in 1950, the building was ready for occupation a year later at a cost of $300,000.[37]

Expansion also had an impact on existing convention departments. Such was the case with the Baptist Bookstore. During the 1940s, this organization changed its emphasis from dispensing Southern Baptist literature to that of educational promotion. Concerned about the state of a world emerging from war, bookstore director H. C. Reavis led a campaign to make people aware of national and international problems and the proposed Christian solution for them. He attempted to accomplish this goal through the establishment of church libraries. Reavis believed that since many communities did not have such facilities, Baptist churches should fill the need.[38] His efforts were also instrumental in providing much of the West with religious material. New Mexico's Albuquerque-based bookstore served Arizona, California, and Colorado for many years. It also assisted in the founding of additional outlets in Phoenix, Arizona, and Fresno, California.[39]

This drive for expansion also impacted the state newspaper, the *Baptist New Mexican*. When Lewis A. Myers assumed the editorship in 1947, he launched a campaign to reach 100-percent circulation among New Mexico Baptists. Myers expanded the newspaper to sixteen pages and used it to keep New Mexicans informed about Southern Baptist activities at home and abroad. Under Myers's editorship, the *Baptist New Mexican* became a voice for conservative Christian beliefs in the fight against "modernism."

Articles and editorials kept readers informed about social issues and how they related to the gospel.

In addition to increasing the scope and content of the newspaper, Myers urged each church to include a subscription for every family in their annual budget. This drive for membership saturation was so successful that by 1955 the state convention no longer needed to subsidize the newspaper. Increased circulation enabled the leadership to more effectively communicate denominational projects and goals. In this way too, the *Baptist New Mexican* functioned as an agent of evangelism and expansion.[40]

Rapid developments among New Mexico Baptists during and after World War II placed strains on the local church and district associations. Southern Baptists are a nonhierarchical people. They organize around a congregational structure in which the principle of local church autonomy is only one step removed in reverence from the Ten Commandments. Historically, associations have formed around the need for fellowship and to conduct evangelism. State conventions are a relatively new development and represent an adaptation to the American political scene.

Expansion and urbanization created programmatic demands that lay beyond the ability and resources of the churches to implement, forcing them to look to the state convention for help. To accommodate the new demands and provide the services required to support a growing organization, the BCNM underwent bureaucratization. An enlarged structure, staffed by an increasing number of trained professionals, produced programs to meet expanding needs, upon which the local churches and associations became more dependent. Slowly, under the increasing pressure of centralization, the power base began to shift from New Mexico churches to the state organization.

Special Projects

Prior to becoming executive secretary, Harry Stagg served as president of the State Mission Board. In that capacity he worked to extend Baptist influence in college education. Even after the loss of Montezuma College, some wanted the convention to try again to establish a Baptist university. Realizing the futility of risking another failure, Stagg built upon an idea tried earlier by Baptists in Texas. He would utilize the presence of Baptist student unions to provide religious instruction on state university campuses. From this concept, the Bible chairs were born.

Dr. Floyd Golden, president of Eastern New Mexico College in Portales, and also a Baptist, became intrigued with the concept when Stagg presented it to him. Working together, they developed a plan whereby the state Baptist convention would supply the instructor, pay his salary, and provide the building. The college would allow the use of its facilities, give credit for the classes, and treat the theology professor as part of the faculty, except for voting privileges. The plan served several purposes. The school obtained a religion department, and the BCNM was back in higher education. The Baptist student union in Portales soon secured proper quarters. Classes began in 1936 under the directorship of Dr. C. R. Barrick.[41]

The idea was an immediate success. Almost half of the students enrolled in religion classes were either ministers or ministerial students. The impact of this program was twofold. First, located on the eastern plains in the center of Baptist concentration, local ministers could receive additional training that would raise the educational level of the clergy. Second, New Mexico youth no longer needed to leave the state to obtain Baptist theological instruction. In some instances, these students could augment their studies by filling the pulpits of small country churches in need of a pastor, a common practice among Southern Baptists.

By 1960, all state institutions of higher education, except New Mexico Tech at Socorro, had similar Bible chairs. Eastern New Mexico University, however, was the only school that provided direct college credit. Here course work could lead to a bachelor or master's degree in religious studies. Hardin-Simmons University in Abilene, Texas, provided the college credits for students of biblical studies at the University of New Mexico, and New Mexico State, Western, and Highlands Universities.[42]

During this same era, education was also the motivating force behind the major undertaking of the Women's Missionary Union (WMU). This auxiliary organization continued to assist the convention with fund-raising activities, support of the Children's Home (New Mexico Baptist Orphan's Home), and assistance with local church programs. But the WMU too had expansionist desires. Director Eva Inlow envisioned a camp that would encourage youth to become "missions minded." Renting a site from the Presbyterians in 1938, by 1940 Baptists had moved into their own facilities in the Manzano Mountains. The primary emphasis of Inlow Camp lay with missions. Inlow intended to use the facility to show children that in God "there was no East or West." This orientation not only instilled evangelistic zeal in the hearts of the attendees, but also exposed them to the world beyond New Mexico. Missionaries from around the world told inspiring stories, leading many to devote their lives to the same cause. By 1960, more than thirty-one thousand campers had used the grounds.[43]

The WMU not only created their own project, but also assisted the state convention in the establishment of the Parkview Medical Clinic in the then-isolated Chama Valley of northern New Mexico. No medical facilities were available within an eighty-mile radius, and any travel required driving over primitive roads. Working closely with the M. C. Oldham family, Stagg, who had originally hoped to be a medical missionary, helped acquire the property. Eva Inlow and the WMU undertook to supply the facility and raised the projected $30,000 needed for operational costs.

Parkview Clinic opened on December 21, 1952. Dr. E. K. Bryan, a returned missionary from China, agreed to serve the clinic, and for five years he and his wife ministered to the physical and spiritual needs of the people. Over time, they initiated youth meetings, started a kindergarten, and eventually established a church in the area. After the Bryans left, the BCNM had difficulty finding a physician who would practice in such a remote location. The clinic closed in June 1963 after state-funded medical facilities moved into the region.[44]

Concern for the needs of others extended beyond denominational projects. Harry Stagg believed that New Mexico Baptists should reach out to society through civic involvement. Through his own membership in Rotary International, Stagg was in touch with leaders in government, education, and business. These contacts helped him in expediting Baptist projects. Conversely, civic leaders also came to him for assistance. One such example was with the Boys' Ranch. Originally, the Kiwanis Club had financed this facility located near Belen, but in 1952, the Kiwanis announced that they could no longer continue supporting the ranch. They appealed to the Rotary organization, which in turn, appealed to Stagg for Baptist involvement. The ranch was $50,000 in debt, and its facilities and equipment needed improvements. The convention chose not to manage the property but did agree to reorganize it. Baptist laymen served on the institution's board, and Walker Hubbard, the director of the Baptist Children's Home, received a leave of absence to supervise the facility until it recovered.[45]

A rapidly expanding convention made quick and practical communication a necessity. New Mexico's vast distances, and in many areas, sparse population, presented a challenge to effective coordination of activities. To meet the demands of a growing work, the convention agreed to purchase an airplane for the executive secretary's use, funded through private donations. Air travel meant that Stagg could make more contacts in less time at a reduced cost. When selling the idea to the convention, Stagg agreed to keep the same travel budget as he would for a car. Between 1957 and 1963, he logged more than six hundred thousand air miles. Not surprisingly, the plane saved $7,000 in salary time alone. On his busiest day, Stagg made six appointments, ranging from

Farmington in the north to Roswell in the south.[46] Utilizing the airplane illustrates the spirit and forward thinking of New Mexico Baptists. Rather than cutting back when overextended, they found new ways to accommodate increased responsibilities. This attitude led to their greatest project—Glorieta, an undertaking so large in scope that it requires its own chapter.

❧

As the depression decade closed, New Mexico Baptists listed 133 churches with 18,500 members. By the end of the 1940s, those numbers had increased to 171 churches with 42,390 members.[47] Evangelism played a major role in this growth. Soul winning by existing churches characterized the thrust of the decade. The figures on baptisms support this. During the 1940s, Baptists registered 20,360 baptisms, with 60 percent occurring between 1945 and 1949. Actually, the decade was more tumultuous than the figures suggest. A total of 72 churches had organized, but redistribution of the population from a rural to urban base caused many to close their doors.[48]

Although turbulent activity characterized the 1940s, the 1950s, on the other hand, represented sustained, controlled growth that manifested itself in church planting. The decade began with 171 churches and ended with 249.[49] Eighty-seven new churches started between 1950 and 1959, and only 5 of these failed to live into the 1960s.[50] Meanwhile, church membership increased 80 percent during the 1950s, averaging 3,377 additions each year. By the end of the decade, convention records reported 77,742 Baptists on church rolls. From 1940 to 1960, Southern Baptist affiliation in New Mexico had quadrupled. Baptisms actually exceeded the total number of new church members by 4,094 or 12 percent.[51]

Just how much did this growth alter the New Mexico religious landscape? The numbers reveal an interesting story. New Mexico is, and has been for nearly four hundred years, overwhelmingly Roman Catholic. In 1939, estimates placed the state's population at 500,000.[52] That year there were 18,500 Baptists, making the ratio of Baptists to the general population 1 in 27. By 1950, the population had increased to 681,187, with 45,604 Baptists, reducing the ratio to 1 in 15. In 1960, residents numbered 951,604, with 77,742 Baptists, dropping the ratio to 1 in 12. Denominational breakdown of statistics for 1960 reveals that of the 462,121 people attending religious services in the state, 301,000 were Catholic; 77,742, Baptist; 38,871, Methodist; and 44,508, all other Protestant denominations.[53] Baptists were just 5,637 shy of accounting for half of all Protestant churchgoers in the state. For every 2.2 Protestants, 1 was a Baptist.

CHAPTER 4

Glorieta

While New Mexico Southern Baptists battled to establish themselves in the state, they also waged a struggle to elevate the importance of the West in the eyes of their own denomination. The Fortress Monroe Agreement with the Northern Baptists in 1894 had opened the door for Southern Baptist expansion, but early efforts outside the traditional boundaries of the South remained meager. Westerners felt detached and isolated. Distances between churches made it difficult for Western associations to function. A preacher could go for weeks, even months, without being able to talk to another member of the clergy. Evangelism encountered new difficulties. Many people in the West did not respond to Southern revivalist techniques, and it was apparent that ministers needed help in developing new approaches. In the 1920s, George W. Truett, pastor of First Baptist Church in Dallas, saw the value of a grand assembly as a means of addressing these challenges. He was convinced that ministers and their congregations needed encouragement, fellowship, training, and a sense of belonging that only such an encampment could provide.

Site Selection

Depression and World War II led to an exodus of Southern Baptists from the South. Many moved west, to search for jobs in the ranching, oil, and lumber industries. Military service and defense industry employment added to this westward migration. These transplanted Southerners longed for contact with their homeland, but to journey back to the Southern Baptist assembly in Ridgecrest, North Carolina, for fellowship and training proved impractical. Expansion also placed strains on the binding power of the Southern Baptist Convention (SBC). A Western encampment might help pull the two sections together, thus providing a center for the continuation of a Southern Baptist lifestyle in a "foreign environment." During the war, pressure for a conference center continued to build.

Texas Baptists were the first to take action. In conjunction with the annual state convention in 1945, an informal group met to discuss the steps necessary to launch an assembly. Representatives from New Mexico, Oklahoma,

Louisiana, Arkansas, and Missouri caucused in a Dallas hotel room at the invitation of their Texas brethren. They saw a Western assembly as part of the growth of the West and crucial to the unity, or possible division, of the Southern Baptist Convention.

Each representative wanted the conference grounds in his state. Harry Stagg, who attended along with W. J. Lites, immediately laid claim for New Mexico. A wealthy Baptist layperson offered $50,000 toward the establishment of the site at Paisano, Texas, where George W. Truett had long held his cowboy camp meetings. When Stagg inquired whether the offer would hold if the location were outside Texas, the answer was affirmative, but the benefactor's untimely death precluded any further development.[1] Meanwhile, representatives passed a resolution calling for the Southern Baptist Convention to appoint a committee to study the feasibility of another assembly at its next meeting in Miami. In 1946, the convention approved the request.[2]

Once Southern Baptists had committed to building another assembly, speculation became rampant as to its probable location. Texans immediately offered the Paisano site and in so doing touched off a debate over multiple assemblies. Recognizing the need for a long-range leadership-training program, the Miami convention specified that such a curriculum be established through the summer assemblies. Furthermore, the sites needed to be located as nearly as possible within a day's automobile drive of those who would be likely to attend.[3] In December 1946, the subcommittee of the Executive Committee of the Southern Baptist Convention recommended the acceptance of the Paisano encampment, which included 960 acres of land and $150,000 in cash. Duke McCall, executive secretary of the Executive Committee, found himself barraged with "opinions." Three viewpoints emerged: (1) establish a facility in Texas and later another in California, (2) construct assemblies in Texas and the Ozarks, and (3) build several regional encampments throughout the West.

Debate once again raised the sectional issue. T. W. Madearis, general superintendent of the Missouri Baptist General Association, felt that "It would be nothing less than a tragedy for Southern Baptists to set up an assembly at great financial outlay anywhere on the perimeter of the territory involved . . . when there are excellent sites central to vast aggregations of our Baptist people."[4] Even though Madearis's letter typified the concern over the geographical expansion of the denomination, westward growth posed yet another problem.

Floyd Looney, editor of *The California Southern Baptist,* favored regional assemblies, but the prospect of possible division alarmed him: "I can see where pinning one 'school of thought' against another could work for broken fellowship."[5] To avoid the problem, Looney proposed a uniform program in subjects and personnel. He envisioned Easterners traveling west and vice versa to bring together the "mature reasoning" of the South and East with the "zest and aggressiveness" of the West.

New Mexico Baptists had hoped to see the proposed assembly established in their state, but the location debate bypassed them. The subcommittee's recommendation to accept Paisano and later construct another facility in the Ozarks appeared to seal the issue. At least this was the way that Philip McGahey, pastor of First Baptist Church in Albuquerque and chairperson of the New Mexico committee to promote an assembly in the state, perceived the decision. In an open letter on December 19, 1946, in the *Baptist New Mexican*, he lamented that the committee had overlooked his state because New Mexico could not compete financially. Behind the disappointment attributed to fiscal impotency lay the deeper issue of the West being treated as a "stepchild" by the national convention. McGahey began his epistle: "Yes, we have no Southwestern Assembly for New Mexico! We could not and did not rate." Expressing a sense of abandonment he continued:

> Our arguments were that it would have helped these Western states to meet the Catholic problem and advance this section of South-Baptist territory like probably nothing else would advance it. But we lost and we will go along with our brethren and do everything that we can to advance the cause of Christ out here in New Mexico and the other Western States.[6]

Behind the selection of a site for the new encampment lay a yearning for recognition of the West as a valued part of the Southern Baptist Convention.

When Duke McCall learned of McGahey's article, he immediately fired off letters to the editors of the other state Baptist newspapers. He requested that they not copy the report and declared it premature. The Western Assembly subcommittee voted unanimously in favor of Paisano. In discussing its decision with the administrative arm of the SBC's Executive Committee, however, the latter body requested that the subcommittee gather more information about additional sites prior to making a formal report to the Executive Committee. A note from McCall to McGahey informing him of his letter to the state editors touched off a spirited correspondence. During this exchange, Western "feelings" again surfaced. Responding to McCall, McGahey wrote: "I never dreamed that one of them would READ or CARRY anything written by a New Mexican. . . . [M]any people in the Western part of the Southern Baptist Convention do not believe that a THOROUGH STUDY HAS BEEN GIVEN

TO THIS MATTER."[7] McCall's statesmanship and a cooling of emotions on McGahey's part helped avert a controversy.

The multiple-site debate that embroiled the Paisano facility also attracted the interest of the Sunday School Board. Since this agency would have to administer the new assembly, its opinion was critical. In a letter to McCall on March 24, 1947, T. L. Holcomb, executive secretary of that body, voiced the board's position and, in effect, derailed the debate:

> Dr. McCall, it seems that there is some sentiment for the Convention to own and operate several assemblies in the West. In our humble judgment it would prove a business tragedy for the Convention to undertake to develop more than one assembly in the West for at least a number of years.[8]

The prospect of only one location worked against the Texans' hopes. Later at its annual meeting in 1947, the Southern Baptist Convention turned down the subcommittee's recommendation of Paisano. Messengers determined that the site was too far South, which would effectively make it a one-state assembly.[9] New Mexicans suddenly had another chance.

The obstacles in bringing the proposed encampment to New Mexico were overwhelming. A newly appointed Western Assembly Committee determined that the presenting state must own the property free and clear.[10] Only recently free from debt, New Mexico Baptists had no property to offer. This minor detail, however, did not deter Harry Stagg. In October 1947, at the state convention's annual meeting he obtained a resolution authorizing the State Mission Board to acquire land for use as a Western assembly site.[11]

Baptists found a suitable property in the Pecos Valley Ranch, just east of Santa Fe. The State Mission Board invited the Western Assembly Committee to inspect the property prior to purchase. On the day of their arrival, however, Stagg had to make a humiliating announcement: The Archdiocese of Santa Fe had purchased the property for $10,000 above the asking price. The owner had reasoned that the convention could not come up with the money prior to the expiration of its option and, therefore, had accepted the Catholic Church's offer.[12]

Undeterred, Stagg refused to quit. In January 1948, he learned from Clint Irwin, pastor of First Baptist Church in Santa Fe, about yet another parcel. The owner of Breese Ranch, located at the top of Glorieta Pass, was about to place her land on the market at half the asking price of the Pecos property. Without hesitation, Stagg took an option on the real estate and placed $2,000 down, with the balance of $48,000 due in thirty days.

His position secure, Stagg now faced the problem of persuading the State Mission Board to approve his action. After four votes, the board finally acquiesced. New Mexico Baptists raised the money for the land with donations from churches and revenue from the sale of the property designated for a new headquarters building. They purchased the ranch on the last day of their option. Had they been unsuccessful in this attempt, a man from St. Louis was waiting in Santa Fe to buy it. The Mission Board invited the Western Assembly Committee to inspect the new site, but they refused to come. Even an offer to pay their expenses failed to elicit a positive response.[13]

Again, Stagg would not admit defeat. Enlisting the cooperation of the Santa Fe, Albuquerque, and Las Vegas Chambers of Commerce, along with various state government agencies, he put together a pamphlet that promoted Glorieta as the logical site for the proposed Western Assembly.[14] Taking the literature to Memphis, Tennessee, where Southern Baptists were holding their 1948 convention, Stagg made sure that every messenger's seat had a copy of the brochure. Such "commercialism" generated a great deal of criticism, but his action kept alive the prospect of a New Mexico location.[15] Missouri and Arkansas were also offering potential sites. The national convention instructed the Western Assembly Committee to recommend a definite location by the time of their 1949 meeting.

New Mexico Baptist hopes lasted but briefly. On September 15, 1948, the committee voted five to four to locate the Western Assembly in Harrison, Arkansas.[16] The Executive Committee accepted the decision and planned to recommend this site to the Southern Baptist Convention when it met in 1949. Throughout 1948 and 1949, friction arose within the Western Assembly Committee. Chairperson Perry F. Webb resented attempts by New Mexico Baptists to lobby for the Breese Ranch site. In a personal letter to Duke McCall, Webb vented his frustration: "It seems to me we must proceed, despite the determined opposition of a determined minority, which opposition is solely based upon the desire to have the assembly in their own state."[17] In March 1949, Webb wrote to McCall, again referring to two or three dissidents who were "determined it shall not be located according to the overwhelming majority of the committee." Webb suggested that because of the attitude of a few, it might be a better procedure to present his committee's findings to the entire convention for the messengers' vote. McCall agreed.[18] In the same correspondence, Webb revealed the issue at the heart of the conflict: "I simply do not believe it should be located out in New Mexico away from every kind of facility and so far removed from our Baptist territory."

At the Southern Baptist Convention's Oklahoma City meeting in May 1949, the Western Assembly Committee presented its decision. Two of the minority members on that committee refused to quit. In a final attempt to salvage the assembly for New Mexico, Philip McGahey and C. Vaughn Rock took their report to the floor, making a direct appeal to the messengers. They were attempting the impossible. No convention had ever turned down a majority report.

McGahey urged the messengers to consider Glorieta's location because it would be "in the center of the greatest mission field on earth." His speech raised questions from the convention floor. An unidentified messenger addressed the majority committee representative and asked if, perhaps, the assembly's location should be farther west. The spokesperson's reply changed the course of Southern Baptist history. He answered, "[T]he committee already had committed the convention to the Arkansas property." One person observed: "He dropped his molasses jug right then." It appeared that the committee was trying to "put something over" on the people.[19]

A major debate ensued. Advocates for the Arkansas property pointed out that the Harrison Chamber of Commerce would make a gift of the land, build a road to the site, and give it a name. Westerners replied that the Baptist Convention of New Mexico (BCNM) already owned the property free and clear. It was on the Pan American Highway, and it already had a name— Glorieta. One man described as a "big, old tall preacher" got up and said, "I came through the Ozarks and the skeeters like to ate me up. You got any skeeters out there?"[20] Otto Hake, an Alabama native but then a resident of Albuquerque, vividly described Harrison's bugs, ticks, chiggers, and stifling heat. When the time came to vote, the convention overwhelmingly chose Glorieta. To the majority on the Western Assembly Committee, "west" meant west of the Mississippi River. As New Mexico Baptist historian Betty Danielson has pointed out, to the messengers who made the final decision, it meant that region reached by covered wagons across a wide prairie.[21]

When the count was announced, Duke McCall leaned over to Harry Stagg and asked if he would have any objections to deferring the vote so that the Sunday School Board could study the feasibility of the site.[22] After years of struggle, New Mexico had won. Now McCall was asking that victory be set aside and the decision postponed. Realizing the need for cooperation in an undertaking of this magnitude, Stagg agreed to the request.

The Southern Baptist Convention may have voted for Glorieta, but McCall's motion effectively placed the decision of the Western Assembly's location in the hands of the Sunday School Board. Thus, when a special committee from Nashville arrived to examine the site on September 1–2, 1949, New Mexico Baptist state leaders were understandably nervous. The committee's thirty-three-point checklist was a special concern.[23]

The committee consisted of T. L. Holcomb, Sunday School Board executive secretary; Harold Ingraham, business manager; and W. A. Harrell, secretary of the Architecture Department. As they inspected the property, Ingraham created a great deal of consternation among the New Mexico contingency. "Cantankerous" was the word used most often to describe him. As business manager, he was responsible for asking questions and looking for reasons why the land might be unsuitable. After supper, the three men sat in their hotel room at the La Fonda in Santa Fe, discussing the project until after midnight. Finally, Holcomb announced that, if they could find sufficient water, he was willing to recommend Glorieta as the place for the Western Assembly.

On the following day, the New Mexico contingent assembled at the Baptist Student Union building near the University of New Mexico. Holcomb called on Ingraham to announce the committee's decision. When he rose to speak, all those assembled thought the answer was "no." Ingraham recounted the experience:

> [W]hen I stood up, I'm just telling you the icicles formed on the chandelier and dropped off window shades. I never felt such a coldness in my life. I suddenly realized what it was, and I never did make more speed. . . . When I made the statement after prayer and consideration, the night before with the one provision that we must test for adequate water that depended on the right answer to that, we were ready, under Dr. Holcomb to go back and recommend to the Sunday School Board that it be accepted and that the Sunday School Board undertake to build an Assembly here. There were tears, tears. Half the men in that room were crying and back of that was something. All this drive that Dr. Stagg talked about, all the sacrificing this state made but even back of that was the yearning of the West for recognition and the realization of some of the leaders that if they didn't get it, the Convention was likely to split. . . . I don't think posterity, or any of us, will ever realize what Glorieta actually meant to the unity of the Southern Baptist Convention and to the saving of the West with all of its potential for Southern Baptists.[24]

Once the Sunday School Board officially approved Glorieta (well drillers had found four artesian wells), victory still eluded its promoters. Another set of obstacles emerged that could still defeat the project. The board announced that they needed seven additional tracts of land to ensure the integrity of the site from potential outside commercial development. They expected the New Mexico Baptists to spearhead the campaign to secure this land, although they did not ask them to pay for it. Stagg again went to work, but before he could begin, private individuals who heard of the requirement purchased six of the seven parcels in anticipation of personal profit.[25]

Prospects looked grave. Writing to Stagg from Nashville, T. L. Holcomb stated the board's position, "It is the definite conviction on the part of each of us that the failure to get this land will absolutely determine the Sunday School Board's interest in the entire project." Duke McCall was of the same opinion.[26] Negotiations proved successful, but Southern Baptists had to pay almost twice per acre what they would have paid had they been able to deal with the original owners.

The final tract presented a unique hurdle. A Roman Catholic living in California owned the seventh parcel. Despite all efforts, he refused to sell his land to Baptists. Stymied, Stagg sought the help of Judge Manuel Sanchez, an attorney from Santa Fe and a friend of the executive secretary. Sanchez journeyed to California, negotiated with the owner, and offered a compromise. Sanchez purchased the land himself and then transferred it to the denomination.[27]

With all land purchases completed, New Mexico Baptists thought their work was finished. Another problem arose, however; they could not obtain clear title to the land. There were no surveys for many of the parcels. Researchers could not find plats, court records, or anything else that would establish boundaries. Stagg invited adjacent property owners to join in having the area surveyed and then to bring suit to quiet title. Most participated, and the denomination paid the share for those who refused.[28] With this issue resolved, they had cleared the last hurdle. In December 1949, Duke McCall notified Harry Stagg that the Executive Committee unanimously voted to instruct the Sunday School Board to take over the development, operation, and ownership of the property.[29]

Erecting an Assembly

Optimistic about their ability to resolve the remaining obstacles, state leaders went ahead with the property dedication in advance of official approval. A car caravan left Santa Fe on October 26, 1949, carrying 250 people to the ceremony. Representatives came from eleven states, as well as Alaska and Brazil. The governor and members of New Mexico's supreme court also attended. Denominational leaders addressed the gathering and reiterated that the assembly would not only be a training center for Southern Baptists, it would also minister to the needs of all Baptist churches in the West.

Impressed by Glorieta's tourism possibilities, the city of Santa Fe prepared its own welcome. The day after the dedication, police barricaded the plaza for street preaching. J. W. Middleton from Atlanta delivered a sermon in front of the Palace of the Governors, commemorating the first Baptist message given one hundred years earlier by Hiram Walter Read.[30] After ceremonies were completed, construction began. Baptist leaders from New Mexico and throughout the South met on April 25, 1950, to devise a strategy for the encampment's development. Among them were E. A. Herron and Harry Stagg. Unlike the Ridgecrest Assembly in North Carolina, which had grown haphazardly, planners forged Glorieta's layout down to the last detail.[31]

Several problems immediately became apparent. Breese Ranch did not lend itself to the block style layout so typical of Southern development projects. Planners determined that the design of the assembly should fit the contours of the land, taking advantage of existing grades and slopes so as to avoid excessive cuts and fills. This decision precipitated a debate over building design. The broken topography made the construction of one central facility impractical. Some advocated building "clusters" of small, self-contained campuses for up to six hundred people, each complete with its own dining hall.

A closer look at this proposal revealed that it would be too expensive for an assembly intended to accommodate 3,500 people. Instead, participants decided to construct one facility, with buildings in alternate locations. This decision allowed architects to design structures around a master plan and to erect them in stages, all of which limited the initial amount of capital required to begin the project. Harry Stagg suggested the installation of a small train system to shuttle attendees between locations and jokingly applied for the job of engineer.[32]

Erecting the assembly at Glorieta proved an expensive undertaking. Although the Sunday School Board was to construct and maintain the property, that agency lacked the funds to fully underwrite the project. In order to "jump start" the building process, the Southern Baptist Convention authorized a "capital campaign" in an attempt to raise several million dollars. Utilizing a brochure entitled, "Presenting Glorieta—In the Land of Enchantment," the convention hoped to encourage individuals as well as state conventions to invest in their denomination's future. T. L. Holcomb pledged the Sunday School Board to match all contributions dollar for dollar up to $100,000.[33]

In a not-too-subtle move to increase contributions, the Sunday School Board decided to name the administration building "New Mexico Hall." Holcomb informed Stagg of this honor and then advised him that the BCNM would have to contribute $100,000 toward the cost of construction. State leaders were furious. Recalling the incident, Stagg remembered: "When I presented that to our state Mission Board in the student center at the university in Albuquerque, I thought they were going to throw me out."[34] The board reconsidered and voted to receive gifts of $100,000 toward building the hall.

Work on the property commenced when Herron took over as manager in June 1950. During the first year, he authorized a property survey, had fences built, wells drilled, sewer lines laid, the sewage plant constructed, electric lines run, and the road plan developed. The second year, 1951, expenditures produced more tangible results. Initial-phase construction began on several structures, including the dining hall, Holcomb Auditorium, and New Mexico Hall. Designers from the Sunday School Board decided to construct the buildings in the Territorial style of architecture, deeming it the most appropriate for the region. As an adaptation of the Eastern Colonial style it might appeal to people visiting from the East as well as those who lived in the West.[35]

Construction proceeded slowly due to inclement weather and the difficulty of obtaining building materials. The Korean War also interrupted regular shipments and, in some cases, caused cancellation of contracts. One bright spot, however, was the cooperation of the Santa Fe Railroad. Glorieta lay along the Chicago to Los Angeles route. Company officials authorized the building of a special siding that allowed delivery of supplies directly to the site.[36]

The slow pace of construction created doubt among Westerners concerning whether the assembly would ever be the mammoth undertaking promised. During the summer of 1951, a train carrying people to the Southern Baptist Convention in San Francisco stopped at Glorieta. Governor Edwin L. Meacham came from Santa Fe to greet them. Herron gave a tour of the facility, showing where the buildings would be. People walked around for about an hour and then got back on the train, apparently unimpressed. In December, possibly with this reaction in mind, T. L. Holcomb suggested a get-acquainted week at Glorieta for August 7–13, 1952.[37]

With only eight months of preparation time, the thought of having the site suitable for even a small gathering seemed foolish to Herron. Nevertheless, he proceeded with the plan, and things went well until a few weeks before the event. In July 1952, union workers struck, protesting the use of nonunion carpenters at half-pay. Southern Baptists had used union labor for all contracted work at Glorieta, but, in addition, the assembly had hired retired carpenters to do small projects around the grounds. These were older individuals who needed jobs but were physically unable to do more than half a day's work.

The strike meant that the auditorium would not be finished for "Pioneer

Week." Undeterred, Herron sent out a distress call to churches in Santa Fe, Los Alamos, and Las Vegas for help in erecting temporary facilities. He ordered lumber from a nearby mill to construct a tabernacle and arranged for a 40 × 60 tent for use as a dining hall.[38]

The day before Pioneer Week began, a union official asked to see Herron. He inquired about what they were going to do concerning the upcoming meeting. Herron told him that they were going to hold it. "Where?" The man asked. Herron pointed to the tent and replied, "Over there." Thirty minutes later the pickets disappeared.[39]

Pioneer Week proved a huge success. It cemented the acceptance of the site as appropriate for Southern Baptist work. Registrants totaled 1,417 people from seventeen states. Conditions were primitive. Women slept on cots in a barn, labeled the "horse lot," and the men slept in a log structure with shavings on the floor, called the "pig pen." Campers also spread bedrolls at the ranch house and on the floor of unfinished Texas Hall. Many stayed in tents, trailers, campers, and station wagons. Shared hardships bind people, however, and at Glorieta's first gathering, East and West came together.

T. L. Holcomb served as presiding officer for the week. The initial meeting focused on the achievements and future plans for Glorieta. The remaining six days featured Bible study and inspirational messages in the morning and evening. Afternoons were open for recreation. (This arrangement established the pattern for the assembly's subsequent programs.) Prominent denominational leaders also attended, including James Sullivan, Holcomb's successor at the Sunday School Board; W. A. Criswell, pastor of First Baptist Church in Dallas; and Duke McCall. New Mexican Baptists were there in force. Stagg reminded his constituency that the eyes of the Southern Baptist Convention were upon them.

Enthusiasm mounted as the people participated in groundbreaking ceremonies for seven more buildings. With the dining hall, auditorium, and administration units already under construction, Herron felt confident that the eight major structures would be ready for the scheduled first full summer of activities in 1953.[40] Pioneer Week, combined with the start of a second phase of construction, cured the skepticism about Southern Baptist commitment to construct a major assembly facility in the West. The troubles at Glorieta seemed finally at an end. The first full season in 1953 recorded 35,758 guest days.[41] Then came the summer of 1955.

The Santa Fe County Assessor's office declared the assembly to be a "resort" and assessed its property value at $10 million. In response, the Sunday School Board filed suit claiming the Glorieta assembly to be a "religious conference center." If the county won, the tax burden would force the new facility to close. During the trial, Harry Stagg gave testimony tracing the history of the assembly to the present day. At the noon recess, the Baptist contingent was having lunch when their lawyer arrived sporting a wide grin. Counsel for the county had requested that the case be dropped and settled out of court. He had told the judge, "I cannot get one answer out of Dr. Stagg which I can use on our side of the case. We will simply have to make the necessary adjustments concerning the requests of the assembly and the Sunday School Board."[42] The Glorieta assembly emerged from the encounter unscathed, but the taxation issue remained a constant threat.

Baptists continued to expand the assembly, finally completing the building program in 1966. By then the grounds had expanded to 2,500 acres with more than two hundred buildings.[43] Guest days eventually totaled as high as 250,000 per year.[44] In addition to the construction of a "city" in the mountains, the tale contains another story, one that turned the assembly at Glorieta into an environmental showcase.

Architects had designed the Glorieta assembly as a place for Southern Baptists to come for training, but it also became a conservation project. Many years of hard use as a homestead had denuded the landscape. The soil needed preserving, so planners introduced a reforestation program. An eighteen-acre parcel near the entrance proved especially eroded. To prevent further damage, Herron had the land terraced. Endeavoring to determine how best to use the parcel, he considered several options and chose to turn the area into a formal garden. The Sunday School Board, however, considered his idea impractical and too expensive. Herron persisted and finally obtained approval for it as part of the overall plan to landscape the entire 1,300 acres. Herron hired C. E. Holland, former state park commissioner, as the landscape engineer. When he died a year later, his friend, Cecil Pragnell, became director of the project.[45]

Pragnell took over in 1954 at the age of seventy-two and spent a year gathering ideas, researching, and planning the garden. He was fond of quoting a line from Elizabeth Barrett Browning: "Earth is crammed with heaven, and every common bush afire with God." Inspired by her poetry, he conceived the Glorieta property as an "outdoor cathedral." Talking with visitors at the assembly, Pragnell described his vision:

This garden must be a living testimony to the goodness of God. It must be dedicated to God; it must be an inspiration to the worship of God. Every tree an inspiration, every lowly clod a lyric, every star a prayer, every peak a stepping stone to God.[46]

Pragnell constructed an Italian Belvedere garden, consisting of nine terraces bisected by a rock-lined fountain that cascaded down 75 feet high and was 1,000 feet in length. On either side were flagstone walkways surrounded by flowers and trees. Within the eighteen acres were numerous specialty gardens. At the bottom lay a pool garden with a 3,600-square-foot pond lined with irises, pansies, and verbena. Pragnell also created a children's garden with plants mentioned in the Psalms, the book of Proverbs, and Song of Solomon. The iris garden, which was the highest in elevation and one of the five largest in the United States, was his favorite project. With the help of the New Mexico and the National Iris Societies, Pragnell planted ten thousand irises, representing more than a thousand varieties.

In addition, Pragnell created a Shakespearean garden, with seeds sent by friends from plants growing in the poet's own garden at Stratford-upon-Avon. For three years, Pragnell also labored to create a "Bible garden" that displayed the herbs, grains, and trees found in the Near East. During this project, he received aid from the foreign minister of Iraq, the Israeli Embassy in Washington, and several Jewish societies in Los Angeles. Other specialty gardens included an herb garden with plants for cooking and healing, a music garden, and a replica of the Garden of Gethsemane.[47]

In creating this outdoor cathedral, Pragnell relied on the handiwork of Hispanic laborers, noting that they had a special talent for working in stone and building with wood. With their aid, he transplanted more than 16,000 conifers, representing more than twenty-seven varieties of evergreen trees. He also included several thousand aspen, cottonwood, Russian olive, elm, acacia, juniper, and apple trees. The greatest challenge for Pragnell was to find plants that bloomed for a three-month period at a 7,500-foot elevation. Friends and interested donors throughout the United States and Europe contributed a variety of flora, leading to the planting of 150,000 perennials. His greenhouses produced an additional 70,000 annuals and developed a new variety of delphinium named "Glorieta." Pragnell used native plants extensively, bringing in every variety that would grow at that altitude. He had especially good results with columbines.[48]

Most visitors to the assembly only knew Cecil Pragnell as that "kind old man" who gave talks about the flowers on Sunday afternoons. Like the Glorieta assembly itself, his story was unique. Pragnell came to New Mexico in 1936 to landscape Los Pablanos Ranch along the Rio Grande. Like so many artists, he fell in love with the state and took the job of Bernalillo County extension agent to enable him to stay. He was no ordinary horticulturist, however; his father had been royal gardener to Queen Victoria and had sailed with Darwin on his epic voyage aboard the H.M.S. Beagle to the Galapagos Islands. As a child, Pragnell learned his craft by helping his father tend the queen's estates. As a young man, he toured Europe and the Far East, studying gardens and researching exotic plants. His command of landscape architecture led to his employment by dignitaries and heads of state, including Edward VII of England and the sultan of Persia. Glorieta was his last project and possibly his finest. By the time he retired at age eighty in 1962, his colleagues referred to his work there as "the finest mountain gardens in the world."[49]

❧

As the Southern Baptist Convention expanded out of the South, the Western Assembly served as a bridge uniting sections and becoming an agent of cohesion amidst increasing diversity. In this capacity, the Glorieta assembly influenced the denomination in numerous ways. First, it helped bring about sectional unity. North, South, East, and West came together around a common Baptist cause. Second, the New Mexico site aided the convention in stepping out from its traditional "Southern mind-set." Expansion brought in diverse groups. The new forms of worship and evangelism deemed necessary to reach these people made Southern Baptists more pluralistic and accepting in their approach. Third, the Glorieta venture helped break down racial barriers.

Through Glorieta, the Southern Baptist Convention experienced the diversity of life outside the South. Slowly, and sometimes jarringly, Southern Baptists adjusted to distinct peoples and cultures. The BCNM, however, encountered heterogeneity long before the rest of the denomination. During the period from 1938 to 1960, the BCNM's growth and expansion required the building of a Baptist identity in the midst of cultural, racial, and religious pluralism. Responding to a different environment forced the BCNM to explore new avenues of ministry and social involvement.

New Mexico Baptists and Social Issues: 1938 to 1960

Not only was the state convention busy building a strong corporate struc-ture and erecting denominational edifices, it was equally active in speaking out on issues of concern to Baptists. Leading this crusade was the *Baptist New Mexican*'s aggressive editor Lewis A. Myers, who directed the newspaper from 1947 to 1959.[1] To ensure that it was not simply a mouthpiece of the Southern Baptist Convention (SBC), Myers solicited articles from New Mexico Baptists who had attended denominational meetings rather than just use press releases from agency headquarters. At the local level, he encouraged leaders and laypersons alike to express their views.

Traditionally, Southern Baptists have made temperance and gambling their primary social concerns, and from 1938 to 1960 New Mexico Baptists followed suit. Charging that drinking was a threat to the welfare of the nation, the state convention passed numerous resolutions protesting the sale and use of alcoholic beverages, calling for an immediate return to prohibition in New Mexico through local option and county option. In 1945, the Reverend C. Paul Rich proposed that a copy of the current protest be sent to Harry Truman along with a letter expressing New Mexico Baptists' regret that as a professed Baptist the president favored the use of strong drink.[2]

Baptists also applied pressure at the state level. The convention petitioned Governor Meacham to use his authority to stop all violations in the issuance of liquor licenses. As a member of the New Mexico Temperance League, Baptists were instrumental in having state law 61-526-27 enacted. This measure restricted licenses to one for every 1,500 people in the state.[3] Baptists took the position that alcohol abuse was a moral problem, not a disease. They charged the liquor industry with propagating the "disease" concept so that they could ask for public funds to take care of the human wreckage caused by drinking. Baptists argued that liquor propagandists used this line of reasoning to separate the use of alcohol from alcoholism.[4]

During the 1940s, the *Baptist New Mexican* ran numerous editorials and articles concerning the devastating effect that alcohol had on people and society, occasionally devoting an entire issue to the subject. This campaign continued into the 1950s, but as the decade wore on the intensity lessened. Still, opposition to the use of spirits continued to be a primary plank in New Mexico Baptist social policy, although by 1960 it no longer occupied the center stage of the convention's social concerns.

Next to strong drink, Baptists considered gambling the greatest destroyer of home life. The Harriman Lottery, proposed in 1938 to endow the Carrie Tingley Hospital for crippled children at Hot Springs (now Truth or Consequences), became the catalyst that provoked concerted action. At their 1938 annual meeting, New Mexico Baptists passed a resolution condemning the bill. In addition, the convention voiced its distress over the possible legalization of gambling on horse racing and called for stricter enforcement of laws prohibiting the use of slot machines. In a letter to Clyde Tingley, Stagg voiced the concern of his fifteen-thousand-member organization, endorsing the governor's decision to defer action on the Harriman initiative. First Baptist Church in Santa Fe, along with several private citizens, also lodged a protest. Determined to meet the challenges to the moral health of the state, the convention appointed a Social Service Committee to watch for actions detrimental to the teachings of the church.[5]

In further action, the convention endorsed the antigambling campaign led by the Association for the Repeal of the New Mexico Para-Mutual Betting Law. In 1960, the BCNM vigorously campaigned against a proposed national lottery.[6] For New Mexico's Baptists, gambling was simply the taking of another's possessions without being accused of theft.

Religious Freedom

Even though issues regarding personal piety received continued attention, it was in the area of religious liberty that New Mexico Baptists expended their greatest efforts in the postwar years. A resurgence of proposed alliances among national ecclesiastical bodies after the war became a source of concern among the clergy. Preaching the annual sermon at the state convention in 1946, the Reverend L. M. Walker spoke on "safeguarding religious liberties." He asserted that Christian unity movements might threaten cherished Baptist doctrines.[7] Ecumenism and its attendant dangers engaged Baptist thinking for the next fifteen years. A constant barrage of editorials and articles appeared in the *Baptist New Mexican,* written by New Mexicans and others throughout the Southern states who championed the cause of exclusivity.

Missions and religious freedom dominated the dialogue. Leaders and laity alike expressed concern that submission to an interdenominational body might restrict their efforts at evangelism. This alone was enough to reject any outside affiliation. To ensure denominational distinctiveness, the New Mexico churches conducted a crusade once each year to stress Baptist beliefs and heritage. At the heart of this fear of ecumenism lay the perception that it might lead to a loss of individual freedom under group pressure.

New Mexico Baptists expressed deep concern about an increasing world movement toward "centralization." They perceived this trend in the realm of industry with its manufacturing associations; in labor, with unions; among farmers, with cooperatives; and in religious bodies through ecumenism. "Such organized groups are a part of our mechanized society," wrote Harry Stagg, and "their domination over the individual conscience must be resisted."[8] Ministers reminded their congregations that they were citizens of the Kingdom of God and that no other influence should divide them into opposing groups.

Not only was church unionism a move toward centralization, with the accompanying loss of distinctive beliefs, it was also a threat to diversity, attempting to produce a "generic religion."[9] Ecumenicism, if accepted, would threaten local church autonomy. Instead of congregations governing their own affairs, they would be subject to a hierarchy that might not share their beliefs. Lack of consensus in doctrine would place authority in the hands of mere human beings instead of the scriptures. For the sake of unity, Baptists would have to recognize as fellow Christians those who denied the virgin birth, deity of Christ, and biblical inerrancy.

Refusing to succumb to this consolidating trend in American Christianity, New Mexico Baptists fiercely asserted their distinctiveness and separateness. In so doing, the state convention rejected what they considered to be the "reductionism" that church union might bring to Christianity. In the drive for church unity, Baptists thought they saw a yearning for political power rather than spiritual strength. Social and political reform needed numbers, and Baptists claimed this was the motivation behind the movement. Sidestepping doctrinal questions would only result in spiritual weakness. Such an organization might tend toward regimentation. Conformity could become an obsession, thus making ecclesiastical bodies less tolerant of minorities and far more dictatorial.[10]

One of the effects of Landmarkism among Southern Baptists was the belief that all members should separate themselves from other denominations to be of one mind. Many New Mexico Baptists adhered to this more rigid doctrine, holding that worship with other groups would result in doctrinal confusion.[11] To maintain their distinctiveness, Baptists vigorously disseminated their beliefs, from the pulpit and in the pages of the *Baptist New Mexican*. Sermons on specific points of theology and articles dealing with Baptist practices, along with Sunday School notes for teachers, were regular features of the newspaper well into the late 1950s.

Commitment to the principle of religious liberty has long fueled the Baptist rejection of ecumenicism. But a separation of church and state issue occurring shortly after the end of World War II made it more than a doctrine for New Mexico Baptists. A conflict between two different religious cultures that had been simmering for almost one hundred years—public education—erupted. For nearly a century, the Catholic Church had acted in alliance with the state to help provide schooling. This practice led to a commingling of funds and personnel. State money supported parochial schools and robed clergy taught in public institutions. Baptists saw in this practice not only a violation of the Bill of Rights but also a threat to freedom of religion since it gave one ecclesiastical body preferential treatment over another. In 1947, concern led to a major confrontation in Dixon, a rural community located in the north-central part of the state. Even though New Mexico Baptists were not a participant in this conflict, they reacted as if it were theirs.

State officials had moved equipment from several public schools in the district to buildings owned by the Catholic Church and subsequently either abandoned or sold the structures without community consent. Nuns had received appointments to teaching positions formerly occupied by secular personnel, with minimal involvement from people living in the area. This policy was prevalent throughout New Mexico where nuns held 122 such posts. Their salaries were paid from public funds. Particularly galling to New Mexico Baptists was that these monies left the state, helping to finance the sisters' sponsoring order. Appropriations for Rio Arriba County, where Dixon was located, amounted to $65,000; the total for the state reached $250,000.

Dixon Protestant parents protested this state of affairs. They charged that Catholic doctrine infiltrated the public school curriculum and that their children's education suffered because of inadequately trained nuns. To provide public education free from sectarian influence, Protestant members of the Dixon community raised funds to construct a new school. A few days before opening, however, officials announced that a nun would head the school and that some of the teachers would also be sisters. Protestant citizens lodged protests with the county school board, but the board refused to act. On September 15, 1947, approximately fifty people journeyed to Santa Fe to attend a state education board hearing on the matter. Upon their arrival, the board voted to turn the meeting into a closed session, with only one member from the Dixon community allowed to represent the group. There was no opportunity to present objections, bring in witnesses, or request changes.[12]

Up to this point, the issue involved only a group of dissatisfied Protestant parents in the community of Dixon where Presbyterians had taken the leading role. Failure to have their concerns properly addressed also led to a limited Baptist involvement.[13] Offers of assistance from individual Baptists, combined with the denomination's reputation as a strong advocate of separation of church and state, led to a meeting at Albuquerque's First Baptist Church. Here it was determined that legal action was the only recourse.[14] New Mexico Baptists offered assistance with expenses. The Protestant parents filed suit on March 10, 1948, naming schools in ten counties as defendants. Included in the suit were state school superintendent Charles L. Rose and members of the State Board of Education, along with 144 Catholics from several religious orders for the purpose of stopping further "religious encroachment in the public schools."[15]

Archbishop Edwin V. Byrne was quick to respond: "The fact is that for nigh a half century Sisters and Brothers have fulfilled the educational needs of certain communities as public school teachers . . . to those public school authorities who felt they could not solve there [sic] educational needs and problems in any other way." After assuring that it was not the Catholic Church's intention to violate the "misunderstood" idea of separation of church and state, he went on to state: "It was only through a sense of duty of her mission to promote the welfare of human society that the church permitted Brothers and Sisters to accept the office of teacher in the public schools."[16]

The trial began on October 10, 1948, and was entered into the court records as *Zellers et al. v. Huff et al.* At the close of the deliberation, Judge E. T. Hensley announced that he would rule in favor of the plaintiffs. The trial established that in certain areas of New Mexico schooling, no separation of church and state existed. The decision required twenty-six schools in the ten counties listed in the suit to conform with the law. The ruling covered seven major points:

1. It barred by name 143 Catholic sisters and brothers from teaching in New Mexico public schools.
2. Required that sixteen Catholic buildings be replaced by publicly owned structures.
3. Necessitated the revamping of the state textbook system.
4. Prohibited the free transportation of parochial students in public school buses.
5. Prohibited the displaying of Catholic insignia in public schools.

6. Determined that present laws were inadequate to provide proper relief for the plaintiffs.
7. Acknowledged that there was no separation of church and state in the twenty-five schools named in the trial.

New Mexico Southern Baptists interpreted the verdict as a victory for the exercise of religious liberty. Concern regarding compliance, however, overshadowed their exuberance. Baptists felt that their best course of action was to monitor whether school districts were adhering to Judge Henley's ruling and to file contempt of court charges if they found violations.[17] Their fears proved prophetic.

The Catholic Church evaded the decision and the New Mexico state government ignored it. Rulings by the attorney general voided many points of the judgment, including the use of tax moneys for textbooks. The legislature passed a bill providing for public funds to be used to transport children to parochial schools. The governor signed the legislation into law, while admitting that it violated the court's decree and the U.S. Constitution. Conflict between Catholics and Protestants broke out again in 1952, this time in an alleged religious liberty violation over access to Jemez Pueblo, and a year later at Zia Pueblo. Both pueblos were fiercely Catholic and resisted any attempts at evangelization by Protestants. At Jemez, Indian converts to Protestantism lived under threat of having their property confiscated. Tribal elders also banned Baptist missionaries. One elder declared: "The pueblo is Catholic and we want no one winning the people away from the faith." At Zia, conditions were more extreme. The Catholic priest told Protestant converts either to recant or suffer penalties. The pueblo government denied converts land and water rights. New Mexico Baptists sought redress in the courts claiming violation of freedom of religion. In both cases, however, the judges avoided the issue, citing lack of jurisdiction.[18] As the decade drew to a close, the struggle for separation of church and state and religious liberty shifted from schools and access to Indian reservations to the upcoming presidential election.

The above grievances served to intensify New Mexico Baptists' opposition to John F. Kennedy's bid for the presidency. State leaders were outspoken concerning their fear that, if Kennedy were elected, the nation would suffer the usurpation of its laws and constitutional guarantees in the same way that Protestants had suffered in New Mexico. A leading advocate of this position was Dr. William D. Wyatt, pastor at First Baptist Church in Albuquerque. In numerous sermons and articles, he contrasted Baptist and Catholic doctrines. Often citing works by Catholic theologians, he sought to demonstrate that the Vatican advocated the state support of religion, a position in direct conflict with the Baptist doctrine of separation of church and state and freedom of worship.[19]

At the heart of New Mexico Baptists' concern over Kennedy's candidacy was the fear that should a member of the Roman Catholic Church be elected it would give that body special representation in the presidential orbit. Baptists in the state feared that in this case the interests of the Vatican might supersede those of the United States.[20] In the Southwest it certainly appeared that this had occurred. State officials had violated the Constitution, said Baptist leaders, by regularly using tax moneys for private education. After a decade of battling the Catholic Church over separation of church and state, leaders and laity were apprehensive. As the election approached, anxiety mounted. When Kennedy won they were disheartened.

Despite their fears, the Vatican did not establish a branch office at 1600 Pennsylvania Avenue. Instead, the battle to secure religious freedom in New Mexico shaped Baptists in ways they had not expected. The struggle actually enhanced denominational identity by forcing them to define their beliefs in relation to the Catholic Church.[21] This battle, in turn, served to motivate the membership's efforts in missions and evangelism, contributing to an increased presence for the convention.

Race Relations

New Mexico Baptists' own religious minority status, combined with living in a pluralistic environment, made them sensitive to racial prejudice. On this issue, the BCNM departed from the denominational mainstream. Less than a week after the bombing of Pearl Harbor, Joseph B. Underwood, a New Mexico pastor, gave expression to this conviction. Writing in the *Baptist New Mexican,* Underwood pointed out that "as Christians we should all remember our guilt and repent of the selfishness in us that is the root of war." He reminded his readers that "God was also the God of the Japanese as well." Derogatory terms such as "wops" and "japs" were unacceptable for Christians since the Japanese were also made in the image of God.[22]

A. C. Miller, another Baptist pastor and contributor to the *Baptist New Mexican,* wrote that each race had God-given gifts for the benefit of all humanity. Therefore, no one race should keep another in submission. He warned Baptists about judging others by making the Bible conform to their own racial prejudices. The Christian position was that God loves all. Christians, therefore, needed to examine their own political, economic, and civic behavior to see that everyone received equal treatment.[23]

This attitude, aired by individual Baptists, became the official policy of the Baptist Convention of New Mexico (BCNM). In a 1948 resolution, that body supported the Social Service Commission's stand against racial discrimination and injustice. Likewise the editor of the *Baptist New Mexican*, Lewis A. Myers, ran a column titled "Commending the Commendable," where he voiced the New Mexico Baptist position on racial issues.

Although some SBC agency actions received approval, Myers was quick to condemn other activities. A special point of contention was the denomination's educational policies. Myers pointed to the hypocritical practice prevalent in Southern Baptist colleges and seminaries of not admitting Blacks. This policy, he said, contradicted the denomination's universalist missionary claims. When it was announced in 1951 that three of the Southern Baptist seminaries would accept Black men for admission, he demanded to know why Black women should not have the same opportunity. Not content to stop there, Myers took the denomination to task over racial intolerance, unfair practices in trade relationships, and the "Dixieite" attitude found across the "Bible Belt."[24]

When the Christian Life Commission passed a resolution supporting school desegregation in 1954, New Mexico Baptists were quick to note that it did not go far enough. When, they asked, will segregation end at the local church? Is separation of the races in any form consistent with the cross of Christ? Were Baptists better than their neighbors and not their brother's keeper? These questions, they asserted, still needed answers.[25]

Within their own ranks, Baptists in New Mexico attempted to reach out to other ethnic groups. In June 1953, an international-interracial youth camp began at Inlow Camp for the purpose of establishing relationships across racial barriers, focusing on the avowed purpose of teaching children to love those who were different from themselves. Riverside and Parkview Baptist churches in Albuquerque, together with the Home Mission Board, sponsored "friendship centers" as a means of reaching all peoples within a specified geographical area. The Reverend Robert Lee Brown, Jr., became the first Black pastor elected president of the Albuquerque Baptist Ministers Association in 1956. All Black Baptist churches in the state had the option of joining district associations. R. Y. Bradford, speaking at the Baptist church in Chama, noted that at a time of racial tension nationwide (1958), in New Mexico, Anglos, Hispanics, Native Americans, and Blacks could sit side by side on Sunday morning without prejudice.[26]

The liberalized racial policy found among Baptist churches in New Mexico might have remained an aberration among Southern Baptists had it not been for the presence of the Western Assembly site in the state. Southern segregation and Western accommodation collided at Glorieta. In 1953, an incident occurred that challenged such openness.

Annie Filmore, a Black woman from Durham, North Carolina, arrived at Glorieta during the summer of 1953 seeking inspirational training. Prohibited from attending Ridgecrest, the SBC's assembly site in the East, she had reasoned that in the West things might be different. Disembarking at the entrance to the encampment from the bus that had transported her across the continent, she walked toward a car parked nearby. Behind the wheel sat Dale Danielson, a teenager from Albuquerque, who was spending the summer helping to build the family cabin at the conference center. He offered to take Ms. Filmore to New Mexico Hall where she could check in. Her arrival caught the staff by surprise. No one knew quite what to do. Observing the turmoil, Danielson later remembered: "At the Assembly offices I could tell a crisis was brewing when she disappeared into the inner sanctums and the door closed. I hung around, fearful of what might be happening." Emerging from her ad hoc meeting, Ms. Filmore asked Danielson to take her back to the gate so she could catch the bus. "They will let me stay only if I stay in Texas Hall all by myself. The room is designed for three and I must pay the triple rate. I don't have enough money to stay."[27]

Refusing to let her depart, Danielson insisted that she stay with his family at their cabin. Reflecting over the event years later, he recalled that what was intended to be an act of kindness toward Ms. Filmore turned out to be a greater blessing for himself and his mother. Ms. Filmore's Bible reading and prayer became an inspiration not only for the Danielsons, but also for the ladies attending the Women's Missionary Union conference, who made Ms. Filmore their favorite guest.[28] Quietly, and without direct confrontation, this action served notice to Southern Baptists at Glorieta that racial discrimination would not be countenanced in the West.

The incident, however, infuriated the *Baptist New Mexican*'s editor, Lewis Myers, who was anything but quiet. He labeled the action of Glorieta's officials one of blatant economic persecution designed to drive her away. "It undid everything western Baptists strove for in getting Glorieta here," he said. "We are a pageant of multiple peoples living together in diversity and sharing. God has made of one blood all nations."[29] Observing a year later that several Blacks had sought entrance to Glorieta and had been accommodated, he wrote: "Out here in the great Southwest where live four dominant races, the world can be shown what Christian amity can do."[30]

CHAPTER 5

Hispanic and Native American Missions

This desire to spread the Southern Baptist message to all races in the state carried over into the missions program of the BCNM. At a meeting held in Prescott, Arizona, on May 26–27, 1947, the BCNM turned down an offer to spearhead SBC work in Colorado, Wyoming, Nebraska, South Dakota, and Wyoming, citing its responsibility to reach the "language people" (people whose native language was not English) of New Mexico.[31] Speaking as director of missions, Gerald B. Palmer stipulated that there was "no difference between the Anglo and the Hispanic or the White man and the Indian." Scripture opened the door to all who believed, making it everyone's responsibility to see that the gospel was presented throughout the state. He noted that ethnic believers were "part of our everyday life—our neighbors, our friends, our relations and, above all, fellow Baptists."[32]

New Mexico Baptist work among Hispanics and Native Americans progressed slowly. Only two missionaries ministered to the Hispanic population in 1938. Ten small churches plus a few missions, with a membership of nearly five hundred persons, represented several decades of effort. Among Native Americans, the situation was even less encouraging. Two churches, one at Isleta Pueblo and another at Alamo (Navajo territory), marked the extent of Baptist work in the state. By the end of World War II, however, both the state and national conventions were financially able to renew their efforts. In 1947, the BCNM resumed publication of the Hispanic and Native American Baptist newspapers. The Home Mission Board provided the personnel. By 1950, fifty-five missionaries to ethnic groups served in the field.[33]

In the early 1950s, the work began to move forward dramatically. Coordinating efforts between the Home and State Mission Boards proved to be the catalyst. Beginning in 1953, all language work (i.e., work among Native Americans and Hispanics) became a cooperative effort between the state and national mission boards. Then in 1960, full operational control was transferred to the state convention. The Home Mission Board, however, continued to supply 88 percent of the funds. This restructuring gave the BCNM a greater role in the development and direction of the work.[34]

Joint operations accelerated missions work. By 1957, 70 missionaries served Indian and Hispanic Baptists and more than half a million dollars was spent on buildings. In addition, the State Mission Board assisted with $110,000 for salaries and expenses. Three years later, monetary and personnel commitments registered substantial gains. Statistics for 1960 show 90 missionaries employed (out of 1,282 nationwide), with an annual budget of $260,000. The Home Mission Board contributed $231,400 and the state the remainder. Despite all these efforts, however, the number of converts was disappointing. By 1960, there were only 1,235 Hispanic and 965 Native American Baptists, accounting for only 2.85 percent of the total membership.[35]

Why were the results so meager? Baptists encountered what the Presbyterians, Congregationalists, Methodists, and United Brethren had experienced decades before. The Native American and Hispanic peoples of the state were proud of their inherited traditions and refused to change. Earlier efforts of evangelization by these denominations through education and Bible reading had failed to bring about any mass conversions to Protestantism. For their part, New Mexico Baptists found that simply proclaiming an open racial policy and evangelizing in a Southern style did not produce any substantial number of converts either. Baptist theology and practice were born in an environment of persecution, where religious liberty was often subordinate to ecclesiastical authority. Such treatment produced a fiercely individualistic form of Christian belief. Baptist polity and beliefs developed more out of a desire to preserve religious freedom than to develop a Christian community. It is not surprising, then, that Southern Baptists failed to effectively evangelize Native Americans and Hispanics, whose societies remained largely communally based.

Realigning Religion

In many areas, the New Mexico Southern Baptist commitment to missions and evangelism collided head on with the state's religious and cultural environment. Unlike many of their ecclesiastical cousins who prior to World War II came to an uneasy acceptance of religious pluralism (that all roads lead to God), Baptists continued to believe that salvation came only through a personal acceptance of Christ. However, historically Baptists had always accepted religious diversity (the right of each person to worship God in his or her own way). This attitude was simply a matter of respecting an individual's freedom of conscience, also very much a Baptist tradition. Of course, unless people had the opportunity to hear the gospel message from a Southern Baptist perspective, their choice of how to worship could not be said to be "fully free." Empowered by this conviction, the BCNM's theology equipped Baptists to take full advantage of the new opportunity that the war offered for denominational expansion.

Postwar evangelism encountered ecclesiastical as well as cultural barriers. At no time in the history of the SBC had Baptists encountered such formidable opposition. Departing from the denomination's traditional role of political passivity (alcohol and gambling excepted), New Mexico Baptists went to battle over their principles of separation of church and state and religious freedom. In the face of Catholic hegemony, Baptists challenged the religious status quo. In the process, they brought changes to New Mexican society.

By 1960, the New Mexico religious landscape had undergone a major restructuring. Baptists contributed to that change in three ways. While still preponderant in the southeastern part of the state, the denomination was no longer restricted to a narrow beachhead along the Texas and Oklahoma borders. Through an aggressive program of church planting, evangelism, and missionary activity, New Mexico Southern Baptists could now be found in all parts of the state. Except for isolated Hispanic villages in the north-central mountains and various pueblos, virtually every community in the state had a Baptist presence. New Mexico could no longer ignore the Baptist influence. Second, legal battles over sectarian influence in the public schools, along with the issue of religious freedom in the pueblos, drove a wedge into the state's historic religious systems. Finally, with the establishment of the assembly at Glorieta, the Archdiocese of Santa Fe had to accept that a western bastion of the nation's largest Protestant denomination was, literally, located in its backyard.

David may not have toppled Goliath, but from 1960 forward, the Roman Catholic Church in New Mexico could not disregard Protestants in general or Southern Baptists in particular. Even though the archbishop was still clearly the most important ecclesiastical personage in New Mexico, he no longer held undisputed sway in the state's religious affairs. After 1960, accommodation would characterize not only Protestant attitudes toward other religious groups, but, especially after Vatican II, Catholic as well. A new era of spiritual détente lay on the horizon. Baptists played a major role in bringing about this change.

Storm Warnings

As New Mexico Baptists basked in their newfound prominence, storm clouds were beginning to gather. In a 1960 open letter to the Southern Baptist Convention, Duke McCall, president of Southern Seminary, commented that spiritual pride had blinded the Southern Baptists to warning flags throughout the denomination. He pointed to an Executive Committee directive that informed SBC agencies not to expect full support from the convention's Cooperative Program for the next year or two. Departments lowered their goals from one fourth to one third those of 1959. Total enrollment in seminaries was down from a peak in 1957. The Foreign Mission Board did not have enough prepared volunteers to make all appointments that it had planned for 1960.[36]

Mirroring this observation, articles had also begun to appear in the *Baptist New Mexican* pointing to the failure of the church to live up to its spiritual responsibilities. People were turning aside from the teaching of scripture and failing to support the programs of the church. Other articles called for a great spiritual awakening if America was to survive. Still others placed the blame on the failure of the church to shoulder its social obligations and that failure to do so weakened the whole evangelistic effort. Lewis Myers commented in the 1958 annual report that many church members now reserved for themselves privileges formerly considered non-Christian. He felt that this portended a moral decline.[37] From the mid-1950s forward, there was a noticeable decline in the number of theologically oriented articles. At the same time, promotional pieces began increasing. Near the end of the decade, the Sunday School lesson was dropped and replaced by a weekly feature on "counseling."

A report by Harry Stagg in 1960 contained even more disturbing news. He noted that the BCNM was barely holding its own in the number of baptisms. Enrollments in the various departments were struggling to maintain the same numbers. There also seemed to be a considerable leveling off in economic conditions and general business activity throughout the state. This downturn had led to a decrease in gifts to the Cooperative Program. To stay solvent, the state convention adopted the 1959 operational plan.[38] For twenty-two years, Southern Baptists in New Mexico had experienced an era of great expansion. As the 1960s appeared on the horizon, however, this great leap forward was about to come to an end.

1. Harry and Alma Stagg in Gallup, New Mexico, late 1920s.

2. New Mexico Baptist Orphan's Home at new location in Portales, 1926.

Baptist College.   ALAMOGORDO, New Mexico.

3. Baptists' first attempt at a college in Alamogordo. Financial difficulties forced its closing in 1911.

4. Baptist Hospital in Clovis, circa 1937. The hospital operated from 1920 to 1939, and closed when the county government built a new facility.

5. New Mexico Boys' Ranch. Originally a Kiwanis project, the BCNM reorganized the facility in 1952.

6. Aerial view of Glorieta Conference Center.

7. Aerial view of Glorieta assembly facilities before the completion of Holcomb Auditorium.

8. E. A. Herron, first manager of Glorieta assembly facilities. Herron was responsible for obtaining appropriations for the gardens.

9. Chama Valley Medical Center (also known as Parkview) in the 1950s.

10. Christian Native Americans. From left to right: Rose Naranjo, Santa Clara Pueblo; Gladys Percz, Hopi; Tillie Holcomb, Navajo; and Viola Brewer, Cherokee.

11. Alamo Indian Mission, 1933.

12. C. W. Stumph with Juan Colorado, age 102, at Alamo Reservation in 1956.

New Mexico Baptists in Turmoil: 1961 to 1974

"The gospel is challenged today as never before."[1] This assertion by Bruce Morgan, professor of religion at Amherst College, graphically described the position in which Baptists found themselves as a new decade dawned. Morgan went on to state that the contemporary age had become "post-Christian" and those who dismissed it as just a period of history did not understand the times. Samuel Miller of Harvard agreed. He claimed that "Christianity may be at death's door, the critical period of no return may have passed."[2]

Speaking in 1969 at the Baptist Convention of New Mexico's (BCNM) annual meeting, Joseph R. Estes of the Home Mission Board (HMB) wrestled with this new situation. He noted that "The eyes of the world upon the church are negative. They do not see that we have been relevant to any of the major issues of life."[3] Addressing the state Women's Missionary Union (WMU) convention, Harry Stagg also agonized over attempts to eliminate Christian teachings and influences from society.[4]

These changes proved almost incomprehensible to New Mexico Baptists.[5] Only a few years before, it seemed that the whole nation was clamoring to join their churches. The fallout from this massive paradigm shift brought about a flurry of analysis among Baptists as they attempted to identify what went wrong.

Horace Burns, editor of the *Baptist New Mexican,* commented that "It is not enough to simply rely upon our faith in God and become oblivious to the world in which we live. There are some things to be done, there are needs to be met. There are hungry people, poor people, and there are millions of people who do not know that New Testament Christianity offers a better way of life."[6] Others advocated intensifying the flames of evangelism. Some thought that the problem lay with the failure to instill the rich American legacy in the younger generation. Cultivating a spiritual heritage of Christ in their hearts would bring restoration. Still others pointed to changing social factors, such as the population explosion, modern trends in education, and new ethics and morality, along with increased leisure time and mobility.

In adjusting to these developments, the denomination underwent radical change, setting the pattern for the rest of the century. The rapid growth rate of the 1940s and 1950s slowed significantly. More disturbing, attendance decreased in Sunday School, Training Union, Brotherhood, and WMU meetings. Worse still, baptisms began to fall.

Change also altered the pastorate. Addressing this issue in 1966, Convention president John Parrott stated, "We do not have the great men of yesteryear, because we are not growing them. . . . Rather, we are turning our preachers into denominational promoters, administrators, executives, public relations men, counselors etc., and we do not give them time nor opportunity to grow to spiritual gianthood."[7] A survey the Southern Baptist Convention (SBC) directed in 1971 added substance to Parrott's observation. Pollsters discovered that ministers spent only thirty-eight minutes a day preparing to preach, but over seven hours on administration.[8]

Bureaucratization of the church paralleled the change from pastor to administrator. Traditional ministries and programs proved inadequate to meet the ever-increasing needs of a diverse membership. In response, churches began to significantly increase the size of their paid staffs. At the same time, a larger percentage of the offering now went to cover local expenses, thus reducing funds available for outreach. As professionals took over more and more of the work, the laity became less involved.

Attempting to function amid the massive turmoil of the decade, and at the same time adjust to the changes in ministry, the BCNM experienced an overwhelming sense of frustration. Speaking to the convention in 1971, president Roy Luper made the following critical observation: "The church has faced crises in every generation but perhaps never before has it faced crises such as we now face in the twentieth century. The church has been persecuted, tried and criticized, but today it is simply being ignored."[9]

A Convention in Turmoil

Seemingly unaware of the approaching storm, the State Mission Board began the decade by revealing plans for increased activity in every department, with a goal to reach one hundred thousand in membership by 1967. It was not to be—1961 turned out to be a terrible year. For the first time since 1938 the BCNM began to record decreases in gifts to the Cooperative Program and missions.[10] In addition, that same year recorded the largest change in personnel in convention history. Joseph Underwood, secretary of promotion and stewardship, left to go to the Foreign Mission Board. Sunday School Secretary W. J. Lites retired. Eva Inlow retired, and her assistant Bernice

Elliott joined the HMB. H. C. Reavis, a bastion of BCNM stability since the 1930s, announced his retirement as bookstore manager effective in 1962.

Internal problems also surfaced. The circulation of the *Baptist New Mexican,* which had reached "saturation" in the 1950s, now began to decline. The nonresident membership problem continued to grow.[11] Southern Baptists nationwide had an absentee affiliation of 27 percent. In New Mexico a random sampling placed that figure at 32 percent.[12] Looking for answers, church leaders proffered two explanations: a lack of denominational loyalty and too much comfort.[13] As the convention grew, complacency set in, reducing the desire to evangelize.

Apathy impacted contributions. During the first three years of the decade, contributions had stagnated. Shortage of funds handicapped the work of many departments, seriously undermining the mission of the convention. Jeff Rutherford, new secretary of promotion and stewardship, pointed out that the convention had not reached a Cooperative Program goal since 1959.[14]

Dismal financial and programmatic conditions continued. A State Mission Board report in 1964 quoted Harry Stagg as saying, "We realize more and more that we are laboring under difficult circumstances. These are days of uncertainty, frustration and turmoil."[15] At the Brotherhood convention, Stagg further enumerated his concerns against a backdrop of declining statistics among Baptist churches in the state, showing losses in all programs except for participants in the music ministry.[16]

Reminiscent of the 1920s, the BCNM, nevertheless, continued to push forward with convention projects despite the deteriorating financial environment. The convention in 1963 undertook to assist Brotherhood director H. C. Sivells in purchasing a 168-acre camp near Cloudcroft for use by the Royal Ambassadors, which became known as Sivells Camp. The SBC had transferred the program from the WMU to the Brotherhood in 1958. Not having a facility of their own, they continued to hold the boys' camps at Inlow Camp. To maintain organizational integrity, the Brotherhood deemed a separate property to be a necessity. The land cost $28,000, and the State Mission Board assisted with $15,000 to help develop the property. In 1963, the first year, 496 campers used the grounds.[17]

Raising the money to pay for the camp's purchase became the responsibility of the Brotherhood. Unfortunately, their fund-raising campaign was unsuccessful. Property costs, along with the equipment and material to develop it, created a financial crisis for the convention. In 1964, the BCNM obtained a loan in the amount of $85,000 for critically needed improvements. Since this amount was not in the budget, the burden fell on the Brotherhood to raise the $1,000 per month for debt retirement.[18]

Once again the organization failed to raise the necessary money. Then in 1965, for the first time, Inlow Camp found itself in desperate need of improvements for its buildings. The Royal Ambassadors' facility similarly continued to need enlargement where expenditures already amounted to more than $101,000.[19]

Conditions continued virtually the same for the next two years, with yet another major turnover of personnel occurring in 1967. There were six departures among department heads along with five changes in office secretaries. In addition, five members of the State Mission Board left the state. Harry Stagg's retirement was also anticipated that year. But to allow him to have the longest tenure of any state executive secretary in Southern Baptist history, the mission board asked him to stay on an additional fourteen months. R. Y. Bradford became the new executive secretary on October 1, 1967, assuming full responsibilities on December 1. Stagg took a two-month terminal leave, with official retirement on February 1, 1968.[20]

Deteriorating conditions and anticipation of Stagg's retirement along with the changes in convention personnel brought about a reevaluation of the entire program. Reporting to the State Mission Board during his first year as executive secretary, Bradford noted that there seemed to be a widespread decline in the spiritual health of the churches. Membership participation continued to be discouraging and giving continued to decline.[21] Audie Wiley, pastor at Del Norte Baptist Church in Albuquerque, observed that "We have heard so many uncertain sounds across the nation from our churches that our people are frustrated and confused. Some have laid their arms down for they know not what to do."[22] Such conditions propelled the convention at its annual meeting to adopt a radical solution. E. J. Bradshaw presented a recommendation calling for the convention to amend its structure in order to meet the needs of the current generation. He proposed that the convention president, the State Mission Board chairperson, and the executive secretary be authorized by the convention to select ten persons from across the state to serve on a study committee. This body would then undertake a comprehensive evaluation of the convention, its organizational structure, and the present functioning and effectiveness of the various agencies and organizations, as well as the mission program within the state. Distribution of Cooperative Program funds and other monies by the convention to its agencies also underwent scrutiny. Finally, the committee undertook to provide job descriptions for all employees and personnel. Instructions called for a report to be submitted in 1969 to enumerate any organizational restructuring, along with recommendations for the elimination of obsolete entities or the creation of new ones where necessary.

In the meantime, the dismal conditions continued. A 1969 letter from Bernard Dougherty, president of the State Mission Board, addressed continuing problems: "The fact remains, however, that from a financial standpoint this has been the most trying year in our recent history. . . . Therefore you see reflected in this report a larger deficit than we have reported in a long time."[23] Indebtedness as of December 31, 1968 totaled $123,669.71. Fortunately, a timely gift of $75,000 bequeathed to the convention from the McKearny estate helped to offset some of the debt and assisted with day-to-day operational expenses. Speaking before the WMU convention in 1969, Bradford commented that: "Every department head . . . has been asked to cut down on their spending for 1970 because God's people are not taking their responsibilities in Christian service. . . . We think it is not necessary anymore to witness to those who need our help because of our own selfish desires."[24] Conditions continued to deteriorate; 1970 became known as the "year of concern."

Programmatic Change

Declining financial conditions throughout the 1960s had led the convention in 1968 to take the drastic step of studying the feasibility and advisability of a complete overhaul of its operation. Similarly, activity within the core church programs followed a similar pattern. Enrollment and participation declined, but procedures followed the traditional pattern until near the end of the decade, when changes in orientation and method began to occur.

Sunday School proved to be the backbone of the core church programs, not only in education but also in outreach. It was the Southern Baptists' primary expansion tool, and it had been used effectively in New Mexico for starting churches. Baptists held training sessions at all three levels of organizational activity: state conventions, associational clinics, and individual church workshops.[25] Minutely organized, these programs required a tremendous outlay of time, money, physical resources, and professional personnel, while at the same time relying heavily upon lay involvement for implementation.

Such a system required social stability to operate effectively. Cultural upheaval in the 1960s caused this elaborate model to become obsolete. When Ed Storm became the new secretary of the Sunday School Department after Lites's retirement in 1962, he found that the old methods had fallen on hard times. Churches no longer used censuses, visitation programs, worker training clinics, and workshops to the degree that they had in the past. Lay participation had dwindled. In 1964, for the first time in its history, the BCNM focused its outreach on adults. Even more significantly, the BCNM directed its efforts toward nonresident members, hoping to enlist them into becoming active participants in church life.[26]

Attempts to revive the old programs continued, but clearly new methods were necessary. Writing in 1967, Storm addressed this slowdown in outreach. He encouraged churches to employ techniques that would open up new areas of ministry such as housing developments, trailer courts, and high-rise apartment complexes that could be done by individuals. Storm stressed that even one person could start a Bible study group, especially if he or she lived within the project.[27] In less than a decade, Baptists had gone from massive enlargement campaigns to individual efforts based upon proximity and preference.

This shift is reflected in attendance. In 1961, convention membership totaled 81,036, of which Sunday School enrollment numbered 62,693, or 77 percent of the members. By 1970, membership had risen to 91,374, but Sunday School participation had dropped to 50,145 or 54 percent of the total.

During this same period, the Training Union program experienced similar negative results. What had primarily been a program for training people in church membership and Baptist beliefs had shifted toward "in-reach" in an attempt to involve inactive members in the fellowship.[28] In the process, the Training Union as a tool for educating Baptists in their own theological traditions began to erode.

Southern Baptists changed the name of the Training Union program to Church Training in 1969, thus underscoring the shift in orientation that was taking place. The program became an instrument to help recapture Sunday night by reshaping it to appeal to the needs of the people. Throughout the decade, attendance at the evening service—once a measure of church loyalty and Christian commitment—declined. As community and leisure activities swelled in popularity, churches encountered an increasing reluctance by members to commit the entire day to religious services. To compete with this trend, the Church Training program was redesigned to be a more meaningful and enjoyable experience. The new approach combined new member orientation and leadership training with a revamped Sunday evening service. The new format consisted of informal worship, with inspirational music and biblically relevant messages, conducted at times that fit people's schedules. Despite the changes, participation plunged. At the beginning of the decade, 25,824 members were enrolled in the program. By 1970, however, even with an increase of more than 10,000 in church membership, enrollment fell to 19,577.

CHAPTER 6

Decline in member participation extended to both service organizations. The WMU, never a large society but extremely important in mobilizing the women of the church, had always experienced enlistment difficulties. The 1960s decade simply compounded the dilemma. Before Eva Inlow's retirement in 1962, she addressed this concern, commenting that "In spite of our efforts we have not succeeded in reaching large numbers of women as members of our missionary societies."[29] Vanita Baldwin, the new executive secretary, inherited the problem.

Programs offered by the WMU remained basically the same through most of the decade, but declining involvement led the national body, and its New Mexico affiliate, to undergo a major restructuring in 1968. Recognizing that the availability of women to work in the churches was declining, reorganization took the form of increasing the flexibility of WMU activities. The traditional model was too large and unwieldy, requiring excessive time and personnel to be efficient under changing conditions. The new system simplified the process, allowing for individual customizing. Members could form groups according to their own interests, based on local needs.[30]

The state WMU had already anticipated this directional change earlier with a pioneering ministry that used literacy classes to teach immigrants English as a tool for evangelism. Many churches throughout the state found this new medium beneficial, and began incorporating these classes into their overall mission program.[31] Despite the alterations, however, participation continued to decline.

In contrast, the Brotherhood began the decade with a nationwide reorganization in 1961, which allowed this body to be more effective in promoting the Royal Ambassadors and personal stewardship throughout the churches. Responding to this change in structure the New Mexico affiliate pioneered a new dimension in youth ministry, known as the "Opportunity Camp." Due largely to the efforts of Perry Denton, the camp reached out to boys aged nine through thirteen who had been placed on probation by law enforcement authorities. Denton recognized that these boys differed from the typical child raised in a Baptist church and so needed different treatment. The solution was to enlist police officers and sheriffs' deputies to serve as counselors. They worked with the boys one-on-one to help them turn their lives around and to show them that a law officer could be a friend if they would allow it. This social ministry turned out to be one of the more successful programs in the state.[32]

Success with the Opportunity Camp, however, did not spill over to the Brotherhood's other activities. Participation in the annual retreat continued to decline. When only thirty-three attended in 1969, the retreat was cut from the state budget. Resurrected a year later under the title "Pastors-Laymen's Retreat," it too failed. No other ministry body undertook a major building project during the 1960s, and the financial problems associated with the Royal Ambassadors (Sivells) Camp severely damaged the organization.[33]

Mission work in the state followed the pattern of the other convention programs. Traditional activity centering on missionary efforts to Hispanics and Native Americans continued throughout the 1960s. Then as 1968 neared, a shift in approach occurred, placing more emphasis on lay participation. Missionaries in New Mexico at the beginning of the decade numbered 47 to Hispanics and 33 to Native Americans. Fourteen years later, those numbers remained virtually the same, though the ratio was different: 37 worked among Hispanics and 45 labored with Indians.[34] Fixed personnel figures, when combined with a widening outreach, indicate a change in philosophy and methods. Such an alteration, in fact, is what occurred.

Mission activity to Hispanics and Native Americans moved away from a missionary-dominant program toward ministry that actively involved the people themselves. Addressing the Brotherhood in 1968, Oscar Romo from the Language Division of the HMB said, "If laymen are to make an impact to the different language groups we must be ready to first guide them and then let them work their own way."[35]

Lay workers became an important tool in mission endeavors. Missionaries went into the field to assist pastors, lay leaders, and dozens of congregations to empower their members to take over responsibility for church work. Under this new plan, individuals received training in teaching and witnessing. This approach proved to be a departure from the traditional pattern of relying on the missionary to conduct these types of activities.[36]

In order to assist Native Americans in assuming more control of their churches, Baptist missionaries developed all-Indian steering committees. These bodies planned Indian revivals, and other evangelistic work, with Anglos serving only in an advisory capacity. Indian-led crusades were very effective in the late 1960s, with the Navajo reservation especially open to presentation of the Southern Baptist message. By the end of the decade, a trend toward inclusion and involvement of native New Mexican peoples was clearly in the ascendancy.

For the Hispanic community, the BCNM directed most of its efforts toward assisting Spanish-speaking churches in attaining self-sufficiency. Many of these congregations were in English-speaking areas, where stronger Anglo churches could help them in developing their own pastoral and lay leadership. Slowly, some congregations did become self-supporting. As the convention was painfully aware, however, Hispanic access to economic opportunity severely impeded such efforts.[37]

Evangelism, like the Sunday School and Church Training programs, was well organized, labor intensive, time consuming, and programmatic. In an ideal year, activities began with the State Evangelism Conference in January, followed by associational clinics. Each of the seventeen associations then held Jubilee Revivals. In the fall, Simultaneous Revivals canvassed the state as pastors north of Highway 60 assisted those in the south and vice versa. At the local level, churches usually held two revivals a year, each lasting one to two weeks. This extremely efficient program, honed to perfection in the 1940s and 1950s, continued into the 1960s.[38]

A denomination-wide revival in 1969 known as the Crusade of the Americas gave impetus to this structure. BCNM embraced the program wholeheartedly, urging its churches to set aside January 12 as a day of prayer for the crusade. Associations held special evangelism clinics during the early part of the year. Dates for the crusade were March 16–30, April 6–20, and April 27–May 11. Churches in each association divided the dates and where feasible held two sets of services. Many congregations conducted training classes for individuals in witnessing. Pastors stirred their members with sermons on the glories of past crusades.

The entire convention mobilized. For example, the Southeastern Association rented the high school auditorium in Hobbs. The Central Association, covering the Albuquerque area, leased the civic auditorium. Also, special preachers such as Jess Moody of First Baptist Church in West Palm Beach, Florida, flew in to serve as evangelists. Statistics revealed the impact of the preparation. Joint services in Hobbs resulted in 328 professions of faith, with 182 rededications. Meetings in Albuquerque, supported by thirty-three cooperating churches, witnessed over 35,000 attending the eight-night revival. "Decisions" totaled 345 conversions (professions of faith in Christ) and 489 vows of renewed commitment to follow Christ.[39] As promising as these results were, the 1969 Crusade of the Americas marked the end of an era. After 1969, the emphasis began to change. Although there would still be major crusades, church efforts turned toward lay witnessing (individual or one-on-one evangelism).

Evangelism, designed to empower the individual, became the primary focus of the 1970s. Promotional activities and training classes mobilized the laity to spread the gospel one-on-one. First Baptist Church of Hobbs, under pastor Bailey Smith, provided an example of this type of total church involvement. In 1970 and 1971, his congregation set new state records, baptizing more than three hundred people per year. According to Smith, his church accomplished this feat by focusing on week-by-week personal evangelism. They promoted heavily and prepared the people for witnessing and outreach.[40]

Emphasis on one-on-one ministry led to the adoption of strategies and techniques designed to reach people "where they were." One such opportunity, resort missions, was particularly suited to New Mexico. In the 1970s, "Ski the New Mexico Sun" became more than just a slogan to attract tourists to the state. Pastors and laypersons figuratively hit the slopes to bring the Southern Baptist message to skiers. Worshippers clad in winter attire could now attend open-air services held on the mountain at Angel Fire Ski Resort, and there was also Bible study for Taos Ski Area employees. Person-to-person witnessing even occurred on the chairlifts.[41]

Not limiting themselves to ski resorts, New Mexico Baptists searched out other recreational areas to carry their message. Tourists and health seekers arriving in Jemez Springs found a summer missionary couple spreading the gospel. Baptists in Los Alamos operated a coffee house. Summer fishermen, as well as overflow skiers from Angel Fire in winter, met evangelicals at Eagle Nest. Beginning with Sunday services, this outreach to recreationalists eventually grew into Moreno Valley Baptist Church. Still others took the message to the campgrounds in Cimarron Canyon just outside the village.[42]

A complete turnaround occurred in the attitude of the laity. The convention annual report for 1972 highlighted the renewed interest in evangelism and in personal witnessing. A year later the same organ noted an increasing interest in Bible study. Chief Lawson, director of evangelism, enthusiastically conveyed to the Brotherhood Convention in 1973 that "Reports of great revivals and soul winning efforts have come from across the state. God has caused the fires of evangelism to burn bright."[43]

This evangelistic upsurge was not exclusive to New Mexico or even to the SBC. A new "spirit of revival" spread across the nation in the 1970s, incorporating both international and ecumenical elements. Responding to a call by Billy Graham and Carl F. H. Henry, Southern Baptists, along with over one hundred other denominations, participated in "Key 73." This movement united evangelicals for a worldwide mission thrust.

Unlike the many departments that experienced difficulties in the early 1960s, the Baptist student unions (BSUs) and the Bible chairs entered the decade on a high note. Unfortunately, it would not end so. Campus operations existed at the University of New Mexico and New Mexico State, Eastern New Mexico State, Western New Mexico State, and New Mexico Highlands Universities. "B-Hi-Us" were also established for high school students in the mid-1960s by the convention's BSU director, Truett Sheriff. Sheriff wrestled with the enviable problem of having so many participants that there was a shortage of workers. As the number of Baptist youth attending state-run universities increased, the services provided by the BSUs assumed greater importance. In 1960, 1,356 Baptist students attended state universities. Nine years later, the number had nearly doubled. With BSUs at five universities, the denomination was convinced that they had covered the college scene. As the state of New Mexico expanded its educational institutions during this era, however, concerns over the need to provide additional facilities faced the state convention.[44]

Local churches provided a partial answer to the problem. First Baptist Church in Socorro began work at New Mexico Tech, and Calvary Baptist in Roswell spearheaded efforts at the New Mexico Military Institute. There still remained, however, the junior college in Hobbs, Eastern New Mexico State University's Roswell campus, and the community colleges in Alamogordo, Farmington, and Carlsbad. Amid these demands, Bruce Sandlin became the new director of the BSU program. He immediately launched an expansion program, and a year later two new BSUs began operations. One facility at Hobbs served the junior college and the College of the Southwest, and the other serviced the campus in Roswell.[45]

Even though BSU growth proved to be a convention bright spot amid a decade of troubles, its ministry could not escape the cataclysmic changes that rocked college campuses nationwide. Speaking at the state convention in 1963, Dr. Frank Stagg, professor of Greek and the New Testament at New Orleans Seminary, warned of serious consequences the denomination must face in the future. He noted a growing tension between professors and laity; and between seminaries and colleges and churches at the national level.[46] His remarks foreshadowed subsequent events.

Tensions erupted in 1970 in Portales, when pastor Ray Fuller of Westside Baptist Church charged that a liberal was teaching in the Bible chair at Eastern New Mexico State. He claimed that the majority of the pastors in the Portales Association wanted the professor removed, but that the BCNM had ignored them. Therefore, the ministers planned to withhold funds from the Cooperative Program. The money would now go to individual projects deemed sound and fundamental to the faith. The teacher remained, but the fallout led in 1973 to the establishment of the Education Ministries Committee. This body examined all texts and classroom materials receiving university credit so as to ensure "spiritual soundness." The committee in turn instructed all BSU personnel to "plan programs, Bible studies, activities and select textbooks in keeping with statements in the Baptist Faith and Message."[47]

Doctrinal squabbles aside, the Bible chairs faced a greater problem. The changes taking place on university campuses had a devastating impact on the convention's college ministry. Students no longer enrolled for Bible classes as they once did. As attendance declined, BSU directors spent more time teaching fewer people, and less on general BSU activities. In light of these factors, the educational programs, except for Eastern's, began to be disbanded. Despite all the denomination's hard work to provide Christian education on state campuses, by the mid-1970s the Bible chairs had become a relic of the past.

In an era where everything seemed in flux and programs in decline, there were some institutions that not only survived but also thrived. One was the Children's Home in Portales. When the Hubbards retired in 1971, Bert Edmundson took over the directorship. The only noticeable change was a slight decline in the number of children in residence. Normally, the facility averaged seventy to eighty children living there on a regular basis. In the 1970s, these figures began to drop and stays became briefer.[48] The property remained in good condition, however, and the home experienced no financial difficulties.

Another convention entity that registered sustained growth during this time was the Baptist Foundation. In 1961, the foundation expanded its operation by establishing the Church Loan Corporation. Churches could issue bonds with the principal and interest guaranteed by the corporation. Assets continued to rise so that by 1973 monies administered amounted to more than $2 million, with distributions on earnings totaling more than $215,000 to a variety of beneficiaries and charitable causes.[49]

While most statewide Baptist programs declined in membership and participation, the Music Department proved to be an exception. It was the only program that registered numerical gains. Burgeoning interest in the 1960s revolutionized its agenda. In 1962, the convention's summer music camp registered 46 participating churches, with 956 enrolled and 1,812 in attendance. Then everything began to explode. Church involvement at the music festival in 1963 increased to 71, with enrollment jumping to 1,617 and 2,690 in attendance. Numbers continued to skyrocket so that a year later the BCNM held two separate music camps.[50]

Calls from churches and individuals expressing interest in the music ministry inundated convention headquarters. In 1965, there were more requests for materials, conferences, and music schools than at any time in the denomination's history. During the same year, music camp attendance increased 75 percent over the previous year. Escalating participation by churches led to the first annual music ministers' retreat in 1969. Demand for training necessitated expansion. In 1970, BCNM offered sixteen festivals, fourteen church music schools, two music camps, one music ministers' retreat, a conference at the Glorieta facility, a "Shaping the Seventies" conference, and nine workshops on the new music methods books.[51]

Since most Baptist programs suffered severe declines in the 1960s, the music ministry's performance offers insights into the nature of the changes occurring during this decade, and the impact they would have on the future ministry of the church. Increased involvement in church music formed part of the larger nationwide emphasis on music in the popular culture. Technology had produced the transistor radio, and with that, music became exceptionally portable. People aged eight to eighty walked around with wires hanging out of their ears. Mass access to rhythm and sound proved an integral aspect of the 1960s. Music excited and soothed the feelings of a confused people. At a time when many inhibitions were cast aside, the performance orientation of music provided a vehicle for a more open expression of the self.

In reference to this phenomenon, Milford Moore, associate secretary of the Church Music Department, observed that "Music is now being used in therapeutic ways."[52] His statement helped explain the impact that the rise of interest in music would have on the church. For any department or ministry to succeed, it would have to place the needs of the individual at center stage.

Reorganization

As ministries altered their approach to meet changing conditions, so too did the BCNM. The results of the study committee's findings in 1968 led to the reorganization of 1970, which took effect in 1971. Recommendations for restructuring centered on four observations. First, BCNM's administration was far more elaborate than other state conventions of similar size. Second, in light of its present responsibilities, the budget was at the operational minimum, leaving no room for expansion. Next, over the years 1960–69, receipts fell below budget requirements by $458,633.97, necessitating a lowering of demands to meet the record of giving by the churches.[53] Finally, the study committee concluded that inability to support such an elaborate edifice required cutbacks.

Under the newly reorganized convention, the executive secretary became the executive director. His duties included responsibility for the operation of the convention, along with direct control over promotion and stewardship. Supervision of daily operations became the duty of the business manager who oversaw the various offices, subordinate personnel, and the camps. Five divisions shared the remainder of the work. The committee deemed such an arrangement to be economically advantageous, as well as more equally distributing the workload and improving managerial efficiency.

The new structure was reorganized along division lines. First, the Division of Special Ministries included the Children's Home and ministries deemed important by the BCNM, such as activities targeting senior citizens, unwed mothers, and juvenile delinquents. The division director also served as superintendent of the Children's Home. Second, the Division of Communication Ministries handled public relations and published the *Baptist New Mexican*, with the editor serving as division director. Third, the Division of Foundation and Church Loan Ministries was comprised of the New Mexico Baptist Foundation and the Church Loan Corporation, also headed by a director. Fourth, the Division of Mission Ministries included cooperative mission work to ethnic groups, association and area mission programs, evangelism, and the work of the WMU and Brotherhood. Personnel consisted of a director and two associates. Fifth, the Division of Educational Ministries planned and promoted the Sunday School, Church Training, and Church Music programs, and was staffed by a director with one associate.[54]

The old system had developed in response to explosive growth by adding offices and personnel as needs dictated. Restructuring sought to address internal concerns created by this ad hoc development. New procedures established job grades and salary scales for all employees. Job descriptions for each position helped eliminate friction caused by overlapping responsibilities. Clarifying committee assignments also helped eliminate encroachment into another's jurisdiction. Reorganization also downsized the BSUs. As an economy move, students and local church leaders assisted the director on a part-time basis. The Inlow and Sivells Camps now functioned under the Camp Ministries Committee, which worked with the business manager in areas of management, development, and program coordination.[55]

This reorganization was unprecedented within the SBC. New Mexico was not alone in experiencing financial difficulties. During this era nearly a dozen other conventions endured similar conditions, but the BCNM was the only convention to restructure because of them.[56]

Promoters of the reorganization plan credit it with saving the convention. In financial terms, such claims appear to be valid. In 1971, monetary growth escalated. Contributions to the Cooperative Program and the Lottie Moon, Annie Armstrong, and State Missions offerings registered increases,[57] with the first three at all-time highs. Both camps operated in the black.[58]

Writing in early 1973, Eugene Whitlow contrasted current conditions with those of just two years before. In 1971, the convention was in debt and baptisms were falling. Locally, offerings declined and many pastors wanted to move. A spirit of pessimism prevailed throughout the membership. Now, with people-to-people extended lay witnessing, ministries rejuvenated. Churches increased their attendance, baptisms, and financial support. Whitlow recalled that in 1970 contention was rampant over the proposed restructuring, centering on the new job assignments, and failure to meet the budget. Two years later, Cooperative Program receipts increased by over $100,000. Income in 1972 was $63,497 over budget.[59]

Bradford's final year turned out to be the best of all. Cooperative Program receipts totaled $829,067.14, an increase of $47,414.25 over 1973. Total indebtedness fell to $16,275.61. The annual financial summary reported that all accounts were current. All ministries were supported as budgeted. There was even an operational reserve that enabled the convention to extend its outreach.[60]

It would appear from the information cited and the claims touted by its promoters that the BCNM's restructuring had brought about an administrative and economic miracle. Closer examination, however, reveals that the restructuring simply occurred at the right time. The rebound actually began a year earlier in 1970. This was the "year of concern." Declining revenue in the first six months had caused alarm, but an upsurge in giving during the latter half turned a potential disaster into the best year for world missions through the Cooperative Program. Receipts broke the $600,000 mark, the highest in BCNM's history. This same economic upsurge, as well as the increase in baptisms, program support, and renewed interest in evangelism, was not unique to New Mexico. Numerous articles in the *Baptist New Mexican* reported similar conditions occurring in sister conventions. The entire SBC experienced the same phenomenon.

The attempt to attribute the convention's resurgence to reorganization falters in the face of statistics. Certainly BCNM recovered financially. But in terms of membership and program participation no rebound occurred. In 1961, constituents numbered 81,036, breaking the 90,000 mark four years later. For the next eight years growth stagnated. The 1973 figures were virtually the same as for 1965. The core programs, however, continued to decline. For instance, in 1965, 66 percent of the membership attended Sunday School, compared to 50 percent in 1974. The same trend occurred in the Church Training program, where the percentage of participants declined from 26 percent in 1965 to 14 percent in 1974.

ᘓᕟ

What happened to the convention in this period is an example of operational divergence. In financial terms, the BCNM experienced rapid growth. In terms of membership and participation in core programs, the former stagnated and the latter declined. Giving increased but participation decreased. What overall impact then did the reorganization have?

Certainly the restructuring made for a more efficient operation by cutting expenditures and personnel. The greatest impact, however, was in orientation. Years later, R. Y. Bradford revealed the intent and purpose behind the reorganization. "Perhaps the greatest weakness was that many churches were not looking to the convention leadership for education, inspiration, motivational direction or assistance. . . . [W]e sought to lead the churches to see that the programs of the convention were extensions of their ministries."[61]

Essentially, the restructuring led to the development of a headquarters mentality by making the churches more dependent on the convention. In the Stagg era, the large staff went out to the churches and assisted them in fulfilling their own goals. Under the reorganization, however, the churches came to the convention for help. It was a subtle difference, but one that over time led to the churches being enlisted to serve the needs of the convention.[62]

"Corporate downsizing" best describes the BCNM reorganization. Thirteen departments became consolidated into five divisions, resulting in a loss of ten convention personnel.[63] At the same time, restructuring increased the workload. For example, the Educational Division formerly employed five workers but now only two covered the same field. Reduced staff and increased responsibility led to loss of contact with the laity. Personal interaction with the people suffered at a time when participation was declining.

Changing conditions also gave rise to a radically altered leadership style. Participants in Stagg's administration characterized it as an extended family, a team effort, an "us-and-our" attitude. Under Bradford, the terms most commonly used were pragmatic, all business, and bottom line, with a "me-and-mine" mentality.

Reorganization also impacted Baptist polity by contributing to the progressive weakening of the association. Changes in lifestyle along with technical improvements in communications and transportation facilities undermined involvement. In a 1965 editorial, Horace Burns expressed concern that the association was no longer the primary avenue of work and fellowship among the churches. Albert Hinkley, pastor of Bethel Baptist Church in Albuquerque, voiced his dismay in 1972 over this issue: "There has been a growing weakness in the total structure of our work for the past several years. This is nowhere more visible than [in] the associations."[64] He stressed that the district association should be the first source of participation among the churches for work. Although certainly unintentional, the reorganization's attempt to make the churches more dependent on the convention worked against active commitment to the association.

Perhaps the most important oversight in the reorganization plan was the failure to address the shift in American thinking that had occurred in the 1960s. In this decade, three hundred years of a Judeo-Christian worldview began to erode.[65] The culture built on that belief system had been the foundation upon which the denomination based its work. Baptists simply assumed that the national foundation was at least functionally Christian and thus that they need only concentrate on evangelism and religious freedom.

When that orientation underwent a shift, as it did in the 1960s, Baptists no longer had a base from which to respond to the revolution that engulfed them. Assuming that their dilemma was administrative, they sought to solve the problem through organizational and budgetary change. Instead of restructuring themselves to function in a post-Christian environment, the reorganization of 1970 was merely an economic document designed to accomplish institutional preservation through managerial efficiency. Inability to adjust to the new conditions not only prevented Baptists from providing an alternative to the direction that the nation had taken, but instead, they became part of it.

New Mexico Baptists and Social Change: 1961 to 1974

Turmoil not only resulted in reorganization, but also altered Baptist relations with the community. Traditionally, public involvement centered on moral issues and institutional development projects, such as orphanages, hospitals, and schools. After World War II, battles for religious freedom and separation of church and state became equally important. Although interest in these issues continued, the upheavals of the 1960s propelled New Mexico Baptists toward constructing their version of a limited social gospel.

Alterations in ministry also worked against ecumenical isolation. Social turmoil necessitated more active public involvement, which opened Baptists to the possibilities of interdenominational cooperation. The erosion of Christianity's privileged position in the public square led to finding points of commonality rather than exclusivity among evangelical groups. Specific conditions in New Mexico kept the Baptist Convention of New Mexico (BCNM) from moving as far in this direction as the Southern Baptist Convention (SBC), yet by the end of the period a less insulated attitude is clearly evident.

In the midst of such change, Baptist beliefs also underwent self-scrutiny. Challenges in theology undermined some cherished doctrines. In the process, traditional Baptist distinctiveness began to erode. Attempting to respond to so many new currents of thought weakened denominational identity. A new type of member began to emerge who lacked the doctrinal convictions of his or her predecessors.

Social and Political Involvement

Although New Mexico Baptists were slow to articulate a position on social problems, the subject remained of profound interest to them. Throughout this era, the *Baptist New Mexican* carried an abundance of articles dealing with societal issues and the denomination's response to them. Occasionally, individuals within the state entered the debate. An examination of the speakers' topics delivered before the state annual convention shows a preoccupation with the subject. Emphasis centered on meeting the needs of a changing

American society.

Across the nation and the state, Baptists deemed the major cause of the nation's social collapse to be a breakdown within the family. Dr. Woodson Armes, speaking to the state convention in 1964, directed attention to the skyrocketing divorce rate: "One marriage out of every three ends in the divorce courts. The first reason for the decline and fall of the Roman Empire was the decline of the Roman home."[1] Lucien Coleman of the BCNM's Brotherhood Commission (a national organization with state-level affiliates) cited similar disturbing statistics.

> No nation can rise higher than its home life. . . . The average Jewish child is taught religion 600 hours per year; the average Catholic child is taught religion 200 hours per year and the average Protestant child is taught religion 13 hours per year.[2]

Many contributors to the *Baptist New Mexican* called upon the church to mobilize its resources to stem the tide of familial decay. The church, they argued, was the only institution in society that dealt with the family at all age levels. Others argued that pastors should relate the truth of the gospel to the problems of society. Acting upon this concern led leaders to stress that the gospel be presented not only theologically but also applied to the practical affairs of everyday life. An article by Samuel Lester admonished Christians to intensify, deepen, and broaden their faith to extend into the community structure. Pastors should relate the truth of the gospel to the problems of society: "We are zealous in evangelism but not in the pursuit of an over-all just and equitable society."[3]

Professor T. B. Matson of Southwestern Seminary in Fort Worth, Texas, was the most noted social commentator in the SBC. As the conscience of the denomination, Matson's observations received special consideration, especially in New Mexico where many pastors had been his former students. His writings became a regular feature in the state newspaper. In an article titled, "Theological Conservatism and Social Liberalism," Matson summed up the emerging Baptist position toward social involvement:

> The majority of Baptists are theologically conservative and also conservative economically, politically and socially. We are traditionalists and defenders of the status quo. Our world is changing from rural to urban and we are no longer exclusively Southern. It's time for us to join the nation and the world. We need to maintain our theological

conservatism but couple it with a social liberalism if we are going to speak effectively to the world in which we live. We must take our conservative theology and unite it with a progressive or liberal spirit regarding the application of Christian truth to the pressing social, economic and political problems.[4]

Editorials in the *Baptist New Mexican* chart this new approach. The uniting of conservative theology with social liberalism that Matson envisioned began to surface. In a 1968 article, newspaper editor Eugene Whitlow urged the convention to become involved:

Everywhere we turn we step on social problems. We are not going to do much for humanity's spiritual problems by getting caught up in the stream of the "social gospel," but we simply cannot hide our heads anymore and pretend that poverty and injustice are no concerns of ours. Let's hope that this new year is just the beginning of our deeper involvement in the social ills of the world.[5]

Adding to this new social concern, Pastor Howard Marsh of First Baptist Church in Gallup took issue with those who placed emphasis solely on evangelism. He said that Baptists should ask themselves about their responsibility regarding illiteracy, poverty, disease, and tyranny. In the book of James, he said, the apostle admonishes Christians to demonstrate their religion by helping those in need.[6]

Two new ministries established by the BCNM in cooperation with the HMB had already begun to address Pastor Marsh's concerns: the Baptist Neighborhood Center and Baptist Friendship Center, both in Albuquerque. The Neighborhood Center began in 1961 at the old Edith Street Baptist Church, a multiracial community located in the downtown area. The facility offered a day care center, after-school Bible studies, music, and recreational activities. On Sundays it became a church with a full slate of services. Unlike the traditional church, however, it functioned as a social and spiritual community center. The Friendship Center, which began in 1958 as the Children's Bible Club at Riverside Baptist Church, revamped its outreach in 1964, offering a weekday ministries program for people of all ages.

Both centers developed extensive programmatic activities. For example, counseling services assisted people in matters pertaining to their homes, finances, and religious concerns. A reading readiness program, similar to Head Start, also helped prepare children for the public schools. Volunteers taught basic carpentry classes and tutored those with academic problems. For $1 per day, working parents had access to a day care center for their children that also provided lunch. Other services included cooking classes, a lapidary shop, art instruction for preschoolers, piano lessons, handicrafts, women's Bible classes, and religious services offered in Spanish.[7]

As the decade progressed, the SBC became very involved in addressing racial prejudice within the denomination. On this issue, however, New Mexicans were at variance with Baptists elsewhere.[8] The BCNM simply continued its traditional policy of ministering to all races. Nevertheless, in an effort to keep in step with the "Southwide" emphasis, the *Baptist New Mexican* did print numerous articles on the subject. The only "in-state" contribution came from Harry D. Brooks, pastor of Hillcrest Baptist Church in Carlsbad, who gave a current voice to the convention's historic position in a series of articles featured in 1971.

Using a text from the tenth chapter of the Book of Acts, Brooks provided a fourfold biblical base for overcoming prejudice. He concluded that racism was not of God and should not be part of a Christian society. He went on to say that the church was to be a complete fellowship of all believers and should never be distorted into a private club of peculiar segregationists. "We had better get used to a common fellowship in Christ here," he said, "for it is but a preview of that which is yet to come."[9]

The host of social issues that engulfed the 1960s proved more than a convention the size of New Mexico's could reasonably address. "Overwhelming" correctly describes the situation. The job of keeping the membership informed fell largely on the state newspaper's editors. To accomplish their task, they printed numerous articles from denominational specialists interspersed with guest editorials. Yet even with this help, churches still experienced difficulty in relating their message to changing conditions. In a 1968 editorial, Eugene Whitlow summed up the problem: "Everywhere you turn you hear about the 'irrelevancy' of the church in the twentieth century. If the indictment is true it's because we have failed to relate the voice and strength of the church to the social and moral issues of the community. We need pastoral leadership that will carry over beyond the pulpit out into the stream of things."[10] Whitlow increased the number of articles dealing with social issues to both raise the consciousness of Baptists in the state and to provide the groundwork on which to formulate their thinking.

Numerous issues discussed in the *Baptist New Mexican* did not receive much attention among Baptists in the state. Topics such as Vietnam, Watergate, the War on Poverty, environmental concerns, aging, the right-to-die debate, and the sexual revolution became the province of denominational spokespersons. Abortion, however, did summon a local response. Reacting to a 1973 Supreme Court decision nullifying abortion statutes in Texas, Whitlow observed that the SBC had never really dealt with this problem. A 1970 resolution approved by the messengers had allowed for abortion in the case of rape; incest; clear evidence of severe fetal deformity; and the physical, mental, or emotional health of the mother. The issue of when a baby begins to exist as a human being, however, remained unanswered. Whitlow invited six New Mexican pastors to address the issue.[11]

Doyle Combs, of Parkview Baptist Church in Albuquerque, responded. Combs took the view that life began at conception. He argued that scientific evidence did not support the six-month theory since the heart began beating at eighteen days and brain activity could be seen at six weeks. The more fundamental question, according to Combs, was whether one had the right to take human life. To ask if a fetus was human simply confused the issue. God, he said, certainly intended to create a human being.[12]

A physician from Alamogordo, R. C. Sherman, took strong exception to the Supreme Court ruling. He charged that the court's decision absolved women of the first duty of motherhood—to keep the child alive. As a doctor, he thought that abortion violated his Hippocratic oath. It also prevented the father from having any say in the decision. Addressing the issue of induced abortion, Sherman used the scripture passage in Ruth 4:13, which states that it was God that enabled her to conceive, to substantiate his claim that life began at conception.[13]

Whereas Southern Baptists had traditionally avoided direct involvement in the political process, and only confronted social issues hesitantly, they began in the 1960s to change their attitudes. A 1973 BCNM resolution reflects this transition. In that document, the messengers urged the membership to become more active and support appropriate pressure groups. Rather than limit themselves to the traditional issues of gambling and liquor, convention leaders sought to push their people into the public arena to make their voices heard.[14]

Separation of Church and State

Although New Mexico Baptists paid close attention to some new social issues, their prime interest lay in their continuing struggle to ensure the separation of church and state. Baptist struggles since the Dixon case (see chapter 5) made them especially sensitive to the prospect of federal aid to sectarian education. In the 1960s, this item reached epic proportions in the nation. But since the new area of conflict eventually centered on the funding of colleges,

New Mexicans watched from the sidelines. The *Baptist New Mexican*'s editors kept the readership informed on every turn in the debate, but not until the State of New Mexico's constitutional convention, beginning in 1964, did they have another opportunity to do battle. The convention did, however, express its position in a 1962 resolution: "Be it resolved that we as Baptists maintain a united front in rejecting all public tax funds, federal and otherwise, directly and indirectly, for all Baptist institutions, whether these be loans or direct grants."[15]

When the call came in 1964 to revise the state constitution, New Mexico Baptists entered the field to champion separation of church and state. According to Dale Danielson, state president of Americans United for Separation of Church and State, the "parochiad" (government aid to sectarian education) interests intended to produce a document that would throw out the church-state provisions of the old constitution. They intended to create a loophole that would allow passage of a bill to appropriate over $2 million for Catholic schools in its first year through tuition vouchers.

Americans United began to lobby against the proposed legislation. They challenged the wording that would create this loophole in close committee votes. Momentum increased. The final vote on the crucial education article was 49 against to 20 in favor. As one participant put it: "Both sides were about as stunned as when David slew Goliath."[16] According to delegate James Martin of Las Cruces, parochiad would not have been an issue if Americans United had not brought the issue to their attention. "It would have slipped by with some of us wondering about the wording but not realizing the extent of the conspiracy."[17]

The proposed new constitution for the state carried over many of the same church-state provisions as the old one. The victory for separation of church and state advocates was Section 4D of the new finance article. This clause combined two sections of the old constitution, Article 4, Section 31, and Article 9, Section 14. The article in the new constitution was largely the result of testimony by two Baptist ministers before the finance committee. J. R. Burnett, pastor of Riverside Baptist Church in Albuquerque, and also vice president of Americans United, suggested the omission of the old wording, "except as otherwise provided in the constitution." His suggestion was followed. W. D. Wyatt, pastor of First Baptist Church in Albuquerque, and a member of the board of directors of Americans United, urged the combining of the two sections, and the retaining of the words "absolute control." His recommendation was also adopted.

The new clause by itself ruled out bus transportation, textbooks, and lunches for parochial students. A loophole in the old constitution had allowed for these exceptions. Under Section 2, however, the new constitution did allow for textbooks. The old constitution allowed for all three under the phrase, "except as otherwise provided." Under the new document, all church-owned business property was subject to taxation. Baptists favored this provision, seeing it as a threat only to what they described as "imperialistic" churches that existed on business income rather than on tithes and offerings. New provisions also closed the old loophole in Article 4, Section 31 that had provided for fifty-seven years of public funds to four religious institutions: St. Vincent's Hospital in Santa Fe, St. Joseph's Hospital in Albuquerque, St. Mary's Hospital in Las Cruces, and the Sisters of Loretto facility in Mora.[18]

In a June 27, 1970, article in the *Baptist New Mexican,* J. R. Burnett noted with regret the narrow defeat of the new constitution. He thought that it would have greatly increased religious liberty by making the wall of separation between church and state even stronger. Burnett expressed concern that Catholic Archbishop John Peter Davies had attempted to breach that wall in a statement before the state legislature's Education Committee on August 18, 1969: "I believe the wall of separation of church and state is a figment of imagination and a fiction of law. I say walls should come down."[19] Burnett warned Baptists that attempts by parochiad interests would continue. He recommended that the BCNM establish an agency patterned after the Baptist Joint Committee on Public Affairs in Washington, D.C.[20]

As the decade progressed, parochiad on the national level became more volatile. Glenn Archer, national president for Americans United, expressed alarm over what he saw as a polarization of American society. Groups on both sides organized to elect and defeat legislators who disagreed with their viewpoint. The issue developed into a conflict between the federal government and many church groups. For example, in 1970 the SBC joined a score of national groups with memberships of over 34 million to oppose school vouchers. The convention perceived school vouchers as an attempt to blur the distinction between church and state.[21]

As the debate raged, tensions increased. Normally cooperative groups began criticizing one another. Baptists became so caught up in the issues that they even clashed with Billy Graham. At the National Conference of Christians and Jews, Graham made the observation that the public schools were so secular that it might be of benefit for his grandchildren to attend religiously oriented institutions. Eugene Whitlow seized upon this remark, arguing that Graham's statement implied the use of public tax money to save private and sectarian schools. Whitlow considered this view distorted and contradictory, especially from one who claimed to believe in separation of church and state.

The *Baptist New Mexican* editor also lashed out at the Graham-led prayer services in the White House. He accused Nixon of wanting to set a standard in religion for the nation.[22]

An article in the state paper by John Parrott encapsulates the BCNM position on religious liberty and separation of church and state. He used for his text Christ's dictum: "Render therefore unto Caesar the things which are Caesar's; and unto God the things that are God's." He added,

> While the legitimate demands of the state are to be recognized, absolute obedience belongs only to God. . . . Such recognition requires the complete independence of the church in relations to the state. It makes clear that any attempt toward exaltation of the state to the sphere of the Kingdom of God must be met with strong and sustained resistance.[23]

This theological position provided a base for New Mexico Baptists to analyze events of the period. Several commentators began to detect a shift of direction in the separation of church and state issue. They argued that the current course of events undermined rather than strengthened the position of religion in the nation. J. Wayland Edwards, pastor of First Baptist Church in Artesia, observed that just because Baptists stood for separation of church and state did not mean that God had no place in government. Edwards reminded readers that God provided the laws by which governments rule. God upholds government, he argued, and therefore Christians have a place in government. Edwards warned constituents that if they wanted to keep their government Christian, they needed to become politically involved or otherwise they could lose it.[24]

Horace Burns took a larger view of what was occurring. He argued that to protect the rights of minorities, the rights and freedoms of every group required protection. In the desire to eliminate anything that would offend "people of no faith," Christians could no longer engage in prayer and Bible reading in the schools. Burns added,

> Are we now going to stop, or will we sooner or later remove every trace of anything religious from every public building or thoroughfare . . . ? We may now be at the place where Christian people find themselves giving up liberties they have cherished. . . . Are Americans who believe in God now to speak of Him only in their kitchen or backyards, lest some unbeliever, who has complete liberty to propagate his godless philosophy,

should be offended . . . ? Surely we can have separation of church and state in America without making reference to God in public institutions illegal. . . . As we arrange to protect the minorities among us, we do well to remember that even the majority may be entitled to certain rights also.[25]

Guest speaker Dr. A. Hope Owen, president of Wayland Baptist University, addressed this issue while speaking at First Baptist Church in Albuquerque. He asserted that there is a distinction between separation of church and state and separation of God and state. Owen argued that it was possible to have a common faith in God without endorsing a common church.[26]

All three of these individuals were uncomfortably aware that something was amiss. Edwards detected a shift in the orientation of government but assumed that the country was still vaguely Christian. Therefore, his solution was to unite believers with the culture through political activism. For Burns, this shift was more than just apostasy: Baptist principles were being used against them. New developments were overturning the culture that the denomination had depended on for their beliefs to be relevant in the public square. Meanwhile, Owen sensed that the country was pulling apart, so he attempted to build a synthesis in a syncretistic environment. All three observations represented the Baptist dilemma. Their traditional world was disintegrating, and no one knew how to restore it. Joseph Estes from the HMB summed up these latent concerns: "We may see in our day the complete nullification of the influence of our church in society."[27]

Ecumenical Rumblings

Changes in society, plus a perceived loss of influence, caused a reversal in Baptist behavior. Cooperation with other churches now appeared more reasonable than isolation. Some Southern Baptists endorsed a proposed North American Baptist Alliance. They argued that the nation was entering a "post-Protestant" era and Baptists needed to reexamine their position. The proposed alliance was not a call for a giant "superdenomination," nor a veiled threat at ecumenicism, but merely an attempt to marshal all Baptist resources for Christ's kingdom.[28]

New Mexico Baptists were not quite ready for this type of engagement. In an article entitled, "The Baptist Position on Cooperation," John Parrott echoed the BCNM's traditional position: "[W]e do not cooperate with other denominations in projects or practices of beliefs which we interpret as being in violation of conscience or in compromise of loyalty to Christ."[29] Nevertheless, pressure for interdenominational cooperation continued to build. Burns complained that ecumenism was increasing because the people were willing to scrap their beliefs: "The cry of unity is louder than the cry for the message of the truth, for truth itself takes a beating when to compromise convictions becomes louder."[30] Finally, in 1966 the convention deemed it necessary to address the issue through a resolution placing emphasis on "the preservation of our great Baptist heritage and doctrines."[31]

Even as the BCNM took its stand, forces within the SBC continued to push for more cooperation with other groups. Jess Moody from First Baptist Church in West Palm Beach, Florida, and a favorite revival speaker in New Mexico, called for a "biblical ecumenicism" to pool resources for worldwide evangelism. He said he was not proposing organic union, only voluntary activity, which was the wave of the future. Such activity would be an alternative to the ecumenical movement that promoted sociological involvement rather than evangelistic belief. Each denomination would maintain its identity, leadership, and organization, with no attempt at merger. By adopting his proposal the people could cooperate with other evangelicals and remove the stigma that Baptists were all "isolationists." Moody said his idea came from the 1966 Berlin Congress on World Evangelism, in which more than one hundred denominations from as many countries discussed alternatives to the ecumenical movement.[32] Not all agreed with Moody's assessment, however. Some saw ecumenicism as the brainchild of Carl F. H. Henry and *Christianity Today*. Fearing the creation of a 45-million-member superdenomination, many Southern Baptists urged that the call for evangelical cooperation collapse immediately.[33]

Nevertheless, the "call" began to penetrate the hard shell of resistance found in New Mexico. Whitlow noted in 1968 that for years Southern Baptists had resisted ecumenical involvement:

> There seems to be no good reason why we cannot cooperate to a reasonable extent with others of different religious beliefs in the matter of fighting social diseases the world has. There seems to be no good reason why this necessarily should or could result in the compromise of cherished Baptist distinctives.[34]

Flirting with evangelical ecumenicism served as a stimulus for venturing into previously forbidden territory—Catholic-Baptist dialogue. The HMB's department for work to nonevangelicals led in this endeavor.[35] The first meeting between the two groups occurred in 1969 at the Ecumenical Institute in

Wake Forest, North Carolina. Nineteen Catholics and thirty-nine Southern Baptists met to promote Christian unity.

Although not as overt as the Wake Forest meeting, relations between Baptist and Catholics in New Mexico also began to thaw. Harry Stagg had several friends who were priests, and many Baptist pastors engaged in their own private dialogue with members of the Catholic clergy. A story concerning Glorieta illustrates the changing relationship between the two groups. Stagg recalled that when the assembly opened for Pioneer Week during the summer of 1952, the Penitente crosses on the surrounding hills vanished in a matter of days. Then, in the mid-1960s, they began to reappear.[36]

Quite possibly the election of President Kennedy became the catalyst that precipitated this thaw in relations. Baptists in the state had campaigned hard against his election, for fear that he would be a puppet of the Vatican. Kennedy's stand on federal aid to education, in opposition to the bishops from his church, however, earned him their undying respect. His death shocked and saddened convention members. Large numbers filled the churches for memorial services. Many pastors in New Mexico lauded him as a great leader.

The growing secularization of American society continued to be a dominant theme behind ecumenical cooperation. In 1972, the campaign for cooperation bore fruit. Jess Moody's plan for an evangelical ecumenicism, disdained five years before, found new expression and acceptance. Southern Baptists now embraced the call for unity issued by Billy Graham and Carl F. H. Henry that brought together over one hundred denominations. Each group retained its independence, but would cooperate to evangelize the world a year later under the banner "Key 73." New Mexico Baptists followed their denomination's lead with pastors serving on Governor Bruce King's state "Key 73" committee.

Maintaining the Faith

The turmoil of the 1960s had caused the structural reorganization of the convention. Unrest had increased social and political activism. Upheaval had also opened the door to at least a willingness to consider ecumenical cooperation. In the area of theology, however, the Baptists rallied forces and held their own. Despite battles threatening Baptist distinctiveness, the Broadman Commentary controversy, and women's ordination, New Mexico Baptists remained committed to their conservative evangelical theology.

Delivering the presidential message in 1962, R. A. Long, pastor of First Baptist Church in Gallup, spoke on "danger signs" in which he challenged the BCNM to look ahead and see where it was going:

The danger of liberalism is plain, they see the Bible as an ancient collection of myths and exaggerations. Southern Baptists cannot conform to the popular pattern of today as accepted by some denominations. We are the bright spot now; however, we should take heed, for if we fail God we will also wind up on the scrap heap. We in New Mexico are where we are today because those who went before us were what they were. Fifty years from now they will be where they are by what we are today. One danger is failing to preach our distinctive Baptist doctrine. Distinctive beliefs are what made Baptists. Let us major on God's truth. That is our challenge and responsibility.[37]

The year before, the messengers had stated their convictions as a resolution. In the wake of the Elliott controversy (see chapter 1), they revised the resolution to read: "Be it resolved that we reaffirm our belief that the Bible is the word of God, *without myth or error,* and that it is sufficient for all matters of faith and practice."[38]

Even though New Mexico Baptists stood firm in their conservative beliefs, they were not unaware of the battle raging around them. In an article titled, "A Sufficient or An Insufficient Religion," Long expressed concern that the church was losing its impact on society. He noted that religious conditions in America made it appear that the church was doing fine. There were more church members than at any time in the nation's history. Money poured in to allow grander buildings. Seminaries turned out educated pastors in larger and larger numbers. Yet despite such progress, social conditions in America indicated a nation in decline. Alcoholism had reached epidemic proportions. Divorce and crime rates continued to escalate. Gang activity rose sharply. The number of unwed mothers continued to climb, and sex crimes registered the sharpest growth of all. Long placed the blame for this paradox on the insufficiency of the religion preached. He said that religious pluralism diluted the gospel. Long denounced the belief that it did not matter what one believed as long as people were "sincere." Such a doctrine, he thought, created a climate for moral decline. The solution was to return to the fundamentals of the Christian faith, that is, a personal God, the deity of Christ, the inspiration of the scriptures, the atoning death of Christ, salvation, and repentance. Up to this point, Long saw Southern Baptists as having escaped the dangers of a "waterlogged" liberalism and a "sterile" orthodoxy. He warned, however, that they must remain true to the Bible in doctrine and spirit.[39]

In the same article, however, Long expressed concern that the elements of denominational distinctiveness were no longer being taught. Too often, he said, pastors had a tendency to soft-soap their doctrines for fear of driving people away. In Long's view, preoccupation with church organization, promotion, and administration prevented ministers from digging into the scriptures to deliver the types of messages people needed to hear. Too many members, Long said, did not even know what Baptists believed.[40]

In New Mexico, the attack against Baptist distinctiveness came to a head in 1967 over the issue of alien immersion. In North Carolina, several churches had begun accepting as members people who had been sprinkled or baptized as infants. These acts raised debates throughout the SBC. Charles Killough, pastor of First Baptist Church in Hobbs, wanted the problem dealt with by altering the convention's bylaws. He advocated limiting convention membership to only those churches that baptized by immersion. In response, the convention established a special study committee to investigate and report their findings the following year.[41]

The "Alien-Immersion" Study Committee rendered its report to the convention in 1968. The committee rejected amendment of the bylaws on the grounds that messengers were already members of churches "which have been regularly received into and cooperating with one of the associations in New Mexico."[42] This action upheld the Baptist conviction that local church autonomy must not be infringed upon by an ecclesiastical body. Traditionally, the matter of discipline remained the province of the churches in the association.

The issue reappeared a year later, when Frank Wheeler of Alamogordo made a motion to amend the bylaws. This time the motion moved to prohibit the seating of any messenger from a church that practiced open membership or recognized baptism by other than a Baptist church. Several pastors voiced their opposition, even though they personally stood against alien immersion. The convention rejected the measure in a floor vote.[43]

The next problem to erupt involved "creedalism." The issue had simmered just beneath the surface since the Elliott controversy in 1962. It exploded ten years later with the publication of the Broadman Commentary by the Sunday School Board. Storm warnings appeared the year before. W. A. Criswell, pastor of First Baptist Church in Dallas, published the book, *Why I Preach That the Bible is Literally True*. His position did not sit well with a minority in the SBC, but what ignited the furor was a subsequent response to his critics. Criswell charged that all who could not subscribe to the 1963 Baptist Faith and Message statement should leave the denomination.

With tempers flaring and tensions increasing, all state editors received a copy of the new Broadman Commentary. At the 1970 national convention, James Sullivan, secretary of the Sunday School Board, had moved that all programs be carried out in a manner consistent with the 1963 statement.

Whitlow observed that the commentary was not consistent with this directive, and sent copies of his editorial to all Sunday School Board members, urging that the commentary be recalled. Only one responded. He denounced the editorial, and told Whitlow to read the commentary first.

Understandably infuriated by the insult, Whitlow continued his attack in subsequent editorials. At issue were the first two verses in chapter 22 in the Book of Genesis. The author of this section of the commentary, Professor Gene Henton Davies, a Baptist theologian from Great Britain, claimed that God did not tell Abraham to sacrifice Isaac, and that Abraham's intent to sacrifice his son was a result of the patriarch's psychology. Whitlow challenged Davies's reasoning, claiming that it had dangerous implications. He said that one could argue that John did not receive a revelation on the isle of Patmos. It could be explained that the uncertainty of the times psychologically conditioned John to imagine the whole thing or that Paul suffered from a guilt complex for having persecuted so many Christians, and that this psychologically prepared him to feel that he had encountered Christ on the road to Damascus. Inerrancy lay at the root of Whitlow's critique. He wrote: "We can live with differences of interpretation of the text, but when portions of the text are thrown out completely and an author's idea of what might have taken place is substituted, we cannot buy it. . . . My simple question is this: Who was inspired, Moses or Davies?"[44]

The SBC met in Denver in June of 1970 under less than harmonious circumstances. "Hostile" was the word most used to describe the attitude of the messengers. The first fallout from the Broadman Commentary issue was a motion to recall the first volume. The motion passed. The denomination began to polarize.

A year later, conditions worsened. New Mexico pastor John Parrott, serving in 1971 as vice chairman of the SBC's Executive Committee, expressed dismay at the turn of events. He said that people were making wild accusations against those in leadership, implying or accusing them of denying the truth of the scriptures. Charles Ashcroft, formerly with the BCNM, warned that the Southern Baptist tradition had now become the criteria by which the Bible was to be interpreted, instead of Jesus Christ. He warned that the denomination was in danger of becoming like the Roman Catholic Church. Aghast at the turn of events, Whitlow urged Baptists to forget about the controversy and go on before they permanently damaged themselves.[45]

The conservative theological position of New Mexico Baptists dampened the impact of the controversy. It also ensured that traditional Baptist principles still functioned in the state. A move in 1973 to require all convention employees to subscribe to the 1963 Baptist Faith and Message statement failed. The BCNM refused to embrace creedalism. Never in its history had the convention adopted a statement of faith of any kind.[46]

The other significant issue impacting the SBC concerned women pastors. In terms of numbers, the problem was miniscule. Only nine women received ordination as ministers by 1974 throughout the entire denomination. Yet the change as a departure from women's customary roles was huge. An avalanche of articles debating the merits of the issue ensued.

New Mexico's reaction paralleled the denomination's. When Burns learned about a woman being ordained in 1964 by a church in Durham, North Carolina, he was extremely upset. He wrote an editorial condemning the event, arguing that there was no New Testament base for ordaining women as ministers. Burns called Carl Scott, pastor of Central Baptist in Clovis, who was also the BCNM president. Scott's reaction typified many in the state: "I am not in favor of that sort of thing at all. I oppose it strongly."[47]

Glen McCoy, BSU director at Eastern New Mexico University, approached the issue by looking at the apostle Paul's concept of women. McCoy said that Paul's supposed restrictions placed on women were dictated by the cultural practices of the society to which he was writing. Whenever Paul gave instructions, it was within the context of the effects the practice would have on the Christian gospel. The problem, McCoy said, was in reading our cultural concept of women back into Paul's day. He admonished readers to follow the apostle's advice in Galatians 3:28: "There is neither male nor female; for you are all one in Christ Jesus."[48] The issue in New Mexico never evolved beyond rhetoric during this period, but it did shape opinion for future altercations.

The three issues described above overtly challenged traditional Southern Baptist practices, but in New Mexico things remained unchanged. Still, attempts to meet the challenges presented by social transformation in the 1960s covertly altered BCNM thinking. Adaptations in ministry moved Baptists toward a limited social gospel, but this new direction did not occur without theological debate. John Parrott and R. A. Long defined the issue's parameters in the pages of the *Baptist New Mexican*. Parrott claimed that many Christian leaders attacked the "social gospel" because it was not faithful to the word of God in requiring a personal encounter with Christ. Unfortunately, he said, this concept led to the belief that any mention of social principles within the context of gospel preaching was out of place. Yet Parrot added, "Jesus dealt with social relationships. He preached, taught, and practiced a social gospel."[49]

Agreeing that the Bible taught about social concerns, Long warned against confusing doctrine with the gospel. Baptism and tithing were important but they were not the gospel. They related to the gospel but were not of it. The gospel, Long asserted, "is the 'good news,' and it is this that is the power of God unto Salvation. Becoming involved in social issues is not the power of God unto salvation."[50]

Other ministers in the state entered the debate. G. A. Magee, pastor of First Baptist Church in Eunice, echoed Long's thoughts. He expressed concern over the decline in regularly scheduled revivals, which he attributed in part to liberal thinking. Magee thought that this orientation elevated social concerns over evangelism, thus causing soul-winning to suffer.[51]

Magee's concern dealt with challenges presented to the external proclamation of the kingdom of God by the "social gospel." In contrast, Kenneth Balthrop of Hoffmantown Baptist Church in Albuquerque examined why people were increasingly ignoring that proclamation. He observed a growing indifference on the part of the masses to Southern Baptist-style evangelism. Meaningful evangelism resulted in a change in the total life of the individual. Balthrop went on to say that the methodology to implement this theology must follow the examples of Jesus and Paul, who always met people where they were. Procedures from the past would no longer work. In a fragmented age, the church had to reach every area of a person's being, and this action required a new style of evangelism outside the walls of the church. He concluded that pastors in the future would have to train the laity to witness on the job, at school, and in the neighborhood.[52]

The debate remained thoroughly entrenched within the theologically conservative camp. It was never a battle between advocates of sociological improvements versus those who stressed individual conversion. Instead, the "social gospel" New Mexico Baptists embraced meant taking their message outside the church, meeting people where they were, and proclaiming the gospel while ministering to their needs.

Internal battles within the SBC and social change in American society had forced New Mexico Baptists to reexamine their doctrines. The fight was not over, however. External challenges to Baptist beliefs also surfaced. Numerous issues threatened the theological status quo. The "God is dead" controversy, situational ethics, and the Jesus Movement all received limited attention. For many, the greatest perceived threat to ministry lay in the phenomenon known as glossolalia or "speaking in tongues." Combating this crisis became a major priority among the pastors in the state.

All semblance of rhetorical decorum vanished in the heat of battle. Some, like J. F. Hopkins, pastor at First Baptist Church in Farmington, saw glossolalia as a form of self-hypnosis, or even demon possession.[53] Parrott, normally a pillar of propriety, could not contain himself: "It appears to me that you [persons practicing glossolalia] are a tool of the devil. You may not mean to be, but your intentions don't make the evil you do any more excusable. You have been caught up in a dangerous heresy."[54] Magee took a more sociological view, attributing the practice to frustrated people in a frustrated age looking for a spiritual high.[55]

Although New Mexico Baptists altered many of their practices during this era, they did not change their position concerning glossolalia. A few within the denomination found positive aspects and points of accommodation with the Pentecostal experience and the larger charismatic movement, but this softening did not occur in New Mexico. New Mexico Baptists continued to argue that Jesus did not teach glossolalia, Paul discouraged its use, and that it was a divisive element in the church.

⌇

During the 1960–1974 period, Baptists felt that their way of life was challenged, and indeed threatened, by all the social changes under way in American society. This attitude is evident in the numerous series appearing in the *Baptist New Mexican*. The volume and variety of concerns proved to be overwhelming. Throughout the 1960s, Herschell Hobbs, a former SBC president, wrote a weekly column titled "Baptist Beliefs." T. B. Matson addressed the "problems of the Christian life" in numerous articles spanning a two-year period. Others tackled issues such as the Christian in politics, Southern Baptists and the race problem, the Jesus Movement, world religions, the occult, and many more. These kinds of articles rarely occurred in the 1940s and 1950s. Issues that dealt with beliefs and practices came out in the form of a Sunday School lesson or sermon notes. That the regular format could not contain the flood of new subjects reflects the extent of the dislocation.

This disequilibrium in Baptist faith and practice led to a transformation in the personal expression of religious belief. Whitlow contrasted the old with the new style of worship in a 1973 editorial:

> For too long church activity was the be-all and end-all of the Christian life. Church attendance was thought of as Christian commitment, and church work was equated with a significant involvement in Christian life. The older generation has been "conditioned" in a world in which their experience of a person or place or thing was not consciously included as a part of knowing. If we saw something and understood it with our minds, we thought we knew it.

But the younger generation has come along to feel that to know something is to see it, feel it, touch it, think it, and experience it.[56]

Whitlow's astute observation highlighted the collapse of the inherited religious system. Sterility characterized the old structure, but the new lacked a transcendent standard that could distinguish pious devotion from an exercise in self-expression.

Wayland Edwards summarized the impact that this disequilibrium had on New Mexico Baptists in an address before the convention in 1969. Commenting on the tremendous transformation that had occurred, he noted:

> The world is almost changing faster than a man can change his emotions. The changing world is all about us and we may not be able to do much about it. How can you update something that is already in tomorrow. We need a new awareness of Christ in our lives.[57]

This momentous change led to a turning inward and with it the loss of a corporate Baptist vision. People still participated in church life, but with a growing sense that it was an individual effort. The "new awareness" that Edwards looked for never materialized. Underneath the fanfare of newly initiated projects and crusades, a pessimism pervaded that translated itself into a "coping mentality" in which institutional preservation became the ultimate goal.

───The Chester O'Brien Years: 1975 to 1984

After the tumultuous 1960s, the Chester O'Brien era became a welcome return to normalcy for New Mexico Baptists. On the surface, the previous
decade seemed like an unpleasant dream, as Baptists returned to their twin
emphases of evangelism and church planting. Elected unanimously, O'Brien
began his tenure in January 1975 under extremely favorable circumstances.

Three factors came together to make this period an era of new growth
for the denomination. First, O'Brien built on a long-range planning process,
begun in 1973.[1] A study committee, begun in that year, laid out goals for
every department of the convention for the period 1976 to 1980. Second,
O'Brien's tenure coincided with the "Bold Mission Thrust" crusade. Sponsored
by the Southern Baptist Convention (SBC), the crusade was a denomination-
wide attempt to evangelize America by the year 2000. Preparations began in
the mid-1970s, with New Mexico feeling the full impact after 1980. The
final determinant was a nationwide evangelical upsurge, culminating in the
election of Jimmy Carter in 1976. Dubbed the "decade of the evangelical"
by the media, New Mexico Baptists experienced conditions similar to those
under Harry Stagg after World War II. The merger of these three elements in
one ten-year period produced another wave of expansion.

Attempts at Revitalization

The long-range planning process climaxed at Glorieta in February 1975.
The committee established comprehensive priority goals to mobilize the
churches in evangelizing the state. These goals covered two areas: increasing
church effectiveness, and assisting churches in establishing new ministries
for expressing Christ among all people.

Many items were a revamping of previous programs, including training
for lay members in Bible study, missions, evangelism, and stewardship. New
areas, however, revealed the impact of the 1960s on Baptist faith and practice.
The convention, with the assistance of the churches, accepted the responsibility
to provide leadership for Christian social ministries. Specifically, they planned

for outreach to meet the needs of drug users, the homeless, institutionalized persons, students, and others outside the traditional church community.

Through these efforts, after more than a decade of stagnation, the convention sought to regain the initiative. Working through the churches, the Baptist Convention of New Mexico (BCNM) pushed forward to place an evangelistic witness in areas where no such ministry had previously existed. They assisted churches in the development of their extension plans and aided them in the acquisition of new building sites. Leadership training for ethnic churches also intensified. The resort evangelism emphasis switched from seasonal to permanent work. The BSUs became resource centers, coordinating their ministry with local churches and serving as bases for special projects personnel.[2] The changes this long-range planning process revealed indicate that Baptists fully embraced the necessity of moving outside the confines of the local church. In so doing, the convention made a "limited" social gospel a part of their institutional structure.

Financial strength gave substance to these plans, as the denomination entered a period of fiscal expansion. During O'Brien's tenure, the Cooperative Program budget rose from $702,329 to $2,290,351.[3] From 1972 through 1981, receipts increased every year. Explosive giving resulted in an "overage," allowing for funding of new projects at an accelerated rate. So consistently did this surplus occur that in 1975 the State Mission Board determined that all future expenditures should be based on current income:

> This means that "overage" previously will become "budget" currently. An "advance" budget . . . pre-determines the causes that will be fostered. This approach leaves no loose ends.[4]

Such an important decision had far-reaching implications. It meant that previous giving now determined all future ministry considerations.

Unparalleled giving led to more spending on direct mission work. Even with the indebtedness on improvements at Inlow and Sivells Camps, plus the work on the BSUs in Las Cruces and Las Vegas, the convention was debt free by 1977. In addition, receipts enabled them to place $122,522.72 in an operational reserve fund, and $84,251.15 in a capital fund.[5] Overages continued. In 1978, BCNM recorded its largest surplus in history, $171,074.45. This extra income allowed the convention to purchase additional lots for the BSU in Las Cruces and greatly expand the facilities at Sivells.[6]

Budget receipts continued to increase, with no sign of ending. Optimism over financial conditions led the convention in 1981 to renovate the Baptist

Building (BCNM headquarters) on Central Avenue in Albuquerque. Authorized to borrow up to $600,000, the BCNM pushed ahead and finished the project in 1982.[7]

A portion of this surplus income also benefited the Children's Home. One of the convention's goals involved a complete campus overhaul. By the end of O'Brien's tenure, that dream had been realized. New construction included four cottages, a grocery building, a shop, clothing and laundry facilities, storage space, administrative offices, apartments for workers, and a day-off cottage. All projects were finished debt free.[8]

The Children's Home not only underwent physical restructuring, the direction of its ministry also changed. During this era, the orphanage sustained its greatest period of financial stability. From this solid base, and in cooperation with the SBC's resettlement program for refugees, the home began in 1975 to accept Vietnamese children. By 1980, outreach extended to émigrés from Laos as well.[9]

The greatest change, however, was neither physical nor ministerial but organizational. During this period, the Children's Home evolved from orphanage to a pass-through "rehabilitation center." In previous decades, children coming to the facility became part of a large extended family. Now, fewer and fewer residents stayed for an extended time. Many new residents suffered from emotional problems or other forms of abuse. Once stabilized, they were sent back to their families. For example, in 1976 seventy-eight children received care, and of these, twenty-three returned to their families. Anticipating an increase in this trend, the home requested in 1977 that the state issue a license permitting it to place children in foster care. The home director's assumption proved correct. In 1984, forty of ninety-seven residents left; only sixteen remained longer than a year, and forty-one were new.[10]

The convention's camps also benefited from the budget surpluses. Expanding programs and additional usage by ethnic groups increased the volume at both Inlow and Sivells Camps. By the end of O'Brien's tenure, the number of campers attending during the summer surpassed the two thousand mark for each facility. Such heavy use required extensive upgrading. During O'Brien's first year, a dormitory and staff building were added to the Sivells facility at a cost of $30,596.56. The following year the convention spent $35,446.86 on a manager's home at the Inlow Camp. Improvements at Sivells in 1978 included a chapel, recreation room, and two small dormitories, totaling $109,568.28. Heavy snowfall in 1983 at Inlow necessitated the rebuilding of a bathhouse and cabin.[11]

Despite increased attendance, the camps continued to be a financial drain on the convention. During the 1975–1984 period, in addition to monies spent on renovation and expansion, the BCNM had to make up a $26,661.70 shortfall in operational expenses.[12] Fortunately, financial prosperity allowed the state mission offering and budget "overage" to carry this additional burden.

Availability of money also allowed New Mexico Baptists to expand their infrastructure and enabled divisions to expand their resources and services. Such was the case with the Baptist Foundation. Rapid change in personnel and capital characterized the period. Gary Inman became the third president of the foundation in 1975, replacing J. D. Ratliff. Six years later, Lee Black assumed control. Foundation assets grew from just over $1 million to nearly $4 million in ten years. Endowments for special projects and ministries, such as scholarships, foreign missions, and camps, accounted for an additional $1 million.[13]

Burgeoning finances clearly increased capital development. It was expansion in the areas of evangelism and missions, however, which highlighted the New Mexico Baptist story during the O'Brien era. Goals established through the long-range planning process combined with substantial income provided the foundation for growth. These two factors came together at the same time that the SBC launched its Bold Mission Thrust crusade. This national campaign to reach all peoples led New Mexico Baptists to concentrate on outreach to ethnic communities in a way they had never done before.

The arrival of Billy Graham in March 1975, within a few months of Chester O'Brien's coming to New Mexico, served as a catalyst for this new round of evangelism and missions expansion. Graham had first visited Albuquerque in 1953 at the request of W. D. Wyatt, then pastor at First Baptist Church. Once again Baptists played a prominent role by hosting an evangelism school. The event drew 650 pastors from 110 denominations. Mayor Harry Kinney of Albuquerque and Governor Jerry Apodaca officially greeted Graham. Former governor Bruce King and his wife were also on the platform. University Arena was filled to capacity every night, and estimates placed total attendance at more than 120,000 people. Graham concluded his stay by addressing the scientific community at Los Alamos.[14]

The Graham crusade stimulated evangelistic efforts lasting the rest of the decade. Coinciding as it did with Bold Mission Thrust led to another round of expansion. A falling baptism to membership ratio beginning in the 1960s led the national body to seek to determine what was causing the decline in growth. Research showed that the denomination had failed to penetrate the emerging ethnic and minority communities. Therefore, the language mission department of the HMB, along with its state counterparts, became directly involved in developing strategies to penetrate a variety of cultural groups.[15] Beginning in 1977, the BCNM distributed information packets to pastors and missionaries that included demographic data by county, highlighting the population by age and ethnicity, in preparation for the upcoming campaign.

The Bold Mission Thrust crusade officially began on June 13, 1979, with a rally at the Houston Astrodome. As a national effort the crusade proved disappointing. Escalating confrontation between denominational liberals and conservatives, growing out of the Broadman Commentary issue, sabotaged the campaign. For the BCNM, however, the overall impact stimulated expansion. Church starts provide the evidence. In 1975, the convention counted 250 churches and missions in the state, a figure that had stayed relatively constant for several years. Ten years later, the number had grown to 340. Although of limited success nationwide, Bold Mission Thrust proved a major stimulus to growth in New Mexico.[16] Not being caught up in doctrinal battles allowed BCNM to expend its energies on evangelism.

In attempting to reach outside the church community, the BCNM used a combination of methods, some of which resurrected old procedures. Saturation campaigns, popular in the 1940s and 1950s, found new applications in the 1970s. Director of associational missions for the Western Association, Roy McKinney, interested three pastors in the Grants-Milan area in this idea. Helpers from as far away as Clovis joined a total of 130 people to conduct the survey. They visited more than a thousand homes. Their efforts led to eighteen professions of faith, fifteen enrollees in Sunday School, and sixty families identified as prospects for the churches.

Regional success in 1977 led to statewide campaigns. All convention departments collaborated with the Evangelism Division to conduct a statewide saturation visitation called "Care and Share" in 1979. The following year, simultaneous revivals blanketed the state. Individual training undergirded this corporate effort, with lay evangelism schools and continuing witness seminars mobilizing the laity.

Even as old methodology enjoyed renewed interest, new applications of that spirit emerged. For example, First Baptist Church in Clovis hosted a David Stockwell revival for youth in a gymnasium, featuring the world's largest pizza supper. Although some churches concentrated on new techniques, others used the evangelism format to approach Christian life issues other than salvation. Hoffmantown Baptist Church in Albuquerque conducted a "Christian maturity" seminar, whereas the Central Association sponsored the "Billie Hanks Conference on Christian Discipleship."[17]

Evangelism generated momentum that spilled across borders, making 1980 a banner year. The BCNM participated in joint efforts with other "energy corridor" states in evangelistic endeavors. They also sent eight bilingual pastors to Mexico to help spread the gospel. A dozen ministers and singers went to the Philippines to participate in crusades and revivals. Since 1978, the convention had helped churches in North Dakota, South Dakota, Montana, and Wyoming with mission projects. In 1981, the Northern Plains Convention asked for further help in establishing ten missions. The Northeastern and Tucumcari Associations responded. They coordinated a church-to-church, association-to-association mission strategy, dealing with financial aid, church building, Vacation Bible Schools, and evangelistic outreach.[18] Preparations also began in 1982 for a massive evangelistic crusade in England, sponsored by the HMB. The following year New Mexico sent forty "seed teams" totaling 233 people across the Atlantic.[19]

Intense evangelism produced direct results. Not since the post-World War II revival had there been such a flurry of church planting. After 1945, Baptists had covered the state with churches. By 1960, the convention had a presence in virtually every part of New Mexico. Where then did they find new sources for expansion? The answer lay in New Mexico's ethnic communities.

Ethnic Outreach

Beginning in the late 1960s, mission policy had changed from ethnic dependence on Anglo missionaries to indigenous leadership. This practice accelerated during the O'Brien era. For instance, in 1978 there were eighty-nine conventional missionaries in the field. After that year, the numbers steadily declined so that by 1984 the force had dropped by one third to sixty-one. Attempts to educate Hispanics and Native Americans to handle their churches continued to gain momentum. In 1976, there were four regional conferences held for Hispanics in Artesia, Las Cruces, Clovis, and Albuquerque, and two for Indians at Fort Wingate and in Albuquerque.[20]

In addition to those wanting more formal education, the convention conducted six seminary extension centers located throughout the state, offering classes toward a seminary diploma. To more effectively impact and empower the Native American and Hispanic leaders who might not feel at home in the traditional classroom, the BCNM held specialized courses more conducive to their specific cultural environment. Known as the Ethnic Leadership Development program, Dalton Edwards ran the center in Albuquerque and oversaw three branches located in Gallup, Fruitland, and Tinian.[21]

Education and training of ethnic leaders to conduct evangelism and manage their churches also led to capital expansion projects. For instance, in 1976 new buildings were constructed at Fruitland and Crown Point on the Navajo reservation. The structure on the Alamo reservation also underwent substantial improvements. First Baptist Church in Gallup donated fifty-nine acres, known as the Black Hat property, for use as an Indian leadership-training center. A year later, pastor Bobby Fuller and the membership from First Baptist Church in Bloomfield helped construct a modular chapel at Nageezi.[22]

New developments in Native American evangelism occurred in 1979. Videotapes of the Navajo Indian fellowship meetings with First Indian Church in Farmington aired on television. It was the beginning of several programs featuring pastor Andrew Begaye, speaking in both Navajo and English. The viewing audience extended beyond New Mexico into Texas, Arizona, Illinois, Iowa, and Wyoming.[23]

Traditionally, "ethnic ministry" usually meant Indian and Hispanic, but in the 1970s this orientation changed. Refugees from Southeast Asia arrived in the state. First Baptist Church in Albuquerque began immediately ministering to these new minorities, sponsoring an Oriental Baptist mission in 1978. Fruit Avenue Baptist Church followed a year later, with a refugee program that distributed furnishings, utensils, and clothing. In 1981, Sandia Baptist Church in Clovis began a Laotian ministry under the direction of pastor Hoyt Welch. That same year, Crestview Baptist Church in Albuquerque started a Chinese mission.[24]

While not all churches were able to sponsor a mission, some chose to become involved in ministry to immigrants through literacy classes provided by the Christian Social Ministries program. One such case was Northridge Chapel in Farmington. A growing Asian population led the church in 1982 to offer language instruction. Others teamed up with the BSUs to conduct outreach on state campuses. To help support this work, BCNM held Interfaith Witness Conferences in five cities across the state. In addition, the convention assisted refugees with personal items, such as furniture, clothing, food, and a relocation service to help reunite families.[25]

All this new work consolidated a shift in the ethnic ministry that had begun in the late 1960s. By the end of the O'Brien era, mass evangelism to ethnic communities, plus intense leadership training, had become the primary focus of the convention's outreach.

Operational Divergence

Clearly, expansion characterized the period. For one, the convention excelled financially. A survey examining individual contributions between 1972 and 1982 revealed that New Mexico Baptists increased their per capita giving by

CHAPTER 8

181.2 percent. Only the states of Alabama, Louisiana, Oklahoma, and Texas exceeded this figure.[26] There were also significant capital improvements at the Children's Home and in the Inlow and Sivells Camps. In addition, the number of churches rose by 26 percent. When combined with the upsurge in evangelism and outreach to ethnics, this decade seemed to echo the Stagg era. The similarity, however, was only in appearance.

Behind the expansion in revenue, infrastructure improvement, and church growth, core convention programs plateaued, and in some cases even declined. What appeared as an anomaly during the Bradford directorship became confirmed under O'Brien's term: operational divergence. For example, the *Baptist New Mexican*, after having achieved saturation in the 1950s, lost that coverage in the 1960s. Despite the upsurge in activity, the paper failed to rebound to its previous level. In 1975, subscriptions numbered 15,348. By 1984, even though the denominational membership increased by more than 17,000, the number receiving the newspaper rose to only 17,254. Much of this increase was because of a policy change in 1982 that offered pastors the eighth page for local church news as a means of expanding circulation.[27]

This lack of involvement among the membership was apparent in other Baptist programs as well. Never a large organization, the Brotherhood nevertheless served an important function by supporting the pastor and galvanizing the men for work. Thus, erosion in participation hurt the ministry of the church. When Chester O'Brien became executive director in 1975, the fellowship numbered only 2,754. Despite the increase in membership, ten years later the organization registered a gain of only 416 persons.[28]

Enlistment problems were not limited to the Brotherhood. The WMU experienced similar difficulties. Despite heavy involvement in prayer projects and missions, numbers stagnated. Starting in 1981, the organization initiated a statewide "enlargement campaign." Statistics for 1980 revealed that out of 322 churches, 76 lacked women's groups. Betty Lindrith began working with these congregations to form WMUs. This campaign was part of a national effort to reach 2 million members by 1984; New Mexico's goal was to enlist 8,024. Two years later, "start teams" came in to help establish thirty-five new units in the state. Despite these efforts, the figures fell miserably short. Having begun the period with 5,793 on their rolls, the WMU discovered that ten years later their numbers had only increased by 123.[29]

This lackluster performance, despite the heavy emphasis on time, money, and personnel, carried over into the educational ministries. For several years, Sunday School program membership remained near the fifty thousand mark. In an attempt to revitalize the program, the Education Division returned to the time-honored techniques of the 1940s and 1950s that seemed to be working for evangelism. For instance, in 1975 the division sponsored small church conferences to help pastors organize their congregations for Sunday School and Church Training activities. On a broader scale, in 1979, through the People Search-Witness program, the BCNM conducted presentations for the churches and associations to assist with developing their base for Bible study. The convention also sent mail-outs to churches with suggested tips on building prospect files. Yet, by the end of 1979, Sunday School rolls numbered almost one thousand less than four years before.[30]

As the new decade approached, an era came to an end. Charles Polston, a leader in the Church Training program, and Ed Storm, leader in the Sunday School program, both retired at the end of 1980. Between them they had given sixty years of service to the state convention. Taking over in 1981, Duane Morrow became director of the Educational Division with W. A. Bradshaw serving as his associate. Coinciding with the change in leadership, the SBC launched their "8.5 by 85" campaign, an attempt to raise the denomination's Sunday School enrollment to 8.5 million; New Mexico's goal was 59,000. From the beginning, however, there was a lack of worker involvement. In fact, "Whistle Stop Workshops," designed to mobilize the troops for action, were a disappointment, with few churches and associations participating. One official complained that people were just not taking advantage of the training.[31]

New Mexicans never reached their goal, falling just over 3,000 short at 55,872. In addition, the percentage of involvement declined. Church membership during the O'Brien era rose by 17,717. Sunday School enrollment advanced by 6,771, or 38 percent of the convention's growth.[32] These figures demonstrate that even though numbers were at an all-time high, the percentage of those actively participating continued to plunge. Despite expansion of the church's outreach during this period, the core programs continued to struggle.

While the Sunday School division at least had posted numerical gains, the Church Training program failed even to do that. Beginning the period with 14,134 on the roles, church training numbers ten years later had declined by 54 to 14,080. All attempts to revitalize this program failed. Declining attendance led in the 1970s to a curriculum change. Known as the Discipleship Training program, instruction shifted to an individualized approach utilizing "equipping centers," which were six- to thirteen-week study courses. The courses included soul winning and doctrine but also brought in social ministries and contemporary issues. Attempts to customize the program to fit the person led to experimenting with new times and days. Despite the new format, however, participation did not increase. In fact, the new individualism worked against social cohesion. The many other activities occupying people's time—school, community events, sports, television, travel, and other recreational possibilities—all worked against these efforts. Obviously, the emerging two-income household forced families to choose between time together or yet another meeting.[33]

The SBC interpreted this social change as a curriculum failure of the old Discipleship Training. This analysis led to the creation of the "Life Curriculum" program implemented toward the end of the decade. The new courses marked a radical departure from the old. Emphasis now switched to "meeting people's needs." Study units covered such topics as financial planning and marriage enrichment.[34] The purpose was to generate interest. In the process, the meetings jettisoned doctrinal training.[35] An unintended consequence of this new series was that it did not communicate Southern Baptist distinctiveness and traditions. People began to lose their spiritual and denominational identity.

These changing conditions had an enormous impact on other BCNM ministries. For instance, the BSUs underwent an educational reorganization. Dropping enrollment and increased emphasis on evangelism in the early 1970s led to the abandonment of the Bible chairs. Now, theological training for credit gave way to "lifestyle" Bible study. The new emphasis stressed fellowship, relationships, and Christian living, evolving by the 1980s into a student-led ministry.[36] Area churches and BSUs coordinated their efforts to increase evangelism by meeting the needs of the college student. Only the program at Eastern New Mexico State University continued to offer traditional religious education.

Déjà Vu

Except for the plateauing of the core church programs, the O'Brien period appeared similar to the Stagg era. External expansion in capital growth, evangelism, and church planting looked very familiar to the 1938–1960 period. Then, as in the later years of Stagg's directorship, conditions began to change. In 1982, the chairman of the State Executive Board, Francis Wilson, wrote an open letter to the convention:

> We must be careful with our financial program, but we must be generous as churches with our giving. We must ever keep uppermost that God has called us to be servants and not conservationists. We must not, at the same time, be wasteful with the resources God has

laid at our disposal, but we must be careful with their use to render a good accounting of our stewardship.[37]

In 1983, for the first time in twelve years, receipts failed to reach the Cooperative Program goal. Although the figures showed only a $4,149 budget shortfall, and receipts were up 7 percent over 1982, everyone felt uneasy. Conditions worsened in 1984. This time contributions fell $172,738.17 behind the projected income, though still above the year before.[38] For the first time, significant budget shortfalls began to appear. Overages that had funded so many projects were no longer available. Convention divisions, although still operating in the black, began to curtail some of their programs. For many this condition was ominously reminiscent of the early 1960s.

At the same time that convention finances turned down, infrastructure problems surfaced. Deteriorating conditions at the camps and dwindling funds had by 1984 produced a crisis. Speaking at a State Executive Board meeting in October, Dale McLesky noted, "[W]e are locked into a position of needing massive amounts of money for camp improvements, have no method of attaining funding, and the camps are in bad shape and deteriorating."[39]

Added to the financial problems of decreasing income and the need to spend massive amounts of money to maintain the camps was the indebtedness on the Baptist Building and the renovation of the Albuquerque BSU facility. Initiation of these projects started as income began to fall, which proved uncomfortably similar to the Stagg era and the problem with Sivells Camp. A BCNM fiscal crisis loomed on the horizon.

Even before these overt fiscal dilemmas surfaced, there were indications of emerging problems within BCNM's operations that would eventually affect the financial health of the convention. The reorganization in 1970 had severely curtailed personnel and put a strain on the ability of the divisions to conduct their ministries adequately. This condition became apparent by 1976 when the State Mission Board appointed a committee to study the issue. A report issued a year later favored staff expansion, but no action resulted. The Policy and Personnel Committee again looked into the feasibility after several individuals and groups expressed concern. The committee's reluctance was clearly fiscal: "These requests have real validity and need to be carefully weighed against our financial ability and our constant need for more dollars to fill Bold Mission Thrust responsibilities and opportunities . . ."[40]

Churches were also caught up in the euphoria, pouring available funds into evangelism, missions, and church planting, often to the neglect of their staff. Pastor Billy Foster of First Baptist Church in Bayard expressed concern over its impact on ministers and personnel. Many suffered financial problems due to "starve-to-death salaries" because "the church is spending the money on buildings or feels overzealous toward sending money through the missions program of the church."[41]

Commitment to growth and expansion had left many issues unanswered. By 1984, serious internal problems beset the convention. The staff needed expanding. Pastors and convention employees' salaries required increases to make them competitive with the private sector. Too many ministers and other workers also lacked proper insurance and retirement benefits. In addition, the debt on the Baptist Building needed retiring. The decaying infrastructure at the camps was a fiscal time bomb.

O'Brien did not ignore these issues. He initiated the initial response to the benefits problem through an annuity program. His primary concern, however, lay with returning the convention to its mission of evangelizing and starting churches. Social turmoil in the 1960s had devastated the Baptist psyche and the people needed a new vision. Attempting to restore that loss absorbed O'Brien's efforts. Solving the internal problems became the work of O'Brien's successor.

⤳

Despite the large areas of growth in missions, evangelism, and church planting, the decline in core church programs caused New Mexico to depart from the pattern of other Western states. During the 1970s, the population in the West grew by nearly 24 percent, while Southern Baptists in those states increased by 40 percent, but not in New Mexico. Instead, the state followed the trend of Southern Baptists in the South.[42]

A BCNM study conducted in 1982 revealed that over the previous ten years, New Mexico's population had increased by 28 percent, while Baptist membership grew only 16 percent. During the Stagg era, denominational growth had exceeded the state's expansion. In Dixie, the population grew by 20 percent, but the SBC increased by only 15 percent. The reason given for this decline was that Southern Baptists failed to keep pace with Blacks and other ethnic groups. Despite all the work to non-Anglos in the state, the BCNM experienced the same results.[43]

New Mexico also followed the SBC in membership and Sunday School enrollment. The denomination in 1982 showed 14 million attending their churches, but 4 million or 28 percent were nonresident. The BCNM fared worse. With 109,220 on the rolls, only 63,504 actually attended. Forty-two percent were nonresident members. In Sunday School, the pattern remained the same. The national body estimated that nearly 8 million of its 14 million members were on the education roster, or 57 percent. In New Mexico, only 51,851 participated in Sunday School, which was only 47 percent of the membership.[44]

Financially, New Mexico followed its parent body. Giving each year continued to set a record. By the end of the O'Brien era, however, receipts began to fall below the proposed budget. This same pattern existed within the SBC. For instance, in 1984 income set a new Cooperative Program high but fell nearly $2.5 million behind projections.[45]

In the all-important category of baptisms, the state convention, like its core programs, plateaued, and when adjusted for the increase in membership, actually declined. In 1975, the BCNM recorded 3,824 baptized. Ten years later, the number was 3,955. In 1982 and 1983, the figures broke 4,000, making them some of the highest in convention history. When this barrier was first exceeded under Stagg, however, the BCNM numbered approximately 75,000, or 1 baptism for every 18.75 members. During the years just cited, the rolls averaged over 110,000, making the ratio 1 to 27.5.[46]

The O'Brien years reaped to full advantage the return to religion after the tumultuous 1960s. This "decade of the evangelical" on a diminished scale paralleled the post-World War II revival that Stagg and the BCNM had used to propel themselves to prominence in the state. Baptists in New Mexico as well as the SBC, however, failed to make gains relative to population growth. The plateauing, and in some cases decline, in core church programs pointed to the possibility of a denominational "swan song."

CHAPTER 9

The Claude Cone Era: 1985 to 1995

The declining years of the O'Brien era foreshadowed a change in the fortunes of Southern Baptists in New Mexico. The evangelical wave of the 1970s stalled in the early 1980s. A new time of trial awaited the convention. Unaware of what was about to happen, Claude Cone assumed the directorship on March 1, 1985. At the first State Executive Board meeting of his tenure, Cone revealed his areas of interest and concern: more support for the Cooperative Program; increased state staff salaries; more pastors in the denomination's annuity program; expansion of the hospitalization and retirement programs for convention employees; and address the institutional needs of the Children's Home, the camps, and the debt on the Baptist Building.[1]

Financial Concerns
Immediately upon assuming the directorship, Cone faced a problem that burdened him throughout his tenure: a shortage of operating capital. A report by the business manager, Ted Roberts, on the proposed budget for 1986 made four suggestions: freeze salaries at the present level, have the convention assume the employees' part of the medical insurance, cut program levels by 10 percent, and keep the budget the same as 1985. The reason for these stringent measures was that even though giving exceeded 1984 by more than $142,000, it fell 4 percent below the funds necessary to operate the convention's programs.[2] This pattern of new budget records, yet the inability to meet projected needs, continued throughout the Cone administration.

For the first time, in 1990, the Baptist Convention of New Mexico (BCNM) scaled back its Cooperative Program goal. Receipts still fell short, although they exceeded the 1989 figures. The following year, 1991, was a time of crisis. The convention operated at 93 percent of budget, but still 6 percent above income. At the same time, a number of capital projects demanded attention. The BSU in Albuquerque required $60,000 for improvement of its facilities. Sivells Camp needed the same amount. Mission New Mexico required $48,000 for land and staff.[3]

According to the business manager, Francis Wilson, income set back from previous years kept BCNM on a sound financial footing. In 1995, the largest budget in history was projected. Giving in the early months, however, forced the divisions to operate at 90 percent. Income did increase and the fiscal year ended in the black, but the denomination still needed an additional $157,345.[4] This continued pattern of record giving, with receipts remaining below projections, hampered the development of new work. Preoccupation with the financial integrity of the convention inhibited its outreach programs.

Besides the problem of budget shortfalls, several specific financial concerns required attention. The note on the Baptist Building proved to be the primary concern. In 1985, the convention's debt for this facility totaled $357,607.84. Refinancing the loan provided some relief. The interest rate dropped from 14.5 percent to 11.5 percent, thus saving the convention $28,800 per year in interest. Also, during this same year, the denomination was able to make a $100,000 lump-sum payment against its obligation. A special statewide mission offering to retire the debt took place in 1986. The $206,007.79 collected was the largest ever received. It enabled the BCNM to pay off the building seven years ahead of schedule, saving $84,000 in interest and removing an annual payment of $68,000.[5]

Success in retiring the building debt ahead of schedule amidst financial difficulties led the executive director to tackle yet another area of concern. Cone sought to increase church involvement in the Southern Baptist Convention's (SBC) annuity program. Figures from 1986 revealed very few participants. The BCNM had paid only $40,143 to the Annuity Board. Under Cone's leadership, that figure more than doubled; by 1990, 46 percent of church staff was covered. Numbers continued to rise so that by 1995, 288 pastors and staff members were enrolled from 155 churches, accounting for 72 percent of those eligible for this type of coverage. Reaching this level made New Mexico first in its region, and fourth in the denomination; nationally, the average was 55 percent.[6]

Coping with budget shortfalls and debt on the Baptist Building were not the only problems facing the convention. In 1986, another financial crisis occurred. Gas wells owned by the Children's Home began to go dry. The home's operational income dropped by $75,000 to $100,000 a year. Compounding the financial problem, that same year the New Mexico Christian Child Care Association placed the facility on probation.

The charges against the Children's Home enumerated deficiencies in several areas, as well as an overall need to strengthen the program. Specifically, the critics required that new procedures be implemented to improve the admission and placement process and strengthen the documentation between the worker and the child. They also cited the home for failure to have proper communication and teamwork among the staff. Required changes included developing working relationships with other service providers so as to supplement the ministry with intensive counseling when needed by any youth. Efforts to comply with the association's recommendations led to the removal of probation two years later.[7]

Meanwhile, the need to deal with the financial crisis led to a recommendation that the convention raise $7 million for endowments. Funds would go to benefit four projects: the Children's Home, Inlow and Sivells Camps, BSUs, and special state missions. Plans envisioned $1 million for the BSUs and $2 million each for the other three ministries. The convention designated the first campaign for the Children's Home, beginning in 1987, to run for three years. The immediate financial needs of the home were met by a record Mother's Day offering. For ongoing support, the BCNM encouraged churches to contribute 2 percent of their gross receipts.

Unfortunately, contributions for the endowment proceeded slowly. By 1990, the drive had only raised $515,942 Extending the campaign three more years brought in nearly another $500,000. When combined with an old endowment, the two together exceeded the needed $2.4 million by 1995. Despite support from the churches and the Mother's Day offering, however, the home still experienced financial trouble.

Rising operating costs were the major problem. The reason was due to the changing nature of the home. Begun as an orphanage, it had evolved into a pass-through rehabilitation center. The state licensing board required changes that contributed to the escalating costs. In 1987, the home spent $10,000 per child per year. By way of comparison, the New Mexico Boys' Ranch spent $2,000 more, and Buckner's youth facility in Lubbock, Texas, paid out twice that amount. By 1995, operational expenses had skyrocketed; the Portales facility expended $25,000 to take care of one child over the course of a year. An average of twenty-six children in residence now required nineteen employees. Even with a $2.5 million endowment paying $130,000 in interest and contributions by the churches, the home still experienced a $70,000 shortfall in its $562,145 budget.[8]

The camps compounded the financial drain. Throughout the O'Brien era, they operated at a deficit and were always sustained by surplus funds. Capital improvements received secondary consideration, while the Children's Home underwent a complete renovation. The Inlow and Sivells Camps' infrastructure had deteriorated to the point that they required massive monetary outlay to bring them up to standard.

Attempts to correct the problem began in 1985 by raising user fees so as to make the facilities self-sustaining. The increase allowed for some physical improvements, and in 1986 the camps operated in the black. The good times, however, did not last, with 1987 becoming known as the "year of snow." Inlow received 276 inches, with damages to three buildings costing more than $40,000 to repair. In 1988, the Environmental Protection Agency forced the replacement of the Manna Dining Hall. The BCNM spent $230,902 to construct a new facility and renamed it in honor of former business manager Ted Roberts. In addition, at the insistence of the Soil Conservation Service, the state convention undertook a flood control project to protect its buildings in the event of severe flooding at Sivells. In 1989, further improvements resulted in a $50,000 allocation for each camp. By 1990, financial pressure forced the BCNM to open the camp facilities for use by non-Baptist groups.[9]

Yet expectations of a new generation of campers made the accommodations appear much less attractive. Responding to this change and hoping to stimulate revenue by appealing to a wider base, the convention decided to build a motel-style facility at Sivells. In 1991, the convention allocated $60,000 for use to build a year-round facility that would appeal to adults. Estimated costs of the project amounted to $300,000. But income fell drastically in 1992, thus requiring the use of surplus funds to make up a $35,126 operational shortfall. Another $64,000 went to Inlow for upgrades. The motel project at Sivells received $50,000 more in 1993.

Operational deficits continued in 1995, with spending nearly $18,000 over generated income. In addition to budget shortage problems, attendance began to falter. Declining numbers caused the cancellation of some camps. Despite renovations, new facilities, increasing fees, and use by other groups, the BCNM was one of the few state conventions left in the SBC still subsidizing its camp program.[10]

Having to use large amounts of funds for institutional housekeeping hampered the work of evangelization and new church planting. Maintaining denominational edifices became a serious problem that consumed large portions of money, draining funds for new work. For instance, between 1986 and 1990, the State Mission Offering totaled $901,139. Renovations at Inlow and Sivells used $437,000 of that amount. In contrast, only $230,000 went into land and buildings for new work.[11]

The problem was compounded in 1991. In addition to $65,000 for the motel at Sivells, the BSU in Albuquerque needed renovation at a cost of over $500,000. A total of $60,000 from the State Mission Offering went to this project, whereas only $48,000 went to Mission New Mexico to help start new churches along the Rio Grande corridor. This pattern continued throughout the 1990s.[12]

Dale McLesky's observation in 1984 concerning the camps now extended to the entire convention. The BCNM had become locked into needing massive amounts of money to maintain its facilities and personnel. Indebtedness, budget shortfalls, and capital needs siphoned funds away from expansion and growth. Emphasis switched from proclaiming the kingdom to preserving the institution. New ways had to be found to fund ministries.

Seeking to address this problem, the New Mexico Baptist Foundation, whose assets had skyrocketed during this era from $4,647,348.53 to $13,487,268.65, took an unprecedented move. Foundation president Lee Black announced in 1995 the launching of "Foundation Ventures," a for-profit land development project undertaken to generate income for ministries. To meet future obligations, income-producing endeavors had become essential.[13]

A Plateauing Convention

Financial problems occupied considerable time and attention, but falling participation created a crisis of its own. Declining enrollments caused departmental alterations to meet the demands placed on the church in the post-1980s world. A major concern centered on preserving a Baptist identity and mobilizing the laity to action along evangelical lines. In the 1950s, the BCNM partially accomplished this goal through achieving 100-percent saturation with the *Baptist New Mexican*. Yet the ability of the convention to keep its constituents informed, communicate goals, and forge identity began slipping in the 1960s. When Cone took over, the subscription level lay at only 13,833 out of a membership of 117,679, or 52 percent of families. Despite all attempts to increase circulation, ten years later the subscription rate had dropped to 12,893.[14] Only half the local Baptists received the newspaper.

Declining enrollment also plagued all programs. The Brotherhood continued the Royal Ambassador camps, but falling numbers stimulated them to increased activity. Three new projects combined social action with missions and church construction. Starting in 1990, this service organization initiated a new program called "Impact." Church youth and a Brotherhood sponsor, working in conjunction with Albuquerque's Office of Senior Affairs, helped senior citizens make needed repairs to their homes.[15]

To customize ministry opportunities, the Brotherhood allowed members to initiate activities based on their own efforts through the organization's Planting Through Community Action program. In 1994, Charles Wilson, who worked at the juvenile detention center in the Carlsbad-Pecos Valley area, started a mission action project. This program began with counseling, self-esteem training, and educational work, eventually extending to include a crafts curriculum with the city paying for the materials. Bible study before each session was a regular part of the agenda. Wilson's effort was so successful that it became a pilot program for the state.

Also in 1994, the Brotherhood formed a new organization titled, "New Mexico Baptist Builders." Its purpose was to assist churches and missions in construction using volunteer labor. Members compiled a list of workers and matched their skills to project needs. Despite these efforts to stimulate involvement, participation continued to decline, from 3,340 in 1985 to 2,138 in 1995.[16]

The WMU also sought to attract members by reorganizing themselves to meet new conditions facing women in the post-1980s era. Speaking before the WMU's annual convention in 1994, Acquilla Brown noted: "It is no longer a time just for meeting; more and more women are in the work force. We must emphasize more and more on small training groups."[17] In keeping with the national reorganization in 1995, the state WMU moved from structured programs to "options." The new orientation placed emphasis on a "hands-on approach." Increased member involvement replaced leader-led meetings. Sessions became more interactive, featuring problem solving rather than simple instruction. Prayer, giving, scriptural memorization, and Bible study continued, but in a less programmatic manner. For those who wanted a lifestyle Bible study, the Sunday School Board offered "Women's Enrichment." The New Mexico WMU blended both. Despite attempts to be more relevant, participation continued to decline, from 6,256 in 1986 to 4,491 in 1995.

Clearly, declining membership lay behind all of these structural changes. Decentralization became a denomination-wide phenomenon. It characterized all Baptist programs, divisions, and departments during this era. Operations went from achievement standards set for the whole denomination to each organization setting its own goals, and even to each church determining its level of participation.[18]

The problem of attracting and maintaining members extended to the Sunday School and Church Training programs. Participation in the SBC's 8.5 by 85 campaign brought Sunday School enrollment up to 60,153 by 1985. But efforts to increase that figure by 11,000 over the next five years were disappointing. Stagnation resulted. Despite all the programmatic effort, attendance declined by 346.[19] Throughout Southern Baptist history, the Sunday School has been the denomination's primary evangelism tool. Realization that the program had plateaued brought about the introduction of new techniques. Seeking to attract larger audiences, the Church Recreation Department, a ministry of the Educational Division, sponsored drama workshops, which trained lay leaders in using this medium for worship and outreach.[20]

The major change, however, lay in the area of family ministries. From 1986 forward, this emphasis was accelerated. The "Parenting by Grace" program typified the new adaptations. This program consisted of enrichment seminars designed to help parents with modern family concerns. Through this curriculum, Baptists attempted to deal with the perceived breakdown in the family unit that was becoming more prevalent in their churches.[21]

Under George Warren, who became director of the Educational Division in 1987, family ministry remained a priority, exemplified in the "Marriage Enrichment" conferences. Eleven of the fifteen state associations conducted "covenant marriage training." Moving into the 1990s, the offerings expanded to include family workshops on such topics as Christian self-esteem, communication and intimacy, and making peace with one's past. In attempting to preserve self-identity and the corporate structure of the family, these programs extended an earlier shift away from theology to emphasizing the social and psychological needs of the individual.[22]

The Discipleship Training program, formerly known as Church Training, also illustrated this trend. The new instruction placed emphasis on "preservation" rather than reaching out in service. The reorganized program consisted of four primary assignments. Two of these reflected a consistency with the past: equipping people for leadership and growth in spiritual maturity. But in the 1990s two new areas emerged: assimilating new members into the church and strengthening family relationships. No longer did a profession of faith mean entrance into a homogenous body where people functioned together based on a commonality of belief. Now there were so many differences that people had to be plugged into their own niches or else the church risked losing them.[23] The traditional Baptist community began to give way to individual involvement.

In the midst of change, the Evangelism Division exhibited the most continuity. The previous decade's revivalist spirit carried over into the Cone era. Under the overarching umbrella of Bold Mission Thrust, the SBC initiated another crusade known as "Good News America" in 1986. Eighty-five churches participated. Following up on the success of this latest simultaneous revival, the denomination spearheaded another one in 1990. Under the "Here's Hope, Jesus Cares For You" theme, 161 churches and missions in New Mexico joined the effort.[24]

Just as revivals characterized the period, so too did conferences. Activities such as the State Evangelism Conference, Youth Evangelism Conference, and numerous others dominated the era. Behind this programmatic consistency, however, the content reflected a trend toward individualism. Building on the lay witness emphasis in the 1970s, this training moved toward equipping people to conduct evangelism through their own unique styles. Instead of following a programmed effort as in the past, the new thrust emphasized the expression of one's personality.

The BSUs also reflected this trend toward personal expression. In the post-1986 era, the organization entered a third stage in its development. Throughout the 1960s, teaching and training characterized the program. In the 1970s, instruction changed to lifestyle Bible studies and fellowship. In the 1980s, student-led ministry became the norm. Through leadership teams, students learned to serve, lead committees, plan activities, worship, share their faith, and organize their private lives.[25] In twenty-five years the organization went from theological instruction to personal empowerment. Only the program at Eastern New Mexico University retained the old structure, but not for long.

Throughout this period, the Bible chair at Eastern continued to offer a master's degree in religious education. Changing educational conditions, as well as Baptist expectations, however, led to its abandonment in 1995. Since its inception in 1936, the program served Baptists in the eastern part of the state as a place to receive a theological degree without having to leave New Mexico. Many studying for the pastorate used the school while serving as ministers in area churches. In its fifty-nine years of existence, the program had produced twenty-five pastors, eighty-two missionaries, and two chaplains.[26] By the 1980s, however, with demographic changes and improvements in transportation, this pattern was no longer viable.

The Eastern New Mexico University Bible chair, which had begun as a Baptist program, soon became the cooperative venture of several Protestant groups, with Baptists and the Church of Christ predominating. When these other denominations' schools began offering master's degrees, the number of students who desired theological education declined. The final factor contributing to the abandonment lay with the lack of instructors with terminal degrees, which led to a crisis in certification.[27]

The changing nature of the BSUs led some in the state to call for the establishment of a Baptist school. In a 1982 state Executive Board meeting, Dale Danielson raised the question of starting a college since so many students left the state to attend Texas universities. Later that year, Chester O'Brien introduced to the board the president of Wayland Baptist University in Plainview, Texas, Dr. David Jester. He spoke about their programs at airbases and state campuses and the possibility of having a New Mexico branch. Nothing materialized. Four years later, Cone received authorization to conduct a feasibility study concerning a Wayland branch campus in New Mexico. Dr. Fred Teague spoke to the need for Christian education and indicated that if the study went well, classes could begin in fall 1987. Economic conditions in Texas, however, prevented this development.[28]

A Baptist college never materialized during this period, but attempts to establish theological education moved steadily forward. Southwestern Seminary in Fort Worth, Texas, set up activities in New Mexico in 1993 to offer the master's of divinity curriculum. Southwestern needed thirty students to operate the center but initially only enrolled twelve. After the first year the seminary abandoned the project, but Golden Gate, another Southern Baptist seminary, took over in 1994. The San Francisco-based school offered a similar degree plan. Unfortunately, Golden Gate had no more success than its predecessor, although the seminary continued to operate an extension program for four more years.[29] Indeed, the history of Christian higher education for Baptists in New Mexico is one of disappointment and frustration. Despite several attempts since 1900, either by their own efforts or through bringing in out-of-state institutions, the results have been the same: failure.

New Mission Strategies

In the O'Brien era, new church starts and ethnic ministries became the twin pillars of Baptist development. But changing demographics during the Cone period required developing new strategies in order to penetrate areas hitherto unreached. John Embery, the BCNM's church development specialist, led the convention in exploring new possibilities. Some of his suggestions included Bible studies in mobile home parks and villages where there had been no evangelical work. People who lived in quasi-isolation, such as ranch hands, offered yet another outlet for ministry. Embery pointed out that there were hundreds of opportunities around the state that would never reach church or mission status but could continue as an outreach effort if local congregations staffed them. In the future, people in the church would have to undertake the work with little or no financial outlay.

Embery realized the need for more lay involvement in penetrating these new areas. At the same time, training and capital outlay had to be limited or volunteers would not be forthcoming. Many in the convention had come to the realization that the Home Mission Board subsidy of $1 million annually could not continue. Ministry, therefore, had to become more self-sufficient.[30]

Acting on these suggestions, the convention developed new means to extend its message. For example, no evangelical presence existed in the community of Angel Fire. In cooperation with the BCNM, a Brotherhood group from Texas sent men to help build a church. Starting with thirteen members, it grew into a stable congregation. The Evangelism Department also assisted

Andrew Begaye, missionary to the Navajo, with a mission trip to sheep camps in the Chuska Mountains. The Central Association likewise helped establish two new Black congregations in Rio Rancho and at Fruit Avenue in Albuquerque. Castle Avenue Baptist in Hobbs began a work in an apartment complex. A home Bible study was started in Placitas. Central Baptist in Clovis sponsored a Korean mission at Canon Air Force Base by enlisting the wives of foreign military personnel. Individuals conducted their own ministry. Mr. and Mrs. Wesley Hay of Roswell assisted Vietnamese refugees on a one-on-one basis with personal needs, housing, and employment. These examples were merely representative of new directions Baptists took in outreach as the denomination sought to penetrate heretofore untouched areas.[31]

Ethnic church starts had entered a period of growth during the O'Brien era and accelerated under Cone. In the 1982–1991 period, new congregations expanded from 57 to 99 or 4.2 new churches per year. Over the next three years, the work intensified resulting in 17 new starts, raising the annual average to 5.66.[32]

Demographic analysis showed that by the late 1980s a new mission field had developed. The population center now lay along a north-south axis between Santa Fe and Las Cruces, known as the Rio Grande corridor. Even though the entire region experienced growth, the cities of Albuquerque and Las Cruces were the primary recipients of new residents. Writing in the *Baptist New Mexican* in 1988, Cone called attention to the west mesa area in Albuquerque that was growing at a rate of ten thousand per year. In Las Cruces, an eleven-mile stretch along Highway 70, desolate only a few years before, now had seven thousand to ten thousand inhabitants.[33] The BCNM targeted these two areas.

Another article in the denominational paper by Donald Seigler gave chilling statistical data regarding the BCNM's failure to keep pace with the population growth. In 1985 there was one Baptist church for every 15,478 Albuquerque residents. Three years later, the ratio had fallen to one congregation for every 16,667 people. Since 1980, the city's population had increased by 80,300, whereas resident membership in Central Association churches had grown by only 9,186.[34] These statistics served to make New Mexico Baptists aware that they were losing the evangelization battle.

Compounding the problem, the churches had no funds for expansion. The large number of staff needed for efficient operation, along with building costs and maintenance, had severely depleted resources once used for outreach. In addition, increasing Internal Revenue Service regulations had become so time consuming that churches had to employ financial secretaries.[35] At a time when a new mission field was opening up, Baptist congregations could not fulfill their traditional role of starting churches.[36] Attempts to find a solution to this dilemma struck at the core of denominational polity.

These conditions led to a new strategy. Since escalating land, building, and staff costs had prevented churches from reproducing themselves, cooperative efforts among congregations and the pooling of resources among convention bodies were put forth as solutions. A new approach emerged from these discussions, officially known as the "Two-in-One" plan. Beginning in 1989, the Rio Grande Association initiated a work on the east mesa of Las Cruces, the fastest-growing section of the city. Anglos and Hispanics populated the area in relatively even numbers. These demographics led to the decision to organize two churches.

The Rio Grande Association, in cooperation with five area churches—three Anglo and two Hispanic—purchased 7.6 acres of land. The development committee decided to have two pastors, one for each ethnic group, but to construct only one building. They secured a modular structure from the BCNM and laid out guidelines for a cooperative relationship regarding accountability, finances, and sponsorship. Next, they called the ministers, with the understanding that they would use the same building. To provide both stability and a base from which to grow, some members from the sponsoring churches became part of the new work.

The two new congregations, Good News Church and East Mesa Mission, planned to hold joint sessions every three months. Shortly after organization, however, they discovered that the modular chapel was too small. With help from the State Mission Offering, the churches very quickly constructed a 3,600-square-foot building. Members from both congregations undertook the excavation and foundation work and erected a metal frame donated by First Baptist Church in Las Cruces. Students from the BSU at New Mexico State University put on the roof. Completion of the project enabled the two churches to continue their joint sessions and youth activities.[37]

Success of the "Two-in-One" approach laid a base for a new paradigm in church planting. Four concepts came together in this east mesa venture that infused a new understanding of the process. Joint sponsorship between churches and the association not only worked, but also proved practical and advisable. The state convention needed to be available with financial assistance. It was possible for more than one church to use the same building simultaneously on an equal basis. Finally, it showed that cooperative arrangements among ethnic groups could work.

From this strategy and the lessons learned during its implementation, the

BCNM extended the concept to the entire state. The convention initiated a program designed to bring together the churches, associations, and the convention. By uniting these three entities in a cooperative effort, the BCNM hoped to combine all available resources to promote new church development along the Rio Grande corridor. Amid much hope and fanfare, Baptists launched "Mission New Mexico" in 1991 at the State Evangelism Conference.

Convention plans called for the establishment of fifty new churches during the following five years. Completion would place a Baptist church within easy reach of every New Mexican. Achieving this goal required the enlisting of 138 existing congregations to partner in sponsoring the new work. At the evangelism conference, Cone presented the statistical data that underlay the effort. During the 1980s, New Mexico's population grew by 220,000, or 16.9 percent, but Baptist resident membership increased by only 2,871 or 4.5 percent. Over the same period, the ratio of churches to people fell from 1 to 5,170 to 1 to 5,684, a 10-percent loss in the church-to-resident ratio. The loss was due to not concentrating on the growth areas of Bernalillo, Sandoval, and Doña Ana Counties, which accounted for 73 percent of the increase.[38]

M. V. Summers, director of Mission Ministries, and John Embery, the BCNM's church planting specialist, conceived Mission New Mexico because churches were no longer starting churches and missions as they once had. In the 1940s and 1950s, church staffs averaged about two people each. Most congregations were not in debt. New churches started by spinning off one hundred to two hundred members from the sponsoring body, and pastors generally knew that they could replace those people within the year. Land and building costs were cheap. By the 1990s, the opposite was true. Thus, the traditional Baptist pattern for church planting no longer functioned effectively. The new program was an attempt to find a strategy that would transcend the problems by still relying on the churches, but jump-starting them with the help of the association and the convention.[39]

Under the new plan, churches could be started in two ways. In one version, local churches might join together to begin a work. They would identify a location, provide members from their congregations, and retain a pastor. The association and convention would provide development money and assistance with long-range planning and building needs. The other alternative switched the initiative to the BCNM and the association, which would determine when and where to start a congregation. They hired the pastor, developed the ministry plan, and called on the area churches to assist with the operation.[40]

Despite the prospects, the churches never embraced Mission New Mexico. By 1994, only ten to twelve congregations had participated. What appeared

130

to be an ideal way to mobilize resources and direct them to the point of greatest need failed to generate an active response. Some in the administration pointed to a lack of consistency in promoting the program. Financially, demands on existing churches prevented both fiscal and human contributions. Most churches were in debt and could not afford to lose members. Another explanation placed the lack of success on an inability to share potential. Success for any expansion effort must engage the support of Baptists in southeastern New Mexico, the state's Baptist stronghold. Many of the facilities there were debt free or nearly so. This region did not need to expand, but it had the money to help fund Baptist operations elsewhere. These churches failed to catch the vision for the opportunity that the Rio Grande corridor provided and never became involved.[41]

Loss of influence is a possible explanation for what lay behind this decision not to join the crusade. The southeast area of the state had declined in importance. Oil, gas, ranching, and farming were no longer the economic mainstays they once were. As a result, the area's residents were much less politically significant. The new population center lay within the Rio Grande corridor. Baptists began concentrating their efforts there, further reducing the southeast's influence. By the 1990s, the region had lost its prominence, and thus, much of its vision.[42]

Another plausible explanation was that Mission New Mexico was more than a new evangelistic strategy to stimulate church growth and expansion. In attempting to combine resources and engage all spheres of work under a single comprehensive plan, the initiative altered denominational polity. Traditionally, churches start churches, not conventions. This struck at the core of the congregational structure germane to Baptists: local church autonomy. Under the new plan, the initiative moved from the individual church to the state body.

Nevertheless, Mission New Mexico altered the way the BCNM established churches. Rising land costs, plus the need to determine accurately future growth areas, led to the establishment of the Advisory Land Council, a group composed of Baptist businesspeople. In cooperation with government agencies and other service organizations, the council gathered demographic material and projection charts as an aid in deciding where to purchase property years in advance. Buying at predevelopment prices enabled the convention to acquire more land than needed. As prices rose, Baptists could sell the surplus property to fund building construction.[43]

Other techniques were adaptations of a previous era's methodologies combined with modern opportunities and technology. Many new churches began without a building. They might rent space in a community center, or use a nearby Seventh-Day Adventist church. Other creative possibilities included office complexes and shopping centers. One congregation began in the training room of a volunteer fire department. Another strategy involved starting a home Bible study group in the target area and piping in the worship service from the nearby sponsoring church. Some new work emerged literally under the roof of the parent church where both used the same facility until the new body gained sufficient strength to break off on its own. This approach was especially effective in the area of ethnic church development.[44]

Attempts at Reorganization

Changes in the relationship between churches and the convention in starting new work brought to the surface an issue that had been simmering for some time: the future role of the association. Since the 1960s, that body had been deteriorating, and reorganization in 1970 accelerated the process. In many cases the association degenerated into fellowship groups of the same people. Isolated rural areas needed the contact but urban areas did not. Churches had slowly moved away from using the regional body because of limited time and financial resources. Instead, church leaders would call Albuquerque and obtain whatever they needed. Therefore, if the association was to remain a vital link in denominational affairs, what role should it have?[45]

This question became the subject of a five-year study by a specially appointed Associational Task Force for the BCNM. This committee concluded in 1993 that it was the consensus of pastors, church staff, and laypersons throughout the state that it was time for a change.[46] According to the task force analysis, three developments required a restructuring and rethinking of associational ministry. The first was the demographic transition from rural to urban. Associations composed of smaller churches in predominately rural locations struggled to support their full-time staffs. Financial resources posed another problem. Escalating costs of operating a church required congregations to retain a larger portion of their tithes and offerings to maintain local ministries. Thus, less money was available to support the association. Finally, Baptists began to realize that many non-Baptists were moving into the state, unlike earlier migrations. Confronting this fact led convention leaders to a painful acknowledgment. They had not been successful in reaching people of other cultures through the traditional Southern Baptist structures and programs. Therefore, the association had to become the key agent of change. Under this proposal, the association's new role was to be the vehicle to assist the churches in their area in developing strategies to reach all people.

The task force consisted of two study groups. Committee A was to make recommendations on the manner in which the association related to the convention and the Home Mission Board. Committee B was to take up the role of each association in its local context. Committee A developed a three-tiered classification system that consisted of demographic profiles indicating different levels of expectancy for all new mission development. Committee B came to the conclusion that because of the lack of financial resources and properly trained personnel, it would be better to reduce the number of associations from fifteen to eight. Enlarging the territory and number of churches would enhance the performance of the director of missions.[47]

Despite agreement on the need for change, the task force recommendations met with little success. Many in the convention interpreted them as another device to centralize control, a threat to the principle of local church autonomy and to the idea that churches start churches. Even more damaging to potential acceptance was the merger of the Plains and Portales Associations. Attempting to implement the suggested merger, each group gave up its organization, personnel, and procedures. The outcome was disastrous, resulting in a loss of vision. With the rejection of the study committee's proposal, the original question that prompted the report remained unanswered.[48]

Attempts at reorganization did not end with the associations. To develop new directions for the new millennium, the SBC initiated the "Contract for a New Century." The BCNM sought to bring itself into alignment with this call by revamping and rethinking its ministry. The state convention appointed a fifteen-member Strategic Planning Task Force in 1995 to bring recommendations on positioning itself for the twenty-first century.[49]

Seeking input from Baptists throughout the state, the task force under-took a convention-wide survey sent to pastors and church staff, along with interviews of BCNM staff personnel. From the information gathered, the study committee drew several conclusions. The strength of the convention lay in its fellowship, stable administration, leadership, and willingness to listen. Many complained of a lack of communication among departments. Some thought that the convention was tied to old programs, resistant to change, living in the past, and too denominationally oriented, causing dissent among the troops. Staff discussions also revealed a concern over too much duplication, confusion, "turfism," and absence of a teamwork atmosphere, resulting in a lack of vision.[50]

Armed with this information the task force issued the following recommendations.

1. Remove the requirement that churches must be members of an association to affiliate with the BCNM.

2. Restrict the Children's Home Board to handling only short-term investments of less than a year, with the Foundation managing all long-term securities.
3. Make the camps separate corporate entities with their own governing boards.
4. Reduce the size of the Executive Board from forty to thirty members. Allow members to serve three consecutive, three-year terms. Require that 30 percent of the board's membership be comprised of laypersons.
5. Change the executive director's title to chief executive officer. Elevate the position of business manager to associate executive director, with authority to make decisions when the CEO was away.
6. Move the WMU, Women's Ministries, Fellowship of Ministers Wives, and the Brotherhood to the Education Division and place them under contract labor.
7. Target all resources and personnel to the Rio Grande corridor for new church starts.
8. Evaluate all Baptist ministries and programming based on their evangelistic and discipleship mission impact.
9. Develop a total team concept among all divisions by focusing on the areas of ministry most critical to Baptists in the state.
10. Establish on a yearly basis convention-wide priorities and goals for unified focus in reaching a culturally diverse state.
11. Disburse all money received by the convention through the business manager's office.[51]

Reaction to the proposed reorganization generated heated debate. Some observers argued that the only way to chart a new course required a break with traditional polity and "sacred" programs. Conflict over the nature of the convention lay at the heart of the issue. Proponents of change challenged what they called the "pastoral-church" concept. They maintained that the BCNM functioned more like an association with the executive director assuming the role of a director of missions. In reality, the convention was an organization and it should be run like a corporation with administrators, not pastors. The current "church-type" structure, when extended to the state level, created semi-autonomous divisions producing "turfism." Furthermore, the camps assumed too great an importance in the minds of the constituency. To speak against them was akin to committing the "unpardonable sin," but financially and programmatically they had ceased to be effective.[52]

Opponents maintained that the 1995 report was to recommend how to move into the twenty-first century. To effect any meaningful change required a redefinition of the ministry, which the task force failed to do. By concentrating on structural rather than conceptual concerns, the task force never answered the fundamental question at the heart of the problem: Which body is the driving force behind evangelism and missions, the state convention or the local church?[53]

By failing to address this issue, the report became a compromised document that failed to lead the convention in a new direction. The only significant changes adopted involved associational membership, the downsizing of the executive board, and the spinning off of the camps to their own governing bodies. What occurred was an attempt to preserve the convention moving into the twenty-first century by tightening control and removing liabilities. Instead of restructuring, the 1995 proposal became a consolidation of the 1970 reorganization.

⌇⌇

Some religious commentators have referred to the 1970s as the "swan song of the evangelicals." If this is true, then the 1980s and 1990s, at least for Southern Baptists, became the era of denominational stagnation. Financial necessity forced the BCNM to turn from outreach to preserving its institutional structure. Despite an impressive list of accomplishments under the Cone administration, the statistical data were clear. The convention and its churches had plateaued.

During the O'Brien era, Baptist churches in New Mexico increased from 260 to 340. Over the next ten years, that number stabilized. Figures for 1995 listed 330 congregations. But Baptist activity was not static. Many new bodies began, while others closed, primarily because of demographic shifts. Ethnic churches significantly increased, reaching a total of 123 by 1995. On a typical Sunday morning, Southern Baptist ministers conducted services in seventeen languages to forty-two cultural groups.[54]

Membership and program attendance reflected the same trend. In 1985, 117,679 people claimed affiliation with the convention. Ten years later, the rolls had declined to 113,122. Sunday School followed suit.[55] Over the same period, participation fell from 60,153 to 57,548. The Church Music program, which since the 1960s had run counter to the trend, failed to maintain its growth, losing 436 participants. The Brotherhood and WMU programs declined as well.[56]

Most critical of all areas, however, were baptisms. It is here that Baptists measure the effectiveness of their evangelism and church programs. Southern Baptists are growth oriented. All denominational efforts have one goal—produce converts. In the early 1960s and again for a short time in the late 1970s, yearly numbers exceeded the 4,000 mark. Through the mid-1980s, annual baptisms consistently ran above 3,000. Then beginning in 1987 baptisms fell below this level, registering only 2,743 in 1995, one of the lowest in several decades.[57] For Baptists, a decline in baptisms means failure.

The convention's stagnation is mirrored in the inability to make conceptual changes that might have moved it forward into the twenty-first century. Mission New Mexico, associational restructuring, and the 1995 reorganization were all attempts to address problems and respond to new conditions. Unable to find workable solutions acceptable to a broad cross section of their constituency, New Mexico Baptists experienced a functional plateau as well.

13. A. B. Hanks, missionary to Blacks in New Mexico in the 1950s and early 1960s.

14. Pauline Camack, missionary to the Pueblo Indians.

15. Sivells Camp.

16. H. C. Sivells, founder
of the Royal Ambassadors
Camp near Cloudcroft.

17. Inlow Lodge, late 1940s.

18. Native Americans from Taos and Santa Clara Pueblos at Inlow Youth Camp, 1943.

19. White Bible ceremony at Inlow
Youth Camp, 1952.

20. Eva Inlow,
WMU director and
founder of Inlow
Youth Camp.

21. BSU building at Eastern New Mexico University.

22. Dr. C. R. Barrick, first BSU director at Eastern New Mexico University and later BSU secretary for the state convention.

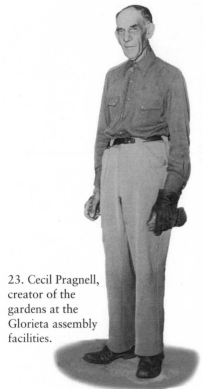

23. Cecil Pragnell, creator of the gardens at the Glorieta assembly facilities.

24. Claude Cone, executive director of the BCNM from 1985 to the present.

25. Chester O'Brien served as executive director from 1975 to 1984, and his wife, Bonnie Ball O'Brien, authored *Harry P. Stagg: Christian Statesman.*

26. R. Y. Bradford, executive director from 1968 to 1974.

27. Harry Perkins Stagg served as executive secretary from 1938 to 1968, at the time the longest tenure of a state convention leader in the SBC.

Continuity and Change: A Redefined Church for the Post-1960s Era

Coping with post-1960s American society led New Mexico Baptists to make fiscal, polity, and structural changes within their convention. Their response affected beliefs and customs, for they had to adapt to a religious climate that seemed to be growing less and less Christian. Adjusting to these new conditions began to undermine traditionally held practices and eroded doctrinal preaching.

By the 1990s, Baptist churches had changed from a "Christian community" that experienced fellowship through preaching, teaching, and singing, to "spiritual shopping malls" catering to the needs of their members through a plethora of specialized programs. Responding to societal pressure to individualize the ministry for self-fulfillment, congregations ceased to be homogenous bodies of believers. Collective worship fragmented into a myriad of mutually exclusive support groups.

These evolving undercurrents slowly altered the outlook of New Mexico Baptists. On the surface, the convention appeared to maintain consistency with its past. In both theological statements and resolutions on historic issues, continuity seemingly prevailed. Yet this outward stance masked an inward change, creating a false sense of stability.

Expanding Political Involvement

In the aftermath of the Dixon case in 1948, Baptists monitored New Mexico public policy issues, looking for infractions involving church and state issues and religious liberty violations. With the defeat of the revised New Mexico Constitution in 1969, J. R. Burnett and Dale Danielson initiated a work informing constituents of impending legislation affecting church and state relations.[1] From 1972 to 1982, Burnett wrote a column during the legislative session titled "Christian Attention to Public Affairs." Through these columns, he alerted legislators to what he perceived as funding hidden in proposed budgets and bills that might assist religious organizations.[2]

The parochiad battle in New Mexico resumed in 1975 when Baptists and Seventh-Day Adventists confronted Catholics over a bill that allowed full state funding of sectarian colleges through grants to their students. The issue raised spirited debate in the state legislative chambers. Senator Alex Martinez of Santa Fe charged that not passing the bill would be discriminatory. It was not exclusive to Catholic schools, he said, but was intended to aid all religious educational facilities. Senator Ray Luger of Las Vegas asked the question: "Do we want to help students get an education or don't we? Separation of church and state is not the issue."[3] J. R. Burnett replied that this reasoning was nothing more than the old "child benefit" theory resurrected. If passed, it would use Vietnam War veterans as a conduit for state funds designed chiefly to float church colleges.[4] The bill died in the House. Proponents tried again the following year, this time in the form of a tuition-incentive grant program. Under the bill's provision, a resident student could apply the grant money to any educational institution, whether church or secular. This bill also failed.

A U.S. Supreme Court ruling in 1975, however, let stand a Missouri court's decision that a tuition grant program for its state colleges did not interfere with First Amendment requirements. This decision gave supporters of government aid to religious education in New Mexico new hope.[5] New Mexico Baptists and Seventh-Day Adventists, along with the American Civil Liberties Union and Americans United for Separation of Church and State, expressed their outrage at the high court's ruling. Nevertheless, subsequent provisions passed in the state legislature.

Having lost the first round in the battle, New Mexico Baptists turned their attention to defeating the state's proposed purchase of the Catholic-owned University of Albuquerque. Under a 1979 proposal, the state would turn the campus into a west-side community college. Baptists expressed concern because the proposed governing board included many trustees and members from the former school. They also noted that many of the faculty from the University of Albuquerque would continue in the same positions at the community college. The issue went to the voters of Bernalillo County in 1979. In a close vote, citizens decided to turn the Technical-Vocational Institute into a community college and the issue died.[6]

Legislative attempts to fund tuition assistance emerged again in 1980, with advocates asking for $3,620,000 for students at independent schools. Baptists and Seventh-Day Adventists addressed the bill's legality, questioning the loopholes in the New Mexico state constitution. This time the measure failed to muster the necessary votes. After these battles, Danielson and Burnett retired, and for the next decade the Baptist Convention of New Mexico (BCNM) operated without an organ to address church and state issues. *Baptist New Mexican* editors attempted to fill this role until 1989 when the creation of a Christian Life Commission took over this function. Yet the parochiad issue served to galvanize the political consciousness of the convention's membership, motivating them to take direct action.

The first such incident occurred in 1977 over a new ABC television show called *Soap,* which dealt with adultery, homosexuality, and transvestitism in a comedy format. Following the lead of Foy Valentine at the Christian Life Commission for the Southern Baptist Convention (SBC), Eugene Whitlow used his position as editor to begin a campaign. Through the pages of the *Baptist New Mexican,* Whitlow provided readers with names and addresses of the executives of all companies that sponsored *Soap.* He urged Baptists to write letters to the sponsors demanding that they withhold support from such an immoral show. Whitlow also urged his readers to participate in the denominational boycott of the sponsors' products.[7]

Whitlow went so far as to call the operations manager at ABC affiliate KOAT-TV in Albuquerque, and requested that the station not air the show. The BCNM also urged its members to send telegrams to all three networks voicing opposition to the unethical and immoral content of programs being shown on American television. This campaign was the first time that the convention had ever engaged in a major operation to bring pressure to bear upon either a public or a private entity. Whitlow summed up the feelings of his constituents: "For much too long now, we American people have been subjected to immoral television programs. It's time that Christians and other concerned citizens unite in order to clean up the television programs that are immoral in any way. It is certainly time to say YES to morality by saying NO SOAP."[8] The nationwide protest had an impact. At least ten of the eleven advertisers scheduled to sponsor the show dropped it, and ABC revised some of the first episodes.[9]

During the early 1980s, an increasingly politicized convention prepared New Mexico Baptists for their next battle: a state-sponsored lottery. The issue surfaced in 1983 when Senator Charles Marquez sponsored the first bill and attempted to move it through the state legislature without hearings. Dale Danielson immediately presented a resolution from the Central Association against the lottery that warned, "[B]y paying back 45 cents on the dollar, the New Mexico Lottery would be a gross rip-off compared to other forms of gambling that pay twice as much."[10] Executive Director Chester O'Brien distributed an article to state legislators that set forth the Baptist position:

(1) lotteries erode the traditional American work ethic; (2) they create an atmosphere in which crime and criminal gaming efforts could operate more easily; (3) lotteries were counterproductive financially, administratively, and socially, as the costs outweighed the benefits from any accumulated profits. Concern voiced by Baptists and other groups defeated the measure.[11]

Senator Marquez reintroduced his bill in 1984. Baptists again went into battle. J. B. Fowler challenged the bill by using studies from faculty members at Michigan State University and the University of Connecticut. He drew on their research to show that lotteries primarily attract the poor, the long-term unemployed, and the less educated. He argued that the lottery as a social institution was a major factor in contributing to the poverty in those states.[12]

As the battle over a lottery became protracted, the BCNM's newly activated Christian Life Committee became heavily involved. Beginning in 1990, the committee set up a statewide network of associations and local churches and utilized a telephone campaign to help defeat lottery and video gaming bills. Pastors mobilized their membership to flood legislators' offices with mail and personal phone calls voicing opposition.[13] Baptists and others opposed to gambling continued their attempts to prevent the establishment of a lottery into the 1990s. In 1992, however, with the election of Governor Gary Johnson, a supporter of the initiative, their efforts went down in defeat.

Throughout the 1970s, Baptists continued to respond to public issues regarding alcohol in their traditional manner, usually by passing resolutions against specific items, such as lowering the legal age limit for purchasing liquor or the expansion of liquor licenses. Not until J. B. Fowler became editor of the *Baptist New Mexican* did Baptists begin to change their approach. Under his leadership, resolutions became proactive rather than merely rhetorical. For instance, in 1984 the convention supported legislation to hold the liquor industry liable for monetary losses suffered by victims of drunk drivers. This stance went far beyond simply moralizing over the evils of John Barleycorn.

Fowler turned the historic anti-alcohol campaign away from platitudes regarding the dangers of drink. Rather, his editorials introduced statistical data and sociological studies as a means to combat the expansion of the state liquor industry. But what galvanized New Mexico Baptists were the deaths of Melanie Craven and her daughters on Christmas Eve 1993 in a drunk-driving accident. The BCNM's Christian Life Commission sent packets to pastors with the names and addresses of their legislators, and they urged church members to petition the legislature and Governor Bruce King for stricter laws.[14]

Ecumenical Relations

Conditions during the 1960s momentarily opened New Mexico Baptists to limited cooperation with other religious groups. Tensions with Roman Catholics in the state even lessened. But in the post-1960s era that momentum slowed. While willing to work with other evangelicals in revivals such as the Billy Graham Crusade, more formal cooperation was not forthcoming. New Mexico Baptists remained consistent in their opposition to affiliation with ecumenical bodies. Pastor Karl Scott of Central Baptist Church in Clovis succinctly stated the convention's historic position in a 1978 article in the *Baptist New Mexican*. Addressing an attempt on the part of the National Council of Churches to bring all denominations under its structure, he said: "Baptists throughout the centuries have believed that every person regenerated by the Spirit of God is a member of the kingdom of God, regardless of church affiliation. . . . Baptists will not now give up this freedom to those who have prejudiced ideas and demand conformity."[15] Baptists in subsequent years have not departed from this position.

Although no official interchange occurred between New Mexico's Baptists and Catholics, relations between the two religious bodies became more cordial. Many Baptists perceived Catholics as becoming more and more like themselves—Christians in an increasingly secular culture. Baptists became more accepting of Catholics because they saw the Roman Catholic Church to be moving in their direction. Beginning in the 1970s, the Catholic Church began using both the Glorieta Conference Center and Inlow Camp to hold meetings. In addition, the archbishop allowed Catholic children to attend Baptist Vacation Bible Schools. After Vatican II (1962–1965), New Mexico Catholics became more evangelical in their approach and placed far more emphasis on Bible teaching and study, which appealed to Baptists.

More recently, Catholics and Baptists supported each other on numerous moral issues, such as opposition to gambling and abortion. Intermarriage between Catholics and Baptists was on the rise, and more Baptist ministers participated in these wedding services. At the same time, Catholics placed a greater emphasis on personal salvation through Christ. Catholics were encouraged to attend evangelistic services and support such events as the Billy Graham Crusade. By the 1990s, New Mexico Baptists and Catholics were no longer "arch enemies."[16]

Women in Ministry

While the BCNM's positions on separation of church and state and nonentanglement with ecumenical bodies remained constant, so too did its attitude toward the presence of women in the ministry. In the 1970s, the idea of female clergy became a major issue within many major denominations, including the SBC. At the national level, some WMU presidents spoke in favor of women's ordination, as did a few seminary professors. In New Mexico, however, the idea received a cool reception.

In this state, the issue centered on the ordination of deaconesses, and the battle was fought in the pages of the *Baptist New Mexican.* In 1975, R. A. Long wrote an article in which he claimed that attempts to read "deaconess" into scriptures would be an improper translation. He argued that no such office existed. On the other hand, J. B. Fowler challenged his interpretation, claiming that deaconesses were valid, although he saw no precedent for their ordination.[17]

Some Baptist churches in New Mexico have had deaconesses. First Baptist Church in Roy has utilized deaconesses for years. This church, a small congregation located in an isolated area in northeastern New Mexico, turned to women because of a lack of men to conduct business. Everybody in the convention knew about the practice, but no one made an issue of it.[18]

The BCNM consistently refused to issue an official pronouncement regarding the ordination of women as ministers. Instead, the convention declared the issue to be a local church matter. Only one congregation chose to exercise that right. In 1992, Heights Baptist Church in Albuquerque ordained two women ministers—Marcia Moore, who served as a chaplain at St. Joseph Hospital in Albuquerque, and Helen Oaks, who worked as a prison chaplain at the Grants facility.[19]

New Mexico Baptist women served on convention committees, executive boards, and in all church positions, except for pastor, deacon, and trustee. Just beneath the surface, however, women performed hidden roles that touch on all these offices. They prepared lessons, wrote articles, published books, and spoke in churches. Such addresses have been termed "devotionals" and not "sermons," to avoid conflict. Thus far, New Mexico Baptist women have chosen not to press the issue, but an expanded role for women lies simmering under the surface.[20]

New Avenues in Social Ministry

Even though Baptist activities in the post-1960s era continued their historic positions, major alterations erupted in the conduct of the denomination's social ministry. In the 1900–1938 period, "social involvement" meant building colleges, hospitals, and orphanages. During the Stagg era, the emphasis switched to the establishment of assemblies, summer camps, and Bible chairs, all structures that provided programming for denominational use. In the post-1960s era, facilities constructed for members gave way to social relief programs for people *outside* the church community.[21]

In the transition to denominationally based assistance programs, Baptist social involvement underwent a fundamental change. From a unified and structured approach that advanced organizational life, the new direction decentralized the ministry. Oriented to diverse people, and administered by numerous individuals, churches, organizations, and agencies, the new focus compartmentalized the work. In the process, social ministry often became the province of individual aspiration rather than being institutionally driven.

The flagship institution embodying this new approach originated in 1967 as a literacy ministry. JaNell Turner, Martha Clauson, and Margaret Norman, in cooperation with Rio Grande Association, established an English as a second language program in the Las Cruces area. Beginning with 6 students, the program grew into the Small World Friendship Center, which by 1993 ministered to 145 students from seventy-five countries. Enrollment included wives of graduate students at New Mexico State University and other women from the local area. Many of those enrolled combined their language instruction with the GED program or citizenship studies. Prayer and Bible teaching formed an integral part of the service.[22]

Expanding on this initiative, the convention began in 1977 to distribute how-to materials in an attempt to stimulate other weekday ministries through its churches. Suggested programs included such areas as mobile home ministry, migrant missions, literacy classes, juvenile prison rehabilitation, goodwill centers, senior adult outreach, and day care centers, among numerous other options. Participation was overwhelming. By 1982, New Mexico Baptist churches had initiated 468 separate programs along these lines.[23]

For example, Calvary Baptist in Hobbs began in 1977 to offer a Meals-on-Wheels program once a week, and soon it served forty to fifty people. In addition, First Baptist Church in Socorro started a "friendship center" staffed by church members, which offered Bible study and handicrafts for area women. The Mesilla Park Church also initiated a prison ministry designed to aid families of inmates.[24]

By the mid-1980s, local ministry efforts had turned in the direction of alleviating various social ills. For instance, Baptist churches in Crown Point and Window Rock established an alcohol-counseling program in 1986. Working together they were able to reach much of the Navajo nation. Many churches, such as First Baptist in Belen, established a food ministry for needy city residents. In another outreach effort, the San Juan Association sponsored the Regain Alcohol Counseling Center in Farmington. First Baptist Church in Gallup began in 1988 the "Renewed Hope" ministry for those suffering from alcohol and drug abuse. Luis Gomez, pastor of El Buen Pastor Church, also in Gallup, processed applicants for legalization through the federal government's amnesty program for undocumented "aliens."[25]

In 1992, Worldchange New Mexico began to involve teens in community service endeavors. In these programs, students paid a fee to participate in an eight-day summer construction program to help the homeless and poor in the state. Projects included renovation of abandoned homes for families and making repairs on occupied property for those unable to bear the expense themselves. Under the SBC's "Hope for Humanity" campaign, the BCNM distributed "How-to-Begin" packets to their churches, with special emphasis on the homeless and on ministering to the poor.[26]

Out of this plethora of programs, one emerged that became an institution. Started by Albuquerque businessman Calvin Horn, this new effort became known as "Noonday Ministries," reflecting the new trend toward individually initiated social action projects.[27] Directed outside the church to the larger community, Noonday quickly moved beyond the bounds of denominational structure.

The ministry began in 1981 when an Episcopal priest, Jeff Wag, circulated a letter that set forth the need for a ministry to the homeless. Horn took the idea to his pastor at First Baptist Church in Albuquerque. Together, with the cooperation of his Sunday School class, they agreed to feed the homeless in the church's fellowship hall. Starting with lunch one day a week, the program quickly expanded to three days. Then, people from outside the church began making donations to help with the expansion. Volume exceeded capacity, resulting in a decision to construct a separate building adjacent to the church, which opened in June 1988.

With the opening of the center, the ministry expanded beyond serving meals, inaugurating a total service operation that included showers, laundry facilities, clothing, telephones, utility and rent assistance, and travelers' aid. Moving past immediate needs, Noonday also assisted people with employment and housing. The ministry even published how-to booklets to help the homeless start their lives again.

According to its director, Dennis Lihte (1998), Noonday provides a valuable social service for Albuquerque. Without it, there would be an additional two hundred to four hundred homeless people on the streets. The ministry serves more than fifty-seven thousand meals annually. Assistance comes from individuals, businesses, churches, and a newsletter that circulates to 1,600 supporters. Approximately 75 percent of the $300,000 operating budget comes from Baptists; the remainder is donated by other evangelicals. Since the ministry functions on the basis of volunteer help and donations, its expenditures are kept to a minimum. Estimates for the city to run such a program place the operational costs at four times the current expense, plus capital for land and construction of a building.[28]

Another area of social ministry, the Neighborhood Center, had its origins in the 1960s under sponsorship of the Edith Street Baptist Church, along with the Home Mission Board. Bob Gross served as director until 1972. Under his leadership, the center became a successful ministry to the community, known affectionately as "Mr. Bob's Place." No other facility like this ministry existed in the neighborhood. Gross established health services, education, crisis counseling, and children's activities, as well as church services. Mr. Bob's Place became the focus for human services in the community.[29]

From 1972 to 1986, a series of directors expanded the work, moving it more toward a neighborhood activities center. Gradually, volunteers installed a woodworking shop, photography room, and offered classes in nutrition, and eventually introduced more than one hundred programs. The City of Albuquerque became involved by using the auditorium for its Meals-On-Wheels program to feed seniors. In 1986, however, the center closed amidst controversy over a proposal to use it as a shelter for the homeless, a prospect that angered people in the neighborhood.[30]

The center reopened the following year, however, under the directorship of Ken and Eileen Goode. The Goodes redesigned the social programs to respond to the needs of the people, as opposed to implementing the ministry designs of the sponsoring organization.[31] Since city health and recreation services were now available, the role of the center became largely one of filling in the gaps. Adapting to existing conditions led to the development of strong daytime programs with camps and children's activities. An amnesty program also taught English and American government to prepare people for permanent residency. A crisis-response ministry provided food, clothing, financial help, and work referrals. Over time, the neighborhood association chose to meet at the center.

Once the city government saw that the community had accepted the Neighborhood Center, it used the center as a contact point for its educational agencies. These included serving government-supplied free lunches, providing a tutoring program to help students stay in school, and offering adult literacy classes. The University of New Mexico conducted an early childhood development program on the premises, and the Amigos Program also used the facilities to provide a drop-in recreation center.

All this activity brought the center into direct contact with various governmental agencies. These entities expressed amazement that Baptists had involved themselves in such types of social work. Since the early 1980s, the government's attitude toward the evangelical "faith community" has slowly changed. Both the city and the state began to realize that churches had a service to offer that government bureaucracies could not, leading to the offering of funds to assist with the work.[32] Still, Baptists have been slow to partner with government agencies in conducting their social work. Their historic emphasis on the local congregation as the agency of ministry and their belief in separation of church and state worked against such involvement. If this type of cooperation continues, however, it will be a major departure for Southern Baptists.

New Trends in Ethnic Ministry

New ideas in social service brought New Mexico Baptists into closer contact with ethnic communities, altering the manner in which their churches conducted minority ministry. Since 1970, the importance of ethnic groups to the SBC has continued to grow. A 1989 report showed that minorities accounted for 40 percent of the U.S. population, but only 10 percent of Southern Baptist membership. Statistical data compiled by the denomination revealed that had it not been for an increase among non-Anglo congregations, the number of Southern Baptist churches nationwide would have declined.[33]

To find a way to reach ethnic communities, the BCNM has had to admit its failings in this area. In addressing the convention in 1987, Claude Cone commented that although 110,000 Native Americans lived in New Mexico, Indian Baptists numbered only 1,500 in the entire state. Hispanics, he said, numbered more than 700,000, yet not one Spanish-speaking church averaged over 200 in its Sunday School. Language Coordinator Abel Becerra expressed concern that the ethnic congregations had plateaued, or even begun to decline.[34]

According to a 1992 report by Language Missions program leader, Gus Suarez, the BCNM had 111 ethnic congregations speaking twelve languages and as many dialects, representing forty-one different cultures. In order to reach the ethnic population in New Mexico—which accounted for 48 percent of the state's population—Suarez argued that Anglos and language pastors must learn how to cross the culture barrier.[35]

Earlier attempts to reach culturally diverse peoples revealed a major deficiency in the historic Baptist approach to missions. Cross-cultural ministry for Baptists usually meant establishing their church program in a non-Southern setting. Recognition that this approach did not work eventually led to a philosophical change. Speaking on this issue M. V. Summers noted:

> I will give you my theological and philosophical concept of missions. We must address the challenge of who we are and where we are. . . . We must move out of the comfort of church and into the world. . . . We don't need to seek to make people like white Southern Anglos. God desires to change the heart of man, not his nationality.[36]

Speaking before the state WMU in 1983, home missionary Betty Eaton commented: "This country has not been a great melting pot, but a pot of rich, flavorful stew. We don't and won't let any people melt into one great melting pot."[37]

These two statements illustrate a major shift in New Mexico Baptist thinking toward ethnic missions. Philosophical change led inevitably to structural adaptation. The traditional language missionary, who sought to reproduce the denomination's program among ethnic groups by trying to get them to adopt a "Southern mind-set," began to disappear in the mid-1970s and was replaced by the regional or catalytic missionary. Actually, this idea owes its origin to the state of New Mexico. While serving in the state in 1958, missionary James Nelson sought a more effective approach for reaching ethnic groups. He conceived of a missionary as one sent into a language field to search out ethnic groups, bring them together, and help them establish their system of worship; hence, the term "catalytic."[38]

Put into practice nearly twenty years later, this type of missionary was a jack-of-all-trades. He or she went into an area and established a complete church program using whatever means necessary, such as camp meetings, Vacation Bible School, or seminary extension, among other possibilities. Ethnic leaders received specialized training and then the missionary turned the church over to the congregation to make it their own.[39]

By the 1990s, the catalytic missionary underwent further refinement, emerging as a "contract worker." This development occurred in response to the desire to make ethnic groups more independent, plus the growing concern over the costs of keeping missionaries in the field. Serving for one year, the new missionary initiated a specific project. At the end of the time period, he or she turned it over to local leaders and moved on.[40]

This altered philosophy, structure, and tactics led to a new approach in planting ethnic churches. The emphasis now involved targeting specific groups and segments within the ethnic communities. Traditionally, Hispanic work had been directed to those at the bottom of the socioeconomic scale. Missionaries conducted services in Spanish because the people did not speak English. The new trend was directed at the upwardly mobile, educated, professional Hispanics, most of whom speak English. A number of second- and third-generation Hispanics are educated, earn higher incomes than their parents, and do not respond well to an unschooled pastor.

The Mexican community along the border, however, is a different entity. In addition, Hispanics in the rural areas of northern New Mexico have their own subculture. Then there are the urban Hispanic "Anglophiles" who want the same programs and resources that the Anglo churches have but that the ethnic churches have been unable to provide. In addition, many of the upwardly mobile Hispanic congregations operate like Anglo churches using very high-tech worship service techniques.[41]

Within the BCNM, Anglo and ethnic churches have begun to organize around occupations. Some cater to blue-collar workers and others to those in management positions.[42] In the 1990s, the convention started targeting subgroups within specific cultures, based on age, education, and job orientation.[43] The process involved creating churches based on demographic characteristics rather than historic beliefs.[44]

There are dangers, however, inherent in this approach. By attempting to establish churches around social, economic, educational, and subcultural classifications, the BCNM may be moving toward a plethora of "nonaffinity churches." Founding congregations on the demographics of subgroups has the potential to cause fragmentation, leading to a form of "Christian tribalism," rather than an historic Baptist community.[45]

Controversy

Theological disputes within the denomination erupted in the 1960s beginning with Professor Elliot's interpretation of origins in his book on Genesis and escalated with Professor Davies's account of Abraham's sacrifice of Isaac in volume 1 of the Broadman Commentary. Debate escalated in the 1970s when Bill Powell and associates sought to rid Southern Baptist seminaries of "liberals." Powell's group was eventually discredited, but Judge Paul Pressler and Paige Patterson of Criswell Bible Institute continued the crusade. Some charged that Adrian Rogers, elected SBC president in 1979, fanned the flames by making partisan committee and board appointments, in a direct attempt to take over denominational institutions for the conservative side.[46]

The situation continued to intensify, forcing the BCNM to express its concern over the expanding hostilities. In 1980, Whitlow wrote an editorial responding to attempts by Patterson to form a political group so as to elect a Southern Baptist Convention president who would side with his group on the inerrancy issue. Patterson had leveled charges against seven seminary professors who wrote literature for the Sunday School Board. Whitlow demanded that the seven men be named and given the opportunity to defend themselves. He received no reply. Then Evangelist James Robinson came to Albuquerque and claimed that liberals had filled the denomination's seminaries. His remarks so inflamed some area pastors that they talked about withholding Cooperative Program funds.[47]

With this threat, the state convention finally took action. The BCNM drafted a resolution expressing its views to the national body. The resolution also served as a framework for containing the debate within its own ranks. As excerpt from the resolution follows:

> For more than two years the Southern Baptist Convention has been embroiled in a battle over the process of electing trustees and committee personnel and certain "brethren" have "avowed" to place their choices in these positions in order to "control" the Convention agencies and institutions in a manner not in keeping with the accepted practices of the convention. . . . A formal movement of resistance to that effort has been formed by other brethren, thus, polarizing and possibly dividing the Convention and further causing disharmony and threatening further disruption of the Southern Baptist Convention. . . . The Baptist Convention of New Mexico encourages the messengers to the Convention and every Southern Baptist Church in the state to seek for harmony and to refrain from actions which would contribute toward a division of the fellowship. . . . The churches of the convention unite in prayer continually for preserving doctrinal integrity of the Southern Baptist Convention.[48]

Messengers to the 1980 convention returned in good spirits. The plea for unity appeared to be working. The debate over the inerrancy issue had not generated the acrimony or contention that had been anticipated. Subsequent events, however, destroyed this momentary optimism. Problems resumed in 1983. The *Baptist New Mexican*'s new editor, J. B. Fowler, took issue when SBC President Jimmy Draper attempted to establish guidelines for Southern Baptist beliefs. Fowler charged that this smacked of "creedalism": "Baptists are too independent minded and too strong in their belief of the priesthood of the believer ever to go for that."[49]

Continuity and Change: A Redefined Church   149

The following year, Fowler protested the nomination of Pressler to the denomination's executive committee. In his opinion, Pressler and Patterson had done more in the preceding five years to divide the convention than anyone since famed Texas controversialist J. Frank Norris. New Mexico pastor John Parrott noted the historical irony. Fifty years before, Norris, who hailed from First Baptist Church in Fort Worth, led a witch-hunt against Reverend George W. Truett of First Baptist Church in Dallas. Now, said Parrot, Patterson, a staff member at the Dallas church, was conducting a similar campaign against Southwestern Seminary in Fort Worth.[50]

Conditions worsened in 1986 with what Fowler deemed a "fundamentalist-conservative" takeover of the convention, with the election of Adrian Rogers as president for a second time. Fowler claimed that Rogers's new coalition turned back every effort by moderate conservatives to place some of their people on the slate of nominees the Committee on Boards presented. Lamenting this course of action, Fowler told his readers that he had no problem with the fundamentalists' theology: "But I sure have problems with their methods, for they have disenfranchised multitudes of lifelong, loyal Southern Baptists whose voice is no longer heard in their beloved convention."[51]

The effects of this struggle began to show among New Mexico Baptists. Whitlow's editorials in the late 1970s received virtually unanimous support. Although very similar to his predecessor's, Fowler's stance generated much criticism. The tone of many letters printed in the *Baptist New Mexican* indicated that at least some viewed the struggle as more than simply a politicized debate. Polarization never occurred, but there were rumblings.

Searching for reconciliation and a basis for cooperation among the opposing factions, the SBC formed the Peace Committee. The committee asked state editors to cease printing articles, editorials, and letters to the editor on the issue so as to give the peace initiative an opportunity to work.[52] New Mexico responded positively to this request, significantly reducing the newspaper space devoted to the crisis. Baptists in the state seemed to take the attitude that it was time to move on to other things.

Compared to many states in the SBC, the theological controversy had very little impact in New Mexico. Many of those reasons are peculiar to the state. Both Chester O'Brien and Claude Cone sought to maintain unity by diffusing any attempts at polarization. They did so by encouraging pastoral dialogue. Ministers talking about the issue among themselves seemed to have a dampening effect. Also, BCNM is a Western convention, which means that it leans toward the conservative position. There were simply not enough clergy with liberal tendencies in the region to present much of a problem.[53]

Work in the West has often been referred to as a "foreign mission field." Typically, those who labor under conditions different from those of their homeland exhibit a more cooperative spirit. In a non-Southern environment, internal battles paled beside the need for proclaiming the Baptist version of the gospel. Therefore, New Mexico Baptists did not see the controversy so much as a "defense of the faith," but rather as a political struggle that interfered with evangelism.[54]

Perhaps the single most important factor that militated against New Mexico Baptists' involvement in the conflict lay with the state convention's dependence on the Cooperative Program. The BCNM has always needed denominational funds to carry out its programs. Controversy threatened that supply line.[55] Writing in 1992, Fowler reminded his readers: "In all the confusion that abounds, New Mexico Baptists need to remember that $850,000 of our operating budget comes from the Southern Baptist Home Mission Board."[56] Two years later, the new editor, John Loudat, echoed similar sentiments. He noted that 75 percent of the budget for the state's Missions and Evangelism Divisions came from this program.[57] New Mexico Baptists could not afford to lose this source of income.

When compared with other states in the SBC, New Mexico experienced little disruption because of the controversy. Under the surface, however, there were repercussions. Some associations in the southeastern portion of the state experienced broken fellowship. Many of the pastors in this region came from Texas, where the battle was especially bitter, and inflamed passions spilled over into New Mexico.[58] Declining contributions, perhaps due to this quarrel, proved to be more damaging. Actual lost dollar amounts are impossible to quantify, but some Baptists in the state seem to have redirected their giving to parachurch organizations because of the conflict. In some cases, individuals went so far as to place revisionary clauses in their endowments, threatening to sever support should the institutions the donors were funding change in their theological orientation.[59]

Attendance at the annual state convention also began to decline. Some observers saw this trend as a byproduct of the inerrancy battle. Although no convention sermons took strong sides, a spirit of disquiet lay beneath the surface. Because the controversy lurked behind the scenes, it prevented New Mexico Baptists from addressing certain issues for fear of embroiling the convention in conflict.[60]

Loss of Distinctiveness

The loss of training in denominational beliefs and traditions may prove to be the most damaging development of this crisis. Since instruction began to decline at a time when the emphasis on theology seemed to diminish among evangelicals, the controversy heightened this phenomenon among Baptists.[61] In attempting to avoid conflict, many ministers preached sermons with less doctrinal content. In the post-1960s era, distinctive Baptist beliefs became increasingly relegated to the periphery of church life. The Bible was deified, but not applied. Baptist theology remained consistent, but it no longer remained at the center of Baptists' Christian expression.[62]

Officially, the BCNM has not veered from its commitment to the historic principles of the Baptist faith. For example, Kenneth Stohner, pastor of Calvary Baptist in Roswell, preached the annual sermon to the convention in 1979 under the title "Going Back to the Basics." In this address he emphasized the need to continue proclaiming Baptists beliefs, affirming that the Bible is the infallible, inspired word of God.[63] Twelve years later devotion to the scriptures had not changed. The theme for the 1991 meeting centered on "celebrating the word." During the gathering, a series of speakers reaffirmed their belief in the divine inspiration of the Bible.

Having affirmed their devotion to the Bible, New Mexico Baptists also displayed equal commitment to traditional Baptist doctrine. From January 23 through April 17, 1982, the *Baptist New Mexican* ran a weekly series on doctrine, featuring commentary from pastors across the state. These articles included topics on God, Christ, the Holy Spirit, sin, salvation, heaven, hell, the second coming, death, and resurrection. No exposition in any way departed from the 1963 Baptist faith and message statement. Despite what many conservatives felt was the "misuse" of the doctrines of soul competency and priesthood of the believer by liberals, the state convention went on record in 1990 as still supporting individual conscience: "We reaffirm our traditional and theological position concerning the autonomy of the believer in scriptural interpretation . . ."[64]

Despite the affirmation, historic Southern Baptist beliefs were not being passed on to the lay membership. Speaking at Golden Gate Seminary in 1986, Joe Stacker of the Sunday School Board observed that doctrinal preaching had declined over the previous twenty-five years. Fowler agreed, recollecting that as a pastor he had always made it a point to preach on what Baptists believed. Few, he said, broached the subject anymore. Since Training Union activities had also ceased being a source for theological education, many Baptist laypersons were without instruction in their faith.[65]

New Mexico pastor John Parrott claimed in 1979 that with over 5 million sermons preached every year, very little had anything to do with the gospel.

Instead of expository messages from the pulpit, he said parishioners received topical sermonettes on anything from "good books to read" to "sex in the Christian marriage bed." Rather than messages that challenged, he claimed that people preferred to be entertained. Southern Baptist historian Walter Shurden noted in 1983 that the denomination used to be a fellowship of kindred minds. Speaking before the BCNM in 1991, guest speaker Joe De Leon summed up the problem: "[W]e are no longer a people of the Book."[66]

This transformation became noticeable in the early 1980s when, according to some pastors, the questions people asked began to change. Many came to the church seeking to use God for personal advancement. Their relationship with the creator centered on what was in it for them.[67] Well into the 1960s, most Southern Baptist churches still emphasized a biblical curriculum. After this period, systematic inquiry quickly declined. The new format dealt with specific issues rather than with a comprehensive approach to life.

A shift became discernible in the subject matter of the typical Sunday morning sermon. Messages often emphasized personal skills, albeit from a biblical perspective, but within a social-psychological context. In an attempt to attract more people, some pastors emphasized the development of self-esteem in the listener, rather than conformity to God. Appropriate subject matter included finances, getting along with others, time management, teen problems, parent-child relationships, and a host of other needs-centered topics. Comprehensive doctrinal study gave way to a band-aid approach that placed emphasis on solving personal problems. Ministers often introduced theology, if at all, through subterfuge. For instance, if the message dealt with the family, the pastor might try to interject Christ's teachings regarding women.[68]

According to some ministers, people now come to church for programs that will meet their personal needs. Overeaters can join a "weigh-down" group and receive biblical encouragement in dealing with their affliction. Would-be stock market moguls can learn how to invest "from a Christian perspective." The physically unfit can "bump and grind" to the latest Christian rock. Flower arranging classes allow people to express their gift of hospitality.

The Discipleship Training program now teaches interpersonal skills, rather than the ideals of how to minister in the church. The old Training Union program once had members memorizing scripture; now they examine sociological issues from a (retreating) biblical perspective. Sunday School has become less a place of Bible study and more a place to share personal concerns and problems. Fellowship, prayer, and a short lesson with a contemporary application usually comprise the modern class. As New Mexico Baptist churches make the transition from a faith community to a sociological center, the historic Baptist message has become more and more diluted.[69]

This decline in theological proclamation and instruction resulted in an unanticipated development for New Mexico Baptists. Soul winning lost its appeal. Recently, Frank Zamora, BCNM president in 1993, asked in a convention address if the churches really wanted to win people to Christ. He said that he was not hearing this concern in their committee meetings or planning sessions.[70] As sermons and programs turned inward to minister to the needs of their members, evangelism suffered. Baptists were no longer reaching out to enlist people as they once had.

Baptists have historically placed an inordinate amount of attention on expansion. Growth drives their evangelism. Increasing their membership especially through Sunday School and new church starts in order to produce more baptisms is the motivating force behind denominational activity. Therefore, Southern Baptists, with New Mexico Baptists following suit, modified their approach to attract more people. Altering content, in turn, changed the theological emphasis even though official statements regarding Baptist doctrine remained the same. Thus, theology remained consistent while being pushed to the periphery of church life.

A Changing Pastorate

As within the realm of theology, where the basic tenets of the faith remained seemingly intact, ministers still assumed most of their traditional roles. Beneath the surface, however, the pastorate also experienced a similar upheaval. The church formerly consisted of three elements: teaching, preaching, and singing. In the post-1960s era, this format changed to programs and therapy. The minister now serves as chief administrator.

In appealing to the modern member, the denomination has responded with a plethora of ministries, programs, seminars, and therapy sessions. As a result, the administrative load on the pastor has greatly increased.[71] A New Mexico Baptist minister quite often works sixty to eighty hours a week. Housekeeping duties require so much effort that the time needed for effective sermon preparation has suffered.

Augmenting this transformation from minister to administrator has been the development of what is known as the "success orientation" of the modern church. To avoid being labeled a failure, a pastor must ensure a steady increase in baptisms and membership. Undertaking an aggressive building project is even better. One sure way to denominational notoriety is to oversee an ever-expanding program. Baptists have had a tendency to equate spiritual well-being with physical growth. Congregational expectations have fed this syndrome, resulting in "preacher buying." Pulpit committees offer large salaries to lure a pastor who they think will lead them to new heights of accomplishment. The pressure for success forces the minister into the role of a CEO who needs to maintain good relations with his shareholders.

To keep people on the rolls, and thus maintain an aura of success, church discipline has suffered. Frank Wheeler, superintendent of Mountain Valley Association, noted in 1975 that in Baptist history individuals were disciplined for adultery, wife beating, and drunkenness, along with other forms of antisocial behavior. In the modern congregation, however, a person can commit these acts without comment; if ostracized by their fellowship, another church will receive the perpetrator with open arms. According to Wheeler, many Baptist churches believe that it is better to hold on to a member than to require him or her to exhibit true faith and practice. The desire and drive for statistical increase has led to the idea "that quantity is more important than quality—a decline in numbers on the roll looks bad on the convention record."[72]

Succumbing to the pressure to be successful has led to gradual erosion in the historic orientations of Baptist churches: evangelism and missions. As individual congregations seek to build up their programs and physical plants to attract new members, they do so at the expense of outreach. Increasing programs not only necessitated an increase in staff, but financial resources as well. Meeting personnel and infrastructure requirements has diverted funds that would normally have gone to starting new churches and other evangelistic projects.[73]

The growth of programmatic ministries, which turned the clergy into administrators, has also spawned the "autocratic leader." Declining lay involvement and expanding staff have "professionalized" the church. In many bodies, a charismatic minister consolidates control of the entire operation under himself. Deacon boards and other committees have little say in the procedure; instead, they function more as "enablement" groups. This hierarchical pattern is disastrous for clergy of modest abilities who may not have the personality skills to implement their will. It also strikes at the core of Baptist polity, for it usurps the idea of a congregation-based operation and replaces it with an ecclesiastical one.

Pressures arising from a changing pastorate have also carried over into ministers' domestic lives. Salaries have not always kept pace with inflation or responsibilities. The need for permanent housing, retirement income, and funds for children's education has forced many ministers to look for other means of employment.[74] Inevitably, all of these factors have led to a crisis affecting the marriages and families of Southern Baptist pastors. The divorce rate among ministers is rising. Although the BCNM provides no statistics, the fact that the convention sponsors seminars dealing with these issues for their pastors indicates that New Mexico Baptist clergy are not immune to national trends.

Saving the Family

The marital and domestic problems experienced by clergy have parallels in the lives of church members. Leaders point to a rapidly changing society that has destabilized the home unit. They see three factors as accentuating the problem: increasing polarization between Christian and non-Christian beliefs, especially as portrayed in the media; economic conditions that have forced people into dual-career marriages; and a perceived decline in educational opportunities for their children. Responding to this situation has created a shift in focus. For many churches, ministry now centers on the family. In the 1980s, the BCNM began conducting workshops to assist ministers in formulating household development projects.

These programs tried to help families learn to live together. Instead of telling parents that they must be "good Christian fathers and mothers," the new curriculum showed them how to practice these ideals. Churches began providing counseling and human resource services as part of their regular ministry, in many cases expanding staffs to include licensed counselors and psychologists. Church recreation also took on an added emphasis. From the athletic leagues and camping programs of the 1950s and 1960s, the emphasis changed to teaching members of a household how to relate to one another through the medium of sports and games.[75]

First Baptist Church in Artesia serves as an example of how extensive such programs can become. In 1988, the church sponsored the New Mexico Congress on Family Living. Seminars covered household-related subjects such as discipline, retirement, money management, and help for the separated and divorced. Other workshops dealt with personal problems that affected the family's ability to function. They included dealing with grief, drug abuse, expressing anger and resolving conflict, intimacy, teen suicide, and sexual abuse.[76] In short, the Artesia church turned itself into a university on family relations.

A Loss of Community

As the church underwent a shift from a community of believers who minister to God, to preserving the Baptist family, so too did its programming. As congregations became "pass-through rehabilitation centers," they have altered the reason for the church's existence. Changing the focus from the divine to the human makes functioning as a unit difficult. Thus, instead of programs that brought people together around a center—God—the church has created a plethora of ministries to meet a wide variety of individual needs.[77] These are recreational, social, and therapeutic, but by being designed for narrow audiences, they compartmentalize and exclude. People come to church not so much to worship God, but to participate in services they deem beneficial to their life. As a result, many individuals treat the church somewhat like a country club. They participate as long as it provides the services desired, or until their children are fully grown. The idea that the gospel might place demands on their lives has become a foreign concept.[78]

In part, this behavior is due to the emergence of a transient society that has lost its family, community, and spiritual roots. Modernity has stripped the individual of attachment to anything but self. Responding to this new type of person, the church has attempted to become "seeker friendly" by giving newcomers what they desire. Instead of people entering into the traditional corporate worship experience, the purpose of which was to lead them out of the realm of the self to an encounter with the divine, the reverse is taking place. Some modern Baptist churches have begun to restructure their Sunday morning service to where the activity is no different than what people experience in the larger culture.

This new approach has led to innovations in the worship hour such as a contemporary format, Saturday night services, drama, puppetry, orchestras, praise singers, and bands.[79] For example, some congregations have worship services on Wednesday night with multimedia presentations. Churches have experimented with new programs, much like a corporation seeking to introduce a new product. Both are appealing to the "consumer mentality" of the potential customer. Although unquestionably unintentional, encountering the "otherness" of God has been sacrificed to make people feel comfortable within their cultural context.

Seeking to attract new people, many New Mexico Baptist churches have become sociological centers. The new programming often ministers to the felt needs of the members and the sermons from the pulpit have often followed suit. Quite frequently the Sunday morning message follows a psychological—"feel good"—format designed to assist individuals in self-actualization.[80] Building the psyche, however, is not without a price. Centering on the human, rather than the divine, has not produced denominational loyalty in the recipients. In New Mexico, it is quite common for a person to attend one church on Sunday morning and another in the evening. Wednesday night finds them at still a different congregation, and other times during the week they might be working with a parachurch organization. Commitment extends only as far as the self has a need.[81]

Disruptive social forces have also altered what individuals look for in a church. The modern work environment has taken a severe toll on many people. They come on Sunday morning looking for something that will allow them to make it through the next week. The sermon or Bible lesson functions as a "therapeutic fix." Instead of developing a relationship with God through a system of belief that would allow them to function under any circumstance, modern parishioners settle for a "dose of Jesus" as an antidote against the ills many have to face. Fellowship with like-minded people has often become more important than worshipping God. No longer able to spend as much time with their children, since economic conditions dictate the two-wage-earner household, many parents now look to the church for assistance. The availability of preschool and children's programs is a major determinant in selecting a place of worship, since they function as a "surrogate family" by teaching values that the adults are unable to impart.[82]

In responding to these concerns, the BCNM conducted a conference in 1987, entitled "Today's Pulpit—Today's People." Speakers advocated moving away from traditional biblical themes and salvation messages. In their place, they urged pastors to preach to people's needs. Adjusting to a needs-based format caused the church to become activity based. By attempting to develop a multitude of ministries, congregations are expanding themselves into oblivion. In the process, cohesion and doctrinal continuity have suffered. Churches are fragmenting into mutually exclusive groups. Staff members are wearing themselves out under exhausting workloads trying to accommodate this diversity. Instead of programs where members interrelate, people are selectively partaking to suit their personal desires.

Not only pastors and staff are beginning to experience burnout; so are the lay leaders and even rank-and-file members. Individuals are becoming overloaded with activities designed to meet increasingly narrow definitions of needs. As one pastor noted, "If our members attend all the services we urge them to attend . . . and they even accept half of the positions which their nominating committee offers them, they hardly have enough time for family life, to say nothing of being actively involved in the political process and the community."[83]

As a result, many New Mexico Baptist ministries are in danger of collapsing. Too many programs and not enough workers have created a leadership crisis. The modern work environment does not leave the laity sufficient time to undergo training, and it greatly reduces the type of projects people can become involved in. Attempting to accommodate erratic schedules, churches offer instruction at odd hours, but this practice adds further stress to an overworked staff. The prospect of failing ministries has turned many churches in on themselves.

Increasing programs and decreasing income forces congregations to cut back on mission expenditures and outreach. Instead, the money goes to protecting, preserving, and maintaining the church's infrastructure.[84] Despite a sizable number of new church starts, the net Baptist growth is minimal largely due to a high rate of failure. Stress among clergy members has brought about the reoccurrence of an old problem: pastorless churches. Nearly 20 percent of New Mexico Baptist churches are vacant on a continual basis. Among small congregations the situation is so acute that the BCNM has set up special orientation programs to help ministers remain in the field.[85]

A Loss of Vision

In 1992, the BCNM sought to address this new state of affairs by sponsoring a seminar entitled, "Shaping the Future of the Plateauing Church." The purpose was fivefold: first, to regroup and rethink the convention's philosophy of ministry; second, to discover why churches were leveling off and not growing; third, to instruct pastors in writing mission statements; fourth, to identify the new types of ministries to start; and finally, to determine what churches outside the SBC are doing.[86]

Emerging from this seminar was the acknowledgment that New Mexico Baptist churches lacked a sense of purpose. There was no vision to invigorate, motivate, and challenge the people to move forward. The root of this problem, however, originated in the 1970s. Speaking to the leadership in 1975, convention president C. L. Bowes said that they needed to "re-excite" the people. The laity, he said, had begun to desert the churches; their interest, commitment, and attendance were all waning.[87] At a 1982 meeting of the State Executive Board, Dale Danielson again brought up this issue: "It would help if we had an overall strategy from our leaders of what we are setting out to accomplish. . . . We need the thrill and excitement to motivate us in the churches."[88] The growing bureaucratization of the convention separated members from their leaders, distancing them from the organization. The sense of being in touch, so characteristic of the Stagg era, no longer prevailed in the state's Southern Baptist churches.[89]

That the BCNM had lost its vision by 1995 is clear. Determining how this occurred is more difficult. Several possible explanations have been put forward. Some have argued that the problem is primarily structural, beginning with the reorganization of 1970. They maintain that the local church gave up its vision to the state convention. Historically, Baptists organized around the local church, but since World War II state organizations have slowly evolved into a headquarters for the denomination within respective geographical areas. Critics assert that a return to the locus of the individual church is necessary, letting it again become the center for vision and ministry.[90]

Organizational direction, however, is not the only factor contributing to the disorientation. Others attribute this loss of vision and declining laity involvement in part to the rising socioeconomic status of New Mexico Baptists. Increasing prosperity in the post-1960s has provided more discretionary income among members. Affluence, in turn, has generated a greater interest in recreation and travel, all of which have competed with the church for attendance and commitment. The reigning abundance has allowed people to fulfill their responsibility by contributing more, but has also absolved them of active participation.[91]

Still another factor may be that the days of Baptist glory in New Mexico are over. During the Stagg years the denomination moved out from its beachhead along the Texas-Oklahoma border and established its work all across the state. In those days, there were projects to build and causes to champion. The Glorieta project mobilized the people for expansion. The Dixon case galvanized them in the fight for religious liberty. To a large degree, since the Stagg era, the convention has channeled its energies toward preserving, maintaining, and consolidating previous achievements.[92] In so doing, the BCNM's vision has lessened.

Quite possibly, safeguarding the operation has turned the BCNM inward. Security and safety have now become the major items of concern for the denomination.[93] The threats of litigation and increased government regulations, improving employee salaries and benefits, and maintaining existing programs and services require an increasing expenditure of time and resources. All these factors have combined to create an attitude of entrenchment and preservation, and such an orientation inhibits growth and expansion. Coping with these conditions has hampered the development of goals that would excite and mobilize the people. In the BCNM's 1995 survey, respondents cited lack of vision as a major concern. Thus far, attempts to address this problem have failed. To solve it may well require redefining the ministry of the church.[94]

CHAPTER II

————Conclusions

Baptist expansion within New Mexico was to a large degree due to the efforts of Baptists themselves, but that growth occurred within a specific historical context conducive to the spread of religion. After World War II, revival radiated across the land for nearly fifteen years. The impact of the depression and war revived interest in the church as an important social institution in the life of the nation. As sociologist Will Herberg noted, however, it was not so much a return to God as it was a celebration of the American way of life in which the Judeo-Christian worldview provided a moral foundation.[1] As a result, virtually all denominations experienced an increase in membership and church construction during this period. In 1940, church membership roles listed 64.5 million parishioners. Twenty years later that number had escalated to 114.5 million, or 63 percent of the entire population. A national poll in 1948 found that 95 percent of the U.S. population claimed to believe in God.[2]

A burgeoning evangelical movement coincided with this "return to religion." Emerging out of "fundamentalism," but shunning its harsher image and anti-intellectual stance, this new evangelism returned respectability to conservative Christianity. A new group of theologians and scholars gave credence to biblical inerrancy, personal salvation, the virgin birth, and the return of Christ.[3] The Billy Graham crusades drew upon America's revivalist past, giving the new evangelicalism an interdenominational appeal.

During the same era, America became locked in what appeared to be a life-and-death struggle with the Soviet Union. The possibility of annihilation fostered a sense of insecurity among the population furthering an acceptance of religion. The Cold War embodied a series of conflicts: democracy against totalitarianism, capitalism against communism, and belief in God against atheism. Anticommunism took on the aura of a religious crusade in which the righteous empire must summon its moral strength to turn back the godless forces of barbarism.

Elements of Growth

These factors combined to create an environment conducive to the growth of religion in America. Baptists in New Mexico participated in, and benefited

161

from, these national trends. What set the denomination apart from other religious groups in the state was their ability to capitalize on these forces. Baptists had a strong evangelical message that they delivered with a passion that comes only from being convinced they were doing the will of God. A dynamic state convention orchestrated its efforts to one end: winning the lost. Zeal and organization produced results.

Another factor that aided Baptist expansion in New Mexico was denominational support. Depression and World War II forced Southern Baptists out of their regional homeland. By 1960, the convention had a presence in nearly every state. This nationwide leap forward benefited New Mexico, not only as the recipient of many new immigrants, but financially as well. To support their scattered membership, denominational agencies restructured themselves to provide the necessary assistance.[4]

War brought economic change to Southern Baptists. As farming became mechanized, those who stayed on the land experienced rising living standards. Those who migrated to the city became laborers or moved into the ranks of professionals, receiving regular paychecks. Blessed with a consistent income, members shared their good fortune with the church. Increased revenue allowed the denomination to support territorial expansion.

Specifically, increased income enabled the Home Mission and Sunday School Boards to sponsor new programs in the West. Money for salaries to support missionaries and evangelists in underdeveloped fields became available. In addition, funds for building construction benefited struggling congregations unable to erect their own churches. Literature provided at special rates connected Baptists anywhere in the country with the South.

Southern Baptists expanded their educational facilities, increasing the number of seminaries to six, with Golden Gate Seminary and Midwestern Seminary located in the West. This expansion had a twofold impact. It raised the educational level of the clergy, and the increase in the number of ministers helped Western churches to escape the itinerant pastor dilemma.

Capitalizing on national trends and denominational support, the Baptist Convention of New Mexico (BCNM) launched its own program of evangelism. Commitment and confidence in Southern Baptist theology undergirded the outreach. Believing that they had the whole truth for the whole world stimulated efforts to propagate the gospel. Aggressive uses of Vacation Bible Schools, Sunday Schools, revivals, census, and visitation and enlargement campaigns spread the Christian message throughout the state. Although migration of Baptists into New Mexico accounted for a large percentage of church growth, it was not the overwhelming factor that it had been in previous years. In the pre-World War II period, individuals moving into the state and affiliating with a Baptist church outnumbered additions by baptism four to one. In the postwar era this ratio fell to two to one.

A positive public image aided this effort during the 1940s and 1950s. Social service projects such as the Children's Home, Parkview Medical Center, and reorganization of the Boys' Ranch created an image of a denomination committed to the larger community, rather than just its own. The Glorieta assembly facilities captured the imagination of people in the state, becoming a source of pride. It was not uncommon for state residents who were not Baptists to take visiting relatives out to see the assembly and its gardens. The place also projected the aura of an innovative organization on the move.

Supporting such a favorable perception of Baptists in the state was the high regard accorded Christianity by the general public during this era. Addressing this issue in 1993, Harry Stagg noted that he would not be able under present conditions to accomplish many of the things he did to advance the convention because of the change in attitude toward Christianity.[5] For example, in the postwar era he was able to obtain a clergy pass on the railroads that enabled him to traverse the state, at a time when the BCNM was unable to allocate money for travel. Chambers of commerce and state organizations backed expansion projects such as the Glorieta assembly by assisting with promotional literature and making financial contributions to the building fund. Public leaders accorded political recognition to the assembly by attending groundbreaking and dedication ceremonies. In turn, Stagg received invitations to attend government meetings and functions. This attitude enabled the denomination to operate in a positive environment, which augmented its growth.

Unity of belief and commitment to Baptist doctrine was another factor that stimulated growth. The Dixon case united the people in their fight for religious liberty. The issue of separation of church and state defined the membership in relation to Catholics, providing a sense of distinctiveness as well as esprit de corps. For those who had recently arrived in the state this was especially important as a means of identification in a new environment.

While many of these factors affected other religious groups in the state as well, one element set Baptists apart: a dynamic leader in the person of Harry Stagg. He was a visionary endowed with an ability to conceive the grand project. Stagg was also able to communicate his goals in such a way that people embraced them as their own and were willing to work for the causes he championed. Besides being a motivator, Stagg possessed administrative skills that kept an expanding convention bureaucracy functioning while making each person feel that he or she was special.

Augmenting Stagg's influence was a superb staff. Throughout this time period there were very few incidents that disrupted harmony. A staff committed to one another and the work at hand resulted in occupational longevity. Unlike the previous era where turnover was rampant, department heads, associates, and secretaries stayed at their posts. Continuity in leadership carried over into consistency in the evangelistic effort.

Collectively, these factors led to the development of a Baptist consciousness. Projects such as the Glorieta assembly, Parkview Medical Center, and Inlow Camp provided physical-geographical identification for the denomination. With every family receiving the *Baptist New Mexican,* parishioners could keep abreast of both state and national Baptist affairs. The newspaper also enabled the BCNM to communicate with its constituents, building cohesiveness between individual members and their churches with the state organization. Standardized Sunday Schools, the Training Union program, and Vacation Bible Schools also built unity among the membership as people across the state received the same teaching and participated in the same types of church programs and growth projects. Stagg's travel and personal contacts rallied people to the standard as they were touched by his enthusiasm and drive. Baptists were able to forge an identity among their people that set them apart as a special group in a land of cultural and religious diversity. No other Protestant denomination came as close as the Baptists to creating a collective consciousness similar to that of the Catholic Church among the Hispanic population.

In many ways, the BCNM's growth paralleled that of the Southern Baptist Convention (SBC). Both bodies had suffered from crushing debt. Stagg had linked both financial obligations and the two conventions emerged from their respective debt loads in 1943 ready for expansion. Depression and war transformed them. As Baptists migrated out of the South, New Mexico benefited. Worldwide conflict increased both the state and national body's income. From a denomination of farmers, the denomination's demographics shifted to include skilled laborers and professionals. Increasing salaries provided the churches with funds for programmatic expansion.

Territorial and financial growth increased the size of both the national and state conventions. In New Mexico, the staff increased from four to thirty-seven. Real property values and organizational net worth escalated. In order to handle the increased workload a professional bureaucracy emerged with more power being vested in the state convention and in Southern Baptist boards and agencies.

Another commonality between the BCNM and the national convention was the presence of strong charismatic leaders emerging from the ranks of pastors. Men such as T. L. Holcomb, James Sullivan, and Duke McCall led the SBC through its time of expansion. Their powerful personalities and strong leadership qualities navigated the denomination through a time of jarring reorganization that could have sent the SBC into dissolution. Instead, they helped keep it on course and expanded the SBC's message nationwide. In New Mexico, Stagg provided the same leadership and guidance, keeping the state on track and leading it to new and greater accomplishments.

Continuity of belief characterized both bodies. They remained theologically conservative and nonecumenical, placing strong emphasis on separation of church and state. New Mexico Baptists became a denominational leader in this struggle through court battles to prevent public funds being used in parochial schools and to gain access to Indian reservations.

Cherished Baptist beliefs such as personal salvation, believer's baptism, local church autonomy, biblical authority, and the priesthood of the believer remained at the core of both conventions' faith and practice. Social involvement still centered on areas of personal piety in relation to alcohol, gambling, and the new issue of pornography. Continuity in doctrinal and social matters was instrumental in holding Baptists together at a time when internal change was altering the educational, social, economic, and territorial landscape of the denomination. This consistency of practice provided a sense of direction and security amid changing times. Commitment to historic beliefs created a unity of purpose that allowed Baptists to move forward and expand across the nation.

Despite the similarities, there were some significant differences between New Mexico Baptists and the national convention. The most striking was over the issue of race. An attitude of acceptance and integration prevailed in the state that did not exist within the traditional boundaries of the denomination. The BCNM, through its resolutions, editorials, associational fellowship, youth camps, and Glorieta assembly policies communicated its belief that all peoples, regardless of color, were equal before God. Furthermore, state Baptists asserted that it was a Christian's duty to see that all races be treated equally and fairly. While the SBC's Christian Life Commission issued similar statements, in New Mexico they became an accepted part of Baptist practice.

Second, New Mexico differed from the rest of the denomination in the area of educational policy and practice. While virtually all Southern and even some expansion states had erected Baptist colleges, the failure of Montezuma led the BCNM to adopt an alternate approach. The state convention chose, instead, to establish Bible chairs through their BSUs at state universities rather than trying again to establish a strictly Baptist school. Except at Eastern New Mexico University, which offered a degree in religious studies, the emphasis lay with supporting Baptist students on secular campuses. As such, the BSUs functioned as a surrogate church with theological training.

A third distinction lay in the dual form of mission activity within the state. In New Mexico, both a foreign and home missions format functions side by side. Distinct language and cultural groups live in the state that antedate the Anglo or Euro-American by hundreds, even thousands of years, who have land, property, influence, and political power. To address this issue, the Home Mission Board in cooperation with the State Mission Board formulated a plan to evangelize the ethnic populations through the employment of missionaries. Personnel and material provided from denominational resources allowed for the conduct of Baptist work as a separate entity to people of a different culture.

A fourth difference lay in the makeup of the Baptist constituency in the state. The SBC has traditionally been a rural denomination. Even in 1960, 75 percent of its churches were still in country locations. New Mexico deviated from this pattern. While in 1940 approximately 75 percent of the Baptist churches were rural, two-thirds of the membership resided in urban areas. By the end of this time period, both the membership and the churches were overwhelmingly urban (87 percent and 58 percent, respectively). The BCNM had become an organization composed of city dwellers. No longer predominately an agrarian people, Baptists in New Mexico had become wage earners, skilled laborers, and professionals.

Finally, New Mexico Baptists differed in their approach to communication. A defining characteristic of the Stagg era was that the leadership stayed in touch with the people. The vast size of the state and the remoteness of many of its towns and villages made maintaining contact difficult and extremely time consuming. To alleviate the problem BCNM personnel took to the air, becoming the only state convention to employ an aircraft in its administrative and evangelistic work.

When all five of the above distinguishing characteristics are analyzed, an interesting pattern emerges. New Mexico Baptists were in advance of trends that would later characterize the SBC. In 1995, the national convention issued an apology to Blacks for their racial policy. New Mexico Baptists spoke out on this issue and were practicing integration decades before. In the field of education, while the national body has over forty colleges and universities, the trend is for more and more Baptist youth to attend secular state and private schools. Anticipating this development, BCNM framed its educational efforts in that direction through the Bible chairs. The BCNM's home and foreign missions approach foreshadowed the rise of multiculturalism and the ethnic and racial diversity now present within the SBC. The Home Mission Board now ministers to over seventy-nine language groups. Only recently has the denomination changed to where its membership is more urban than rural. New Mexico made this transition by 1950. In summary, Baptists in New Mexico during the Stagg era served as forerunners of denominational practice that developed decades later.

Growth in the post-World War II period, however, did not occur without affecting the BCNM and its membership. In the areas of beliefs, polity, and fellowship, the nature of Baptist life in the state underwent restructuring. While a large number of issues remained the same, expansion altered their practice.

During the Stagg era, theological beliefs remained consistent in doctrine and practice. New Mexico Baptists placed great emphasis on maintaining their distinctiveness. The teaching of doctrine dominated the pulpit ministry. Baptist beliefs regarding personal salvation, soul competency, believer baptism, church autonomy, religious liberty, the lordship of Christ, and biblical inerrancy, as well as separation of church and state, were inculcated into the membership. This instruction in the faith occurred through a rigorous program of biblical teaching in Sunday School, Training Union activities, and in the theological section of the *Baptist New Mexican,* as well as through expository sermons.

Although Baptists accepted the right of all people to worship God in their own way, they did not accept religious pluralism in the sense of the plurality of truth. They believed that they had the whole truth for the whole world in the person of Jesus Christ as revealed in the scriptures. As in the previous era, this belief undergirded their evangelism. During the Stagg era, soul winning was still the dominant emphasis of Baptist activity.

While core Baptist theological teachings remained consistent with the past, there were some changes in its expression. Beginning in the mid-1950s, a reduction in theological coverage in the *Baptist New Mexican* is discernible. Printed sermons became more organizationally oriented and less doctrinal. The Sunday School lesson commentary was no longer included. The percentage of copy reserved for biblical teaching decreased. Articles using a psychological/counseling approach that linked Christian truth to specific topics became more common.[6]

There was also a decline in articles dealing with liquor, gambling, and other social behavior concerns. At the same time, the religious freedom issue that in the earlier years had led to numerous articles delineating the differences in beliefs between Catholics and Baptists became more politically oriented as the 1950s progressed. Newspaper articles increasingly dealt with the practice of religion in a democracy, and as the 1960 election neared, reasons for not electing a Catholic. There was also a shift in the nature of the articles, from a more research-oriented, intellectually thought-provoking writing to a more promotional type of piece that projected a favorable denominational image. Baptist beliefs retained their conservative theological base and were filtered through the church programs and pulpit; nevertheless, slight changes in the presentation and nature of that doctrine began to appear.

Structural change in the state convention is more apparent. Physically, the BCNM underwent a major transformation as it expanded from rented office space consisting of two rooms and four workers, to a large bureaucratic structure with its own headquarters building. Financially, the organization entered a previously unfamiliar dimension. Emerging from debt in 1943, Baptists had never experienced what it was like to not have to work under financial constraints. Fiscal solvency and surplus income constituted a new state of affairs. New Mexico Baptists became accustomed to expansion during this era. Unprecedented growth fostered an attitude of confidence and belief in the future. Such good fortune, they felt, must be the result of being blessed by God. Church property and the net worth of the convention increased rapidly, reflected in the size of the annual budgets and escalating gifts to the Cooperative Program.

The number of churches also escalated in this period, increasing by over one hundred. Even more significantly, only a handful fell away. Geographically, Baptists moved out of their eastern beachhead to expand across the state. Associations increased from eight to fourteen, reflecting this movement. Of greatest importance, the shift in membership to the Rio Grande Valley had its origins during this era.

Issues that had affected the local church in previous periods became relics of the past. The problem of pastorless churches no longer stifled the convention. The increasing size of the congregations brought about this change in affairs. The average Baptist church in New Mexico by 1960 numbered three hundred people. Churches now had the membership base to afford a pastor. Another persistent problem, that of not having a place to meet, also nearly vanished as larger congregations and funds from the Baptist Foundation and Church Loan Corporation alleviated this concern. The increase in Southern Baptist seminaries and a national body that was expansion oriented helped produce a cadre of educated ministers. This factor, when combined with the larger congregations that could support them, meant that a more professionally trained clergy was available to staff New Mexico's churches. All of these changes combined to make the most significant alteration of all: Southern Baptists became the largest Protestant denomination in the state and second in size among all religious denominations only to the Roman Catholic Church. They rose from being a small religious group struggling to stay alive to a position of ecclesiastical dominance in twenty-two years.

Some things, however, did not change. Each church retained its autonomy even though the state convention expanded to where it could with some legitimacy be called a headquarters. The state convention leaders saw their role as supporting the individual churches rather than having dominion over them. Despite centralization the congregational style of organization remained intact. As a corollary to this polity, the associational form of affiliation not only continued, but also expanded in numbers and in directing evangelistic efforts. Revivals and promotional campaigns filtered through both bodies. In New Mexico, there was a threefold division of responsibility. The Home Mission Board's concern lay with language ministries. The churches underwrote the associational activity and the state convention dealt with special projects.

Continuity characterized the establishment of denominational edifices. Only the Children's Home survived into the post-World War II period. But projects such as the Glorieta regional assembly were extensions of the Montezuma and Ruidoso assemblies. The Baptist Hospital in Clovis preceded the Parkview Medical Center. The Bible chairs were an adaptation from lessons learned by the previous failure of two colleges.

The third and final area of distinctive Baptist development in New Mexico is in the form and organization of fellowship. The BCNM continued its home missions approach, due to the heavy influx of Anglos migrating into the state. Incoming Baptists still accounted for the largest number of additions to the churches. Ministering to new members occupied the convention's time and resources. Evangelistic efforts to Hispanics and Native Americans with the assistance of the Home Mission Board never achieved the desired results. Efforts to alter the BCNM's composition from a racially homogeneous to a heterogeneous body never occurred. Despite attempts at change by advocating a policy of integration in both church and society, Baptists in New Mexico remained an Anglo island in a culturally and ethnically diverse sea. Like missionaries from an earlier era who thought that educating people to read the Bible would win converts to Protestantism, Baptists discovered that passing resolutions and declaring an open racial policy would not integrate the church.

Southern Baptists became the largest Protestant denomination in New Mexico as a result of several factors. The social climate in the nation after

World War II favored religious expression, especially Christianity. Depression and war had forced many Southern Baptists to leave their homeland, and a large number migrated to New Mexico. The SBC supported territorial expansion, funneling money, material, and personnel into states like New Mexico. During these years the BCNM was led by a dynamic executive secretary who was a visionary capable of motivating people to make his dreams their own. The convention became a well-oiled evangelism machine in which every church program was orchestrated to the "winning of souls." The membership received a strong theological education, which produced a constituency who knew what they believed. Training in Baptist distinctiveness and participating in the comprehensive Baptist program, along with involvement in special projects, helped to develop a Baptist identity and sense of community among the members. Finally, Baptists had a vision. As Baptists, they knew who they were and where they were going.

Plateau

During the Stagg era, New Mexico Baptists departed from the SBC in several ways, most notably in racial policy, education, and urbanization. Recent changes in the fellowship, structure, and theology of New Mexico Baptists, however, have brought the BCNM in the post-1960s era in line with trends in the national body. The denomination now classifies New Mexico as an old-line expansion state, as opposed to the other Western conventions, the majority of which developed after 1940. As it matured, the BCNM grew to resemble its parent. Both bodies are plateauing.

After 1940, the Southern Baptist growth rate exploded from just over 5 million to nearly 10 million by 1960. Baptists in New Mexico quadrupled their numbers during that time, averaging around 3,000 additions per year. Over the next thirty years, the SBC grew by another 5 million, reaching 15 million in 1990, but has hovered near that figure ever since. The BCNM added just over 41,000 new members, reaching its peak in 1990 at 119,852. For both conventions, the growth rate slowed after 1960, but unlike the majority of the mainline denominations in America that went into decline, Southern Baptists continued to grow, but at a much slower rate.

New Mexico Baptists continued to improve their position relative to the other Protestant denominations in the state, and in 1993 they had more members than all the others combined. Most of this growth occurred in the 1970s and early 1980s as Baptists reaped the results of the evangelical tide sweeping the nation. The number of Baptist churches increased from 260 to 340 during this period, remaining fairly constant since then. Increased emphasis on ethnic ministries set the BCNM apart from other religious groups in the state, as the state convention in partnership with the SBC sought to broaden its base. Nearly a fourth of the Baptist churches in New Mexico by 1995 were non-Anglo.

Even though the growth rate slowed after 1960, averaging about 1,350 additions per year, New Mexico Baptists grew in other ways. Financially, the convention burgeoned. Giving increased over 400 percent since the 1960s with new Cooperative Program records being set every decade. Despite numerous hardships, the convention placed its infrastructure on a sound physical, financial, and legal footing. By the 1990s, the BCNM had been able to bring the salaries and benefits of its staff and members up to parity with other denominations, an area in which Baptists had always lagged.

Despite the ability of the SBC and the BCNM to defy trends and to improve their position in relation to other denominations, that ascendancy may be ending. Since 1990, the BCNM has lost ground, falling to 113,122 in 1995, or a 6-percent loss over five years. While membership and church growth continued throughout the 1970s and 1980s, participation in core church programs began to decline. Even though budget receipts rose, they failed to keep pace with expenses. As of 1995, New Mexico Baptists had plateaued and were possibly entering a period of decline because the changes in their fellowship, structure, and theology had caught up with them.

If historical forces created a climate of growth for Southern Baptists in New Mexico, they have also contributed to the convention's plateauing. Social convulsions in the 1960s brought about a collapse of the old society by jettisoning its values and mores. The sexual revolution, drug culture, situational ethics, and a perceived generation gap brought about a transformation in American morality.

At the same time, the Vietnam War, inflation, the civil rights movement, and federal government attempts to abolish poverty caused a disruption of society. Criticism and protest changed the nation's image of itself from an idyllic, homogenous society with shared values, by exposing social, civil, and moral wrongs underlying that superstructure. In the midst of this convulsion, the religious makeup of the nation also underwent a transformation. The "God is dead" movement cast doubt on the idea of a transcendent being by suggesting that such belief was a social construct that had outlived its usefulness. Concurrently, dissatisfaction with the sterility of much theological content in the churches that seemed to appeal only to the cerebral spawned the "charismatic" phenomenon as people sought to experience God through signs and wonders, fulfilling deep-seated needs for personal empowerment. In the process, many

Americans discarded Christianity altogether. As Harvard theologian Harvey Cox observed, many turned to the East for spiritual fulfillment.[7]

In the 1960s, nearly four hundred years of Protestant hegemony as the nation's religious center came to an end. According to John Neuhaus, religion in general and Christianity specifically were driven out of the arena of public discourse regarding societal issues, contributing to the privatization of belief, leaving a "naked public square."[8] In contrast, a decade before, Paul Tillich had been the darling of the intellectuals, and no educated person was unfamiliar with the writings of the Niebuhr brothers. In the post-1960s world, Christian consciousness seemed to abandon the field of intellectual discourse. For purposes of public debate, one had to assume a secular frame of reference.[9] Religious practice retreated to the realm of personal morality and spiritual development.

Bereft of a center, much Christian expression became politicized. The emergence of such issues as abortion and homosexuality under the rubric of "family values" polarized the nation. People of faith split into liberal and conservative camps regardless of denominational affiliation. Even those with no spiritual convictions could not escape what became known as the "culture wars." Rather than reestablish Christian thought on cultural matters, however, conflict made religious faith an even more private affair.[10]

Pluralism and diversity attempted to fill the public square. Multiculturalism, based upon the nation's ethnic and cultural differences, emerged as the new "civil religion." As each group and subgroup celebrated its separate identity, each demanded acceptance of its distinctiveness. The "melting pot" that was supposed to have characterized America disintegrated into mutually exclusive tribalism. Tolerance of all beliefs, values, practices, and personal conduct became the new public policy. Spirituality could exist as long as its teachings posed no standards of behavior based on objective, absolute principles derived from transcendent truth. Emphasis shifted from corporate religious values to individually constructed beliefs.

The impact of this societal transformation on New Mexico Southern Baptists was dramatic. For the previous 150 years, Baptists had been in step with the nation. In the 1960s, that marriage broke asunder. The country made a ninety-degree turn, but the denomination kept moving in the old direction. Although urban in membership, the rural mind-set of New Mexico Baptists seemed quaintly out of place in the "secular city." Their fierce separatism, both individual and corporate, represented a democratic ethos of a bygone era. Devotion to eternal principles as matters of conscience belonged to a different age when people, according to sociologist David

Reisman, were "inner directed." Religious exclusivity in the new relativistic environment made them appear intolerant and even un-American.

Southern Baptists in the state lost their cultural base in the 1960s. In so doing they also lost their sense of direction. Never able to identify what had gone awry, New Mexico Baptists instead developed a "coping mentality" in which they reacted to culture rather than challenging it. Unwittingly, they adopted society's new direction by focusing on the individual. In the process, they became even greater captives of mainstream culture, while at the same time criticizing the course society had taken.

Social transformation led almost immediately to a change in Baptist practice. The denominational program had evolved into an extremely labor-intensive and time-consuming format that depended on laity involvement to function. Church work was designed around a rural environment that presupposed a household comprised of one wage earner in which women did not work outside the home. When women began to enter the public workforce, as they did in ever-increasing numbers in the 1960s, the church lost its volunteer base needed to keep activities operating.[11] As women went to the office, men had to assume more domestic duties, reducing the amount of time they could spend at the church. The rise of single-parent households added to the problem. At the same time, school functions, recreational opportunities, and entertainment possibilities forced churches to compete for people's time, money, and attention.[12] In an attempt to maintain themselves and recruit others, Baptists reorganized their ministry to appeal to the individual. This development would have major ramifications on Baptist theology, structure, and fellowship.

Baptists began to downplay their theology and speak more to the psychological and emotional needs of their members, providing a form of biblical therapy, in an attempt to become "more relevant." They did this by switching their emphasis from centering on God to concentrating on the person. Sunday School and Training Union program activities began to focus more on problems faced by members, rather than biblical teaching and instruction in functioning as a corporate body. In the process the church community changed. No longer united around the concept of worshipping God, corporate ministry fragmented into special groups designed to meet an increasing number of human needs. Each required a separate program and support group. The church became more of a spiritual shopping mall rather than a fellowship of believers.

As governmental services replaced traditional church social ministries such as schools, orphanages, and hospitals, New Mexico Baptists embraced a modified social gospel. They went out of the churches and into their communities implementing ministries that dealt with problems such as drug and alcohol abuse, amnesty programs, and literacy classes. By meeting the needs of those outside its religious community, the BCNM hoped to bring them into the church.

Functionally, this internal change brought about an alteration in the fellowship of the church. As the denomination moved away from focusing on God to preoccupation with the individual, personal need rather than the fellowship of a community of believers ministering to a transcendent being received primary attention. This shift in emphasis carried over into the structure of the church. Programmatic offerings, which had concentrated on teaching and training, now extended to therapy and support groups requiring a plethora of ministries. Biblical principles and truths became tools to heighten self-awareness rather than to increase knowledge of the divine.

The vehicle that changed the fellowship in the post-1960s era was the attempt to combat the perceived demise of the nuclear family. Switching from God to people caused fragmentation in the programmatic offering. Identification of problems within the family unit led to an exponential growth in the number of ministries required to meet the ever-increasing list of needs. As these ministries grew they became further subdivided by psychological, emotional, and physical categories, which in turn separated people in the church from one another.

Developing ministries in order to meet diverse needs led to churches for specific classes of people. Congregations began to cater to age, vocation, educational, and ethnic demographics with programs that further subdivided these groups. Unlike an earlier time when people of all types of backgrounds had fellowship together around a common bond, the emerging Baptist church is retreating into a self-imposed isolation that mirrors the fragmentation found in the larger society's inability to find a common center.

As religion in America polarized into liberal and conservative camps, many people left other denominations and joined Southern Baptist churches. In some New Mexico Baptist congregations, over half the membership consisted of people who formerly attended or grew up in other fellowships. These more recent additions lacked an understanding of Baptist theology and practice. With the changes in programmatic offerings, training in Baptist distinctiveness had declined, resulting in a membership that in many cases had no comprehension of corporate traditions. Previously, Baptists had built cohesiveness among their people through a shared belief system communicated through Sunday School and Training Union activities. However, the new practices have eroded that common identity. Not knowing exactly who they are, New Mexico Baptists are losing their sense of Christian community. Baptist churches in the state are in danger of becoming nonaffinity bodies, consisting of estranged members, leading to a congregational "Shelaism."[13]

At the same time that the nature of fellowship was changing, so did the structure of the churches and the state convention. Changing social forces reduced the number of members available for work in their congregations. This development occurred at precisely the same time that these local bodies were trying to attract more people with new programs that required more workers than ever before. As a result, to fill this need churches began employing larger and more professionally trained staffs to meet the demands of their expanding ministries. New and varied curriculum required more training and education to meet ever-increasing specialized needs. This practice further reduced the number of laity that could become involved, making the churches even more dependent on paid professionals.

Declining laity involvement and increased programmatic offerings bureaucratized the churches. Reliance on a professional staff swelled the payroll. Expanding ministries led to greater demands on the physical plant to accommodate a more varied usage. Financial needs escalated. Churches began to resemble business enterprises as trained staffs sought to manage human and material resources in the most cost-effective manner, while producing a product line that gave the greatest customer satisfaction. Some congregations hired a church administrator; in others, the pastor assumed the position. Under this emerging new pattern, the membership's involvement in running church affairs declined. While the traditional congregational framework remained, in practice it began to erode.

This shift to bureaucratization and professionalization turned the pastor into more of a CEO than a minister of the gospel. Business standards of success applied to the church dictated that there must be a continued increase in giving, baptisms, and membership. Physical expansion through the construction of new worship centers and educational buildings to enable the church to house new programs and ministries has become almost a necessity if pastors are to advance their career. The congregation demands it, and denominational leaders expect it. The transition from a locally governed fellowship to a professionally managed organization has undermined the traditional manner in which Baptists relate to their church. While still congregational in structure, churches are becoming less so in function. Intentional or not, more and more control of church life has passed into the hands of an emerging ecclesiastical hierarchy.[14]

This functional change in structure has also affected the state convention. The demands of urbanization, specifically the growth of the Rio Grande corridor, called into question the congregational form of polity regarding church planting. Traditionally, Baptist churches start new churches. Changing economic and demographic conditions have rendered this practice nearly impossible. The necessary planning, the cost of land, and the difficulty in replacing members lost from the sponsoring church mean that rarely does one congregation have the resources necessary to initiate a new work. Attempts by the BCNM to adjust to these new conditions through "Mission New Mexico," however, met with little success, because the new paradigm was too drastic a departure from conventional Baptist thinking. Nevertheless, polity change will come as New Mexico Baptists watch their church-to-population ratio continue to decline. As the demands of urbanization intensify, the pooling of resources at a central location is inevitable, turning the emerging "headquarters mentality" into a functional reality.

The reorganization of 1970 was the first step in this process. Changing the structure to enhance managerial efficiency initiated a move toward a more bureaucratized and professionalized state convention. The 1993 associational restructuring also followed this trend by attempting to reframe the association by making it part of the greater corporate body and less of an independent entity. The 1995 reorganization was a clash between proponents of decentralization, who insisted on local church autonomy, and those who championed centralization of power in the face of new realities.

These changes in the fellowship and structure of New Mexico Baptists eventually spilled over into their beliefs. Despite the vaunted return to religion in the post-World War II period, theology had ceased to engage the culture. Rather it rested upon it.[15] When society seemed to break apart in the 1960s, Christian doctrine appeared disconnected and irrelevant to the times. People began to look for something that had more meaning in their lives. Sermons often failed to relate biblical truths to the practical affairs of everyday living. Failure to supply the membership with a Christian foundation for life took its toll on the churches. Southern Baptists responded by intensifying their commitment to their conservative orthodoxy. In New Mexico, that position has remained to the present, unlike the experience of some state conventions where separate fellowships have formed.

Yet in attempting to adjust to the new emphasis on the individual and the restructuring of the church's programs to accommodate this change, the practice of theology likewise underwent a transformation. While many members continued to receive the traditional "salvation" message, more contemporary-minded clergy structured sermons that ministered to the "felt needs" of the congregation, which too often were long on humor and short on substance. Instead of religious discourse that provided a foundation for Christian living, more frequently the parishioner received a psychological "fix" to help him or her "make it" through the week. This development, when combined with the decline in church training, resulted in a growing biblical illiteracy that paralleled the nation's, despite official protestations of devotion to the Bible.

⌘

In the 1960s, the nation's commitment to the Judeo-Christian worldview changed irrevocably. Baptists are fond of saying that the method may change but the message remains the same. What they failed to comprehend, however, is that what transpired in this decade was not an aberration that time and new tactics would cure. Beneath the Anglo-Protestant melting pot, a growing pluralism and diversity had simmered throughout the twentieth century exploding onto the national scene in the 1960s. The churches, which had become so identified with the dominant culture, were unable to effectively address this new state of affairs.

Historically, Baptists have never developed a Christian response to culture. They were content to leave social, political, and economic issues alone, concentrating instead on the freedom to worship in their own way, simply assuming that the society was Christian. Even in New Mexico, the BCNM never effectively addressed multiculturalism because the pattern of Baptist growth in the state allowed them to create a cultural South.

When Baptists shifted their orientation to the individual, they unwittingly followed the change in direction taken by the larger culture. By implementing techniques that used the Christian message to heighten self-awareness through ministering to the felt needs of their members, Baptists inadvertently incorporated the new values into their church life. Instead of developing a Christian community that teaches its people how to think and act in a Christian manner in a non-Christian environment, Baptists in New Mexico are in danger of becoming like everyone else. While on the surface they are holding to their theology and polity, they have adopted a functional pluralism to accommodate the diversity of their increasingly individualized fellowship. In the process, New Mexico Baptists have lost their vision and sense of direction.

Epilogue: 1996 to 2000

Without a doubt the greatest change that has occurred within the Baptist Convention of New Mexico (BCNM) over the last five years has been a renewed emphasis on church planting. Conversely, the greatest continuity in the convention during the same period has been the plateauing and continued decline in core church programs.

In reaction to the BCNM Strategic Planning Committee's survey citing lack of vision as a primary problem, leaders began seeking solutions. Interestingly, it was the association that led the way.[1] Directors of missions took upon themselves the drive for a renewed purpose. Combining their work with similarly inclined pastors, they began holding "visioning" clinics to help congregations reach out from themselves.

Spilling over into the state convention, the BCNM began holding "Basic Training for Church Planting" workshops. Held twice a year, these weeklong sessions became a boot camp for church multiplication. Other offerings included a mentoring program, in which older pastors assisted their younger counterparts in learning how to start new works.[2]

Three major elements have contributed to the drive for visioning. Foremost is the heritage of Mission New Mexico. While failing a decade ago, the strategies that this program developed have found acceptance today due to economic necessity and the harsh realities of church planting under current conditions. The realization that churches can rarely duplicate themselves anymore without assistance has led to a greater role for the state convention. Typically, new starts combine a BCNM initiative linked with a sponsoring congregation.

A new program beginning in the latter part of the 1990s, known as "Start Something New," strove to enable churches to expand their horizons.[3] Even if another church or mission was not necessary in the area, there was always a need for some type of evangelistic outreach. This initiative frequently led to offering the traditional format at times and places that catered to "lifestyle" options, such as using the church facility for services on other days of the week for people with occupations that prevented attendance at Sunday morning worship services.

The Missions Division, under its directive, "every church and mission a missionary congregation," became the driving force behind new church starts. Building on the work of former missions director, M. V. Summers, and church planting specialist, John Embery (the developers of Mission New Mexico), the new director, Gus Suarez, galvanized the convention to "catch the vision."

Concomitant with the emphasis on visioning is the realization that new work will primarily have to occur along the Rio Grande corridor, between Santa Fe and Las Cruces. What Mission New Mexico attempted a decade earlier is now accepted policy. Between 1996 and 2000, this impetus resulted in the starting of ninety-one churches, missions, preaching points, and Bible study groups. On any Sunday morning, the Baptist message is heard at 401 sites throughout the state.[4]

One of the major areas where this work is occurring is in multi-unit housing developments, specifically apartment complexes and mobile home parks. Beginning with Bible studies in an individual's residence, many have expanded to the facility's multipurpose recreation rooms. By the year 2000, thirty-six of these ministries existed in various stages of development within the state.[5]

Three factors have undergirded this increase in church planting. Throughout the first decade of the Cone administration, the convention experienced financial shortfalls. New records in giving frequently fell below budget projections resulting in monetary constraints. During the last half of the 1990s, however, fiscal conditions improved. For instance, in 1996 the BCNM only met 96.7 percent of its projected revenue, which left a shortfall of $61,180, compared to a $164,085 shortfall in 1995. In 1997, the convention met its goal and a year later exceeded it by .75 percent. While giving leveled off in 1999, prudent fiscal policy resulted in a $20,000 overage. Then in the year 2000, Cooperative Program giving reached $3,224,887, which was $144,994.00 or 2.5 percent above the projected budget. In addition, beginning in 1997 the convention saw a three-year decline reversed in the State Mission Offering. In 2000, for the first time in its history, the BCNM exceeded the $200,000 mark, with total gifts at $203,016.[6]

The Children's Home, which had been a financial millstone since the O'Brien years, also experienced a turnaround. The earlier decision by the convention to allow the home to have its own board and manage its finances paid dividends. Able to solicit funds and disburse monies in-house led to fiscal stability. In 1996, the home's endowment stood at $2,894,405. Five years later it had grown to $3,738,713, with an operational account balance of $99,285.[7]

Success with one Baptist entity led in 1997 to extending the idea to Inlow and Sivells Camps. In that year both bodies received their own boards, although the business manager for the BCNM continued to manage camp finances. The opening of the nineteen-room motel honoring Chester and Bonnie Ball O'Brien in 1996 completed the upgrades at Sivells. After decades of operating in the red, that facility has shown operational surpluses in recent years. The Inlow camp, on the other hand, needed a major structural overhaul. In 1997, the state body issued a call for sixty churches to contribute $1,000 a year for the following three years to assist with needed improvements. The dedication of the Claude Cone Multi-Purpose Complex in 1999 was a major move forward, although income is still falling behind expenses.[8] Once again, there is interest in starting an endowment as a long-term solution.

A second factor that has undergirded the increase in church planting is the absence of doctrinal controversy. In other states, most notably North Carolina, Georgia, and Texas, splits have occurred. New Mexico has in part avoided this problem by including moderates and conservatives on all state boards, refusing to play exclusion politics. Many new pastors in New Mexico are from Texas, where the battle is especially brutal, and they are glad to leave the struggle behind.[9] Avoiding internal political upheavals has enabled the BCNM to focus on increasing its presence.

Assisting the state's new vision for church planting has also been a renewed interest by the national body. Spearheaded by the North American Mission Board (formerly the Home Mission Board), the Southern Baptist Convention has focused its resources on helping state conventions and associations to expand their ministries. Interestingly, this domestic emphasis is paralleling the same interest internationally. A recent *Baptist New Mexican* article dealt with the worldwide church planting movement that is sweeping Africa and parts of Asia and Latin America.[10] This phenomenon is reminiscent of the evangelism explosion of the 1970s that affected the entire world. Once again, a strong economy resulting in fiscal renewal combined with support at the national level is undergirding expansion in New Mexico.

While church planting is moving ahead at a brisk rate, the BCNM continues to plateau and its churches' core programs to decline.[11] Membership, which began falling in 1990, has not abated. Totals in 1996 stood at 112,066, down from a high of 119,852. By the year 2000 member numbers totaled 102,020, a 9-percent drop. Resident rolls have remained a little more constant, showing a loss of only 1,746, representing a 3-percent decline in the total membership count. This variance is due in part to some churches, but not others, purging their membership rolls. Nevertheless, the picture is clearly one of a convention that not only has plateaued, but also is failing to maintain its membership to population ratio.

Baptisms are still a source of concern. The 3,000-plus per year objective has still not been achieved. The last time baptisms totaled more than 3,000 per year was 1986. In the 1996–2000 period, baptisms per annum ranged from 2,678 to 2,960, indicating a plateauing in the effectiveness of evangelistic outreach.

While there has been a tremendous increase in new work in recent years, a number of churches have closed their doors. Many eastern counties, a traditional Baptist stronghold, are losing population as people move either out of state or to the Rio Grande corridor, offsetting gains in new starts. Also, nearly two-thirds of the new work is in ethnic congregations and these have an attrition rate of around 25 percent, compared to 7 percent for Anglos.[12] As a result, the church and mission count have remained constant, rising from 337 in 1996 to just 340 by 2000.

The core church programs have fared much worse. Sunday School enrollment continued to decline, falling from 56,630 in 1996 to 47,590 in 2000, a drop of 16 percent, with average attendance only slightly better at minus 15 percent. The Discipleship Training program is dying rapidly. Registering 18,456 participants in 1996, the rolls plunged to 13,107 in 2000, a 29-percent decrease. Even the Music Ministry, the one bright spot in the post-1960s era, has not been able to reverse a decline that began earlier in the decade, falling 33 percent during the five-year period.

The declines in the men and women's service organizations, the Brotherhood and WMU, have reached critical proportions. In 1997, the Southern Baptist Convention dissolved the Brotherhood Commission as a separate entity, with the Evangelism Division picking up the work at the state level. Participation fell 57 percent by 2000, with only 1,341 registered in what is now called the Men's and Boy's Ministries. While maintaining institutional integrity, the WMU has suffered similar attrition, losing 37 percent of its membership with only 2,557 currently on the rolls.

While it is too early to make a definitive determination, the decline in core church program attendance does not necessarily mean that members are failing to participate in church activities. It may indicate a rejection of the traditional programmatic offering in favor of more people-centered alternatives. During the 1990s, a growing trend toward small-group or "cell" activity was discernible in many Baptist churches in the state.[13] Like-minded individuals are coming together for fellowship and Bible study, which often extends beyond just a Sunday morning gathering.

Some claim that this new manifestation is nothing more than the way Sunday Schools should function. On the other hand, in many respects it is a revolt against the old system that brought people together as a large group, and then split them up into classes based on age and sex. The new emphasis is far less labor intensive, more spontaneous, and less bureaucratic. Instead of being plugged into a program with a preformulated agenda, participants have the option of determining their own direction.

The danger this poses for the corporate body, however, is that it can lead to fragmentation. It is easy for such groups to emphasize a particular interest or problem and concentrate on those issues, while neglecting the doctrines and teachings of the faith. The potential is certainly present for the further development of mutually exclusive special interest groups, leading to an accentuated intra-church tribalism. In many respects, this phenomenon is a logical extension of the emphasis on needs-centered ministry. Channeling these energies and legitimate desires for a more responsive approach to living the faith into one that builds up the church as an organic body through centering on Christ, may well be the overarching challenge for pastors leading their flocks into the twenty-first century.

Baptist Beliefs

Baptists trace their roots to early seventeenth-century England during a period of political turmoil. A product of the Protestant Reformation, Baptists sought to return to a New Testament-based church. In the process, they developed a system of beliefs that set them apart as "religious radicals." Faithfulness to the Bible was of great concern. Baptist advocates accused the Church of England of having departed from the scriptures, and therefore, of forfeiting its legitimacy. Searching for a new foundation, Baptists developed what they perceived to be a return to Biblical truth that centered around seven doctrines. These convictions, enumerated below, have become the basis of Baptist fellowship, and knowledge of them is a prerequisite to understanding how the denomination has functioned in American society.

1. *Biblical authority.* For Southern Baptists this means that the Bible is the word of God. It is the supreme authority for faith and practice, is divinely inspired, and speaks with authority to all areas of a believer's life.
2. *Lordship of Jesus Christ.* Jesus Christ is the creator of the world and all things are subject to Him. The church and the individual are therefore to be in submission to Christ. This fact determines Baptist relations with society.
3. *Salvation by grace.* Spiritual regeneration is a gift from God through faith in Jesus Christ. As such, salvation is an act of the will, not the result of good deeds or conferred by the state or church.
4. *Believers' baptism.* Baptists protested against the common practice in most Christian countries of baptizing a child as an infant, thus making him or her a member of the parish. The belief in salvation by grace invalidated this practice. The church is comprised of members who have experienced salvation based upon their commitment to Christ, and baptized in obedience to that decision.

5. *Evangelism and missions.* Christ's command to take the gospel to the whole world became the basis for denominational cooperation. Evangelism for Baptists involves living a Christian life and sharing their faith with those around them. Missions are the formal sending out of individuals to teach and preach the Bible at home and abroad.

6. *Priesthood of the believer.* Regenerated persons have access to God through Christ, and therefore, have no need for a human mediator. All Christians are priests before God and minister one to another, sharing the love of God with the rest of the world.

7. *Soul competency.* Since each believer relates directly to God, he or she has the right to interpret scripture according to the dictates of conscience, without coercion from any ecclesiastical authority.

These beliefs have formed the traditional bedrock of Baptist practice and shaped the denomination's structure. Faithfulness to the Bible, as exhibited in early seventeenth-century England, produced conflict with monarchical and ecclesiastical authorities. Baptist convictions required that believers disassociate themselves from any church or government that demanded a greater allegiance than to Jesus Christ. To support their stand, Baptists developed a polity that asserted freedom from hierarchical control, which is manifested in the following three themes.

1. *Religious liberty.* Baptists maintained that individual conscience was free from any civil authority when pertaining to religious matters. If Christ was the Lord of a person's life, then there could be no human lord claiming superior allegiance. This idea carried over into freedom from ecclesiastical control and politically into "separation of church and state."

2. *Local church autonomy.* Emphasis on religious liberty expressed itself in the freedom of the local church to govern its affairs. Each congregation may associate with like-minded churches, but no association, convention, or other religious body can dictate what a church must believe or determine how its corporate worship be conducted. To do so would be a violation of biblical authority and interfere with the principle of the "Lordship of Jesus Christ."

3. *Congregational worship and accountability.* Among Baptists, the church is a covenant between God and humanity. Believers enter into a relationship in which they are accountable to God and each other for their behavior, spiritual life, communicating the gospel, and ministering to one another within the life of the church.

Because Baptists place such emphasis on biblical authority and the lordship of Christ, to the exclusion of civil and ecclesiastical authority, it is not surprising that they are noncreedal people. They have no written dogma to which individuals or churches must subscribe. For Baptists, accepting such a binding statement was "extra-biblical." A creed would mean that both the Bible and Christ would be subject to it. Instead, Baptists have "confessions." Confessions are statements about what the denomination believes as a group at a particular time in history. But they have no binding control over the individual or local church.

—————Notes

List of Abbreviations
Annual New Mexico Baptist Annual (1900–1911), and
The Baptist Convention of New Mexico Annual (1912–1995)

BCNM Archives   Baptist Convention of New Mexico, Historical Archives,
                           Albuquerque
BHH   *Baptist History and Heritage*
BNM   *Baptist New Mexican* (Albuquerque)
Dargan Library   E. C. Dargan Research Library, Sunday School Board
                           of the Southern Baptist Convention, Nashville, Tenn.
SBHC   Southern Baptist Historical Commission, Nashville, Tenn.

Preface
1. Foy Valentine, "Baptist Polity and Social Pronouncements," *Baptist History and Heritage* 14 (July 1979): 53. (Hereafter *Baptist History and Heritage* is cited as *BHH*.)

Chapter 1
1. For a discussion concerning the diverse theories of Baptist origins, see Robert G. Torbet, *A History of the Baptists* (Philadelphia: Judson Press, 1950), 59–61. See also J. M. Carroll, *The Trail of Blood* (Lexington, Ky.: Ashland Avenue Baptist Church, 1931), for a popular account tracing Baptist origins to the time of Christ.

2. M. R. Watts, *The Dissenters: From the Reformation to the French Revolution* (Oxford: Clarendon Press, 1978), 49.

3. Torbet, *History of the Baptists,* 71–81.

4. Walter B. Shurden, *Not a Silent People: Controversies That Have Shaped Southern Baptists* (Nashville, Tenn.: Broadman Press, 1972), 13.

5. Torbet, *History of the Baptists,* 75–81.

6. Earle E. Cairns, *Christianity Through the Centuries: A History of the Christian Church,* rev. ed. (Grand Rapids, Mich.: Zondervan Publishing House, 1970), 396–97.

7. Torbet, *History of the Baptists,* 226.

8. James E. Carter, "A Review of Confessions of Faith Adopted by Major Baptist Bodies in the United States," *BHH* 12 (April 1977): 77–79.

9. Torbet, *History of the Baptists,* 261.

10. Robert A. Baker, ed., *A Baptist Source Book with Particular Reference to Southern Baptists* (Nashville, Tenn.: Broadman Press, 1966), 20.

11. Bruce Shelley, "Isaac Backus," in *Eerdmans' Handbook to Christianity in America,* eds. Mark A. Noll, et al. (Grand Rapids, Mich.: Eerdmans, 1983), 117–18.

12. Torbet, *History of the Baptists,* 261.

13. J. Wayne Flynt, "The Impact of Social Factors on Southern Baptist Expansion, 1800–1914," *BHH* 17 (July 1982): 26–27. See also Nathan O. Hatch, *The Democratization of American Christianity* (New Haven, Conn.: Yale University Press, 1989) for an in-depth analysis of religion and popular culture during the antebellum period.

14. Torbet, *History of the Baptists,* 271.

15. Edward L. Wheeler, "An Overview of Black Southern Baptist Involvements," *BHH* 16 (July 1981): 3–4.

16. Ibid., 4. Additional details on the life of Lott Cary can be found in Leroy Filts, *Lott Cary: First Black Missionary to Africa* (Valley Forge, Pa.: Judson Press, 1978).

17. Shurden, *Not a Silent People,* 37–38.

18. Ibid., 46–47. The shift from the predestination of Calvinism to the free will of Arminianism was not unique to Baptists. It was in step with the democratic mood in the country. See George S. Marsden, *The Evangelical Mind and the New School Presbyterian Experience: A Case Study of Thought and Theology in Nineteenth-Century America* (New Haven, Conn.: Yale University Press, 1970), and Winthrop S. Hudson, *Religion in America: An Historical Account of the Development of American Religious Life,* 4th ed. (New York: Macmillan, 1987).

19. William Wright Barnes, *The Southern Baptist Convention: 1845–1953* (Nashville, Tenn.: Broadman Press, 1954), 12.

20. Willie Greer Todd argues in "The Slavery Issue and the Organization of a Southern Baptist Convention" (Ph.D. diss., University of North Carolina at Chapel Hill, 1964), 115–21, 151, that as abolitionism intensified, Baptists in the South shifted their position from apologizing for slavery—defending the institution—to concluding that it was a positive good. This defense of slavery that the clergy formulated was accepted by the politicians and became the rallying point around which Southern nationalism crystallized. Southern Baptists thus not only defended slavery but, in so doing, were buttressing a Southern "way of life."

21. Barnes, *Southern Baptist Convention,* 306.

22. John Lee Eighmy, *Churches in Cultural Captivity* (Knoxville: University of Tennessee Press, 1972), 39. Eighmy is not the only historian to offer this explanation for Southern Baptist Convention missionary efforts to Blacks. Dwight C. Dorough in *The Bible Belt Mystique* (Philadelphia: Westminster Press, 1974), Winthrop Jordan in *White Over Black* (Baltimore: Penguin Books, 1969), and H. Shelton Smith, *In His Image, But . . .* (Durham, N.C.: Duke University Press, 1972) concur, citing religious instruction for slaves that promoted this end. Recently, this view has been challenged. Emmanuel L. McCall in "Home Mission Board Ministry in the Black Community," *BHH* 16 (July 1981): 29–40, acknowledges that such a use of the gospel existed, but that it is insufficient as a total explanation for the interest of Southern Baptists in the spiritual welfare of Blacks. Using the Southern Baptist Convention minutes, he compiled a list of Home Mission Board activities that began in 1848. The board's aim was the spiritual development of Blacks, not the promotion of their docility.

23. Wheeler, "Black Involvements," 7–8.

24. Russell Begaye, "The Story of Indian Southern Baptists," *BHH* 18 (July 1983): 30–32, 35.

25. Lee N. Allen, "Southern Baptist Home Mission Impact on Ethnics," *BHH* 18 (July 1983): 12–15.

26. Torbet, *History of the Baptists,* 384.

27. Barnes, *Southern Baptist Convention,* 306.

28. Flynt, "Social Factors," 22–23.

29. Eighmy, *Cultural Captivity,* 55.

30. Shurden, *Not a Silent People,* 71–78.

31. Barnes, *Southern Baptist Convention,* 306.

32. H. K. Neely, Jr., "The Territorial Expansion of the Southern Baptist Convention, 1894–1959" (Ph.D. diss., Southwestern Baptist Theological Seminary, 1963), 199.

33. Leon McBeth, "Expansion of the Southern Baptist Convention to 1951," *BHH* 17 (July 1982): 32–33.

34. Neely, "Territorial Expansion," 179–80.

35. Barnes, *Southern Baptist Convention,* 306.

36. W. David Sapp, "Southern Baptist Response to the American Economy, 1900–1980," *BHH* 16 (January 1981): 5–6.

37. G. Thomas Halbrooks, "Growing Pains: The Impact of Expansion of Southern Baptists Since 1942," *BHH* 17 (July 1982): 44–45.

38. Allen, "Impact on Ethnics," 16–18.

39. McCall, "Home Mission Board Ministry," 40.

40. Halbrooks, "Growing Pains," 49.

41. Ibid.

42. James L. Sullivan, "Polity Developments in the Southern Baptist Convention (1900–1977)," *BHH* 16 (July 1979): 27–30.

43. J. Wayne Flynt, "Southern Baptists: Rural to Urban Transition," *BHH* 16 (January 1981): 25–56.

44. Sapp, "Response to the American Economy," 4.

45. Flynt, "Rural to Urban Transition," 33–34.

46. Flynt, "Social Factors," 23–25.

47. Foy Valentine, "A Historical Study of Southern Baptists and Race Relations: 1917–1947" (Th.D. diss., Southwestern Baptist Theological Seminary, 1949), 214–22.

48. Wheeler, "Black Involvements," 9–11.

49. Sullivan, "Polity Developments," 26–27.

50. Larry McSwain and Walter B. Shurden, "Changing Values and Southern Baptists, 1900–1980," *BHH* 16 (January 1981): 52.

51. Timothy George, "Southern Baptist Relationships with Other Protestants," *BHH* 25 (July 1990): 31–32.

52. Glenn A. Igleheart, "Southern Baptist Relationships with Roman Catholics," *BHH* 25 (July 1990): 39–42.

53. James J. Thompson, Jr., *Tried as by Fire: Southern Baptists and the Religious Controversies of the 1920s* (Macon, Ga.: Mercer University Press, 1982), 81–82, 124–25. "Higher criticism" is an attempt to apply the scientific method to biblical interpretation that concentrates on determining the authorship and dates of books, corresponding literary documents underlying them, and their historical dependability.

54. James E. Carter, "The Bible and 20th Century Southern Baptist Confessions of Faith," *BHH* 19 (July 1984): 2.

55. Shurden, *Not a Silent People,* 104–5.

56. Carter, "Review of Confessions," 90.

57. Nancy Tatom Ammerman, *Baptist Battles: Social Change and Religious Conflict in the Southern Baptist Convention* (New Brunswick, N.J.: Rutgers University Press, 1990), 67.

58. For an in-depth look at the issues from the fundamentalist viewpoint, see James

Notes

T. Draper, Jr., *Authority: The Critical Issue for Southern Baptists* (Old Tappan, N.J.: Revell, 1984). From the liberal side, see Alan Neely, ed., *Being Baptist Means Freedom* (Charlotte, N.C.: Southern Baptist Alliance, 1988). See also the articles by E. Glenn Hinson in *Are Southern Baptists "Evangelicals"?* by James Leo Garrett, Jr., E. Glenn Hinson, and James E. Tull (Macon, Ga.: Mercer University Press, 1983), 129–94, 209–14. For a sociological analysis of the two groups, see Ammerman, *Baptist Battles*, 126–67.

59. David T. Morgan, *The New Crusades, the New Holy Land: Conflict in the Southern Baptist Convention, 1969–1991* (Tuscaloosa: University of Alabama Press, 1996), x, xi, 9–12.

60. Robert A. Baker, *The Southern Baptist Convention and Its People: 1607–1972* (Nashville, Tenn.: Broadman Press, 1974), 494.

61. Morgan, *New Crusades,* 155.

62. "Summary of Churches by State Convention: 1994," Baptist Sunday School Board, Strategic Information and Planning Section, MSN 118, 1995, E. C. Dargan Research Library, Sunday School Board of the Southern Baptist Convention, Nashville, Tenn. (hereafter cited as Dargan Library).

63. McBeth, "Expansion," 43.

64. Statistics from Extension Section, cited by Bill Graham, in interview by author, tape recording, Albuquerque, N.Mex., 21 February 1996. At the time of the interview, Graham was director of the personnel department, Southern Baptist Home Mission Board.

65. For an analysis of Southern Baptists during this stage of development, see Ellen M. Rosenberg, *The Southern Baptists: A Subculture in Transition* (Knoxville: University of Tennessee Press, 1989). Unfortunately, this necessary study is marred by the author's derogatory attitude toward her subject.

Chapter 2

1. Dale Danielson and Betty Danielson, "New Mexico's First Protestant Preacher," *Impact* (*Albuquerque Journal* magazine), 30 June 1981, 9.

2. David H. Stratton, *The First Century of Baptists in New Mexico: 1849–1950* (Boulder: University of Colorado Press, 1954), 4.

3. Lewis Myers, *A History of New Mexico Baptists* (Albuquerque: Baptist Convention of New Mexico, 1965), 4.

4. A mission society paid a colporteur (peddler of religious books) to distribute literature as a means of spreading the gospel. This individual often was instrumental in starting churches and usually preached wherever he was on Sunday, but, as a rule, he was not an ordained minister.

5. Stratton, *First Century,* 14.

6. Ferenc M. Szasz, *The Protestant Clergy in the Great Plains and Mountain West, 1865–1915* (Albuquerque: University of New Mexico Press, 1988), 144.

7. Stratton, *First Century,* 12–16. Some evidence indicates that Shaw remained until 1870.

8. Ibid., 19–20.

9. Ibid., 22.

10. Betty Danielson, "One Hundred Forty Years of Baptist Associations in New Mexico: 1852–1992," paper presented at meeting of associational clerks of New Mexico, Glorieta, N.Mex., 4 May 1992, Dale and Betty Danielson, private collection, Albuquerque.

11. Ibid., 8.

12. Stratton, *First Century,* 27.

13. Danielson, "One Hundred Forty Years," 7.

14. *New Mexico Baptist Annual* (N.p.: New Mexico Baptist Convention, 1900), 18. (Hereafter the *New Mexico Baptist Annual* and *The Baptist Convention of New Mexico Annual* are cited as *Annual* or *Annuals.*)

15. *Annuals* (1900–1920).

16. Danielson, "One Hundred Forty Years," 12; Stratton, *First Century,* 45.

17. *Annual* (1908), 27–28; *Annual* (1909), 34, 36.

18. *Annual* (1900), 18; *Annual* (1926), 5.

19. Myers, *History of New Mexico Baptists,* 91–98.

20. Ibid., 105, 147, 654.

21. Edith R. Wright, "Early Navajo Mission Work," *Baptist New Mexican,* 16 December 1948, 7. (Hereafter the *Baptist New Mexican* is cited as *BNM.*)

22. Stratton, *First Century,* 35–36.

23. *Annual* (1916), 27–28.

24. *Annual* (1919), 29–30.

25. H. K. Neely, Jr., "The Territorial Expansion of the Southern Baptist Convention, 1894–1959" (Th.D. diss., Southwestern Baptist Theological Seminary, 1963), 24–25.

26. Danielson, "One Hundred Forty Years," 14.

27. Neely, "Territorial Expansion," 26–27.

28. Ibid., 39.

29. John P. Masterson, "Interest in Early Baptist History in New Mexico," *BNM,* 11 November 1948, 7.

30. Neely, "Territorial Expansion," 34; Stratton, *First Century,* 57.

31. E. B. Atwood, "Controversy," *BNM,* 15 April 1948, 5.

32. *Annual* (1912), 5.

33. *Annual* (1920), statistical tables.

34. *Annual* (1926), 25.

35. *Annual* (1921), 29–30.

36. Dr. J. W. Bruner, quoted in Myers, *History of New Mexico Baptists,* 358.

37. *Annual* (1922), 46.

38. *Annual* (1924), 37.

39. Myers, *History of New Mexico Baptists,* 363.

40. Stratton, *First Century,* 65; Betty Danielson, "Leadership of Beulah Fonville Impacted WMU and Children," *BNM,* 17 October 1987, 13.

41. Betty Danielson and Dale Danielson, "Baptist Hospital," in *1981 Baptist Appointment Calendar,* First Baptist Church, Albuquerque, Baptist Convention of New Mexico, Historical Archives, Albuquerque (hereafter cited as BCNM Archives).

42. *Annual* (1921), 32.

43. Stratton, *First Century,* 66–70.

44. Luis Gomez, "Gomez Views Hispanic Work in New Mexico," *BNM,* 17 October 1987, 7.

45. *Annual* (1923), 26–27; *Annual* (1924), 35–36; *Annual* (1925), 16; *Annual* (1926), 36; *Annual* (1927), 27–28; *Annual* (1928), 43; *Annual* (1929), 29.

46. Myers, *History of New Mexico Baptists,* 104, 205.

47. *Annual* (1929), 29.

48. David McKenzie, "Baptist Ethnic Work in State Shows Growth," *BNM,* 17 October 1987, 7.

49. *Annual* (1924), 36; *Annual* (1925), 16; *Annual* (1927), 26; *Annual* (1928), 45; *Annual* (1929), 32.

50. Begaye, "Story of Indian Southern Baptists," 30–32, 35.

51. C. W. Stumph, "Baptist Activities in New Mexico," pamphlet, Baptist Convention of New Mexico, 1927, 6, BCNM Archives.

52. Stratton, *First Century,* 78.

53. Harry Stagg, "Stagg Reviews Work in State from 1938–1967," *BNM,* 17 October 1987, 15.

54. *Annual* (1929), 55.

55. Myers, *History of New Mexico Baptists,* 405.

56. *Annual* (1929), statistical tables; *Annual* (1934), statistical tables.

57. *Annual* (1937), statistical tables.

58. *Annual* (1935), 19–20; *Annual* (1936), 11, 12, 19.

Chapter 3

1. Myers, *History of New Mexico Baptists,* 415.

2. Dissension caused by the closure of Montezuma led a minority to establish a private junior college in Hobbs, which is still in existence, but it has never been affiliated with the Baptist Convention of New Mexico.

3. Harry Stagg, interview by author, tape recording, Albuquerque, N.Mex., 2 April 1991; Stagg, interview by J. B. Fowler, video, Albuquerque, N.Mex., 26 September 1990.

4. Stagg, interview, 2 April 1991.

5. Bonnie Ball O'Brien, *Harry Stagg: Christian Statesman* (Nashville, Tenn.: Broadman Press, 1976), 106.

6. Stagg, interview, 2 April 1991.

7. *Annual* (1937); *Annual* (1939).

8. U.S. Bureau of the Census, *Census of Population* (Washington, D.C.: Government Printing Office, 1960), 33–35.

9. Stagg, interview by author, tape recording, Albuquerque, N.Mex., 21 May 1996.

10. *Annual* (1942, 1948, 1950, 1958).

11. *Annual* (1940, 1950, 1959).

12. U.S. Bureau of the Census, *Census,* 33–35.

13. "Rural Churches," *BNM,* 14 March 1940, 2.

14. *Annual* (1946), 40–41.

15. *Annual* (1946), 42; *Annual* (1950), 44.

16. Unless otherwise cited, numerical data have been extrapolated and compiled from the statistical tables of BCNM *Annuals* for 1940, 1950, and 1960. Statistical data were coordinated with data from the U.S. Bureau of the Census, *Census of Population* (Washington, D.C.: Government Printing Office), 1940, 1950, 1960.

17. *Annual* (1940), 10.

18. *Annual* (1940, 1950, 1960), statistical tables; Carl A. Clark, "The Rural Contribution," *BNM,* 11 February 1960, 2.

19. Harry Stagg, "Ten Weeks' Victories," *BNM,* 6 March 1941, 9.

20. Ed Storm, interview by author, tape recording, Albuquerque, N.Mex., 21 May 1996.

21. L. D. Ball, "My Observation of the 1955 Simultaneous Crusade in New Mexico," *BNM,* 19 May 1955, 10.

22. Dale Danielson and Betty Danielson, interview by author, tape recording, Albuquerque, N.Mex., 30 March 1991. At the time of the interview, the Danielsons were historians of the BCNM.

23. *Annual* (1938, 1960), statistical tables.

24. *Annual* (1938, 1960).

25. *Annual* (1959), 37.

26. Baptist historian for the state of New Mexico, Betty Danielson, recalls that in the 1940s and 1950s it was not uncommon for more than six hundred people to attend Training Union activities on Sunday night at First Baptist Church in Albuquerque.

27. *Annual* (1938, 1960), statistical tables.

28. A transfer of letter allows a current member of a Baptist church to move his or her membership to another Baptist church without going through the process of making another statement of faith or being baptized again.

29. Statistical data on baptisms, transfers of letter, and statements of faith were compiled from associational annuals from 1938 to 1960.

30. According to Ed Storm, without the aid of the Home Mission Board, the Baptist Convention of New Mexico could not have carried out its programs. Storm, interview.

31. Myers, *History of New Mexico Baptists,* 477–78. An evangelism department had previously existed but was terminated in 1931 because of the depression. In 1937, however, the position of state evangelist was reinstated, with John W. Williams filling the post.

32. "Denominational Matters," *BNM,* 15 February 1945, 4.

33. The Royal Ambassadors was an activity organization for boys that included camps, outings, Bible study, and general training for church work and missions.

34. "Capturing History—Brotherhood," *BNM,* 30 May 1957, 12; Myers, *History of New Mexico Baptists,* 632.

35. "Capturing History—Stewardship Department," *BNM,* 30 May 1957, 13; Myers, *History of New Mexico Baptists,* 512–13.

36. *Annual* (1947), 19; *Annual* (1949), 23.

37. Stagg, interview, 26 September 1990.

38. "Capturing History—Baptist Book Store," *BNM,* 30 May 1957, 4; *Annual* (1952), 51.

39. *Annual* (1955), 40–41.

40. "Capturing History—BNM," *BNM,* 30 May 1957, 3; *Annual* (1953), 30; *Annual* (1955), 25.

41. Stagg, interview, 26 September 1990.

42. Truett Sheriff, interview by author, tape recording, Albuquerque, N.Mex., 9 April 1991. Sheriff is a former Baptist student union director for the state convention.

43. Myers, *History of New Mexico Baptists,* 522.

44. *Annual* (1952), 49–50; *Annual* (1963), 22.

45. Stagg, interview by author, tape recording, Albuquerque, N.Mex., 4 April 1991.

46. Stagg, interview, 26 September 1990.

47. *Annual* (1949), 17.

48. *Annual* (1945–1949).

49. *Annual* (1959, 1950).

50. Myers, *History of New Mexico Baptists,* 525.

51. *Annual* (1940–1960).

52. *Annual* (1939), 13.

53. *Annual* (1960), 31.

Chapter 4

1. Luther D. Mitchell, "The History of Glorieta," 7–8, Dargan Library; Stagg, interview, 2 April 1991. Stagg recalled the name of the individual who offered the $50,000 as a "Mr. Kokernut," but could not remember a first name, nor was he sure of the spelling.

2. A great deal of confusion existed concerning who was to appoint the committee, and two such groups emerged. The Executive Committee recommended that the committee they appointed meet jointly with the one nominated by the Southern Baptist Convention, and both committees convened in December 1946. Duke McCall to C. H. Bolton, 20 September 1946, Western Assembly File, Southern Baptist Historical Commission, Nashville, Tenn. (hereafter cited as SBHC); Duke McCall to John A. Ellis, 21 September 1946, Western Assembly File, SBHC.

3. "Report of subcommittee of the Executive Committee of the Southern Baptist Convention concerning site for Western Assembly," December 1946, Western Assembly File.

4. Medearis recommended a new committee with a representative from each state west of the Mississippi River to study the geography and populations involved. The convention adopted his suggestion. T. W. Medearis to Duke McCall, 18 April 1947, Western Assembly File, SBHC.

5. Floyd Looney to Duke McCall, 1 January 1947, Western Assembly File, SBHC.

6. Philip C. McGahey, "Western Assembly in Texas," *BNM*, 19 December 1946, 4.

7. Philip McGahey to Duke McCall, 7, 18 January 1947; Duke McCall to Philip McGahey, 20 December 1946, 13 January 1947; Duke McCall to state editors, 20 December 1946, Western Assembly File, SBHC.

8. T. L. Holcomb to Duke McCall, 24 March 1947, Western Assembly File, SBHC.

9. Mitchell, "The History of Glorieta."

10. McGahey was the New Mexico representative on the new Western Assembly committee, and thus, Stagg, through him, spearheaded the pursuit for a New Mexico site. In fact, he was the only one in a position to do so.

11. Stagg, "Glorieta Assembly," *BNM*, 2 September 1948, 2.

12. Stagg, interview, 2 April 1991.

13. Stagg, interview, 26 September 1990; Southern Baptist Convention (SBC) and Baptist Convention of New Mexico (BCNM) officials, "History of Glorieta," group interview by Hubert B. Smothers, transcript and tape recording, August 1967, SBHC. The transcript of this group interview also quotes Stagg as saying that the committee refused to come, but he adds that individual members could come if they wished. On the tape, but not in the transcript, Stagg says that three of the nine came.

14. In 1946, McGahey had also enlisted the aid of chambers of commerce and businesses. They sent telegrams to Nashville, promoting New Mexico as the place for the Western Assembly.

15. Stagg, interview, 4 April 1991.

16. SBC and BCNM officials, interview transcript, 12.

17. Perry F. Webb to Duke McCall, n.d., Western Assembly File, SBHC.

18. Perry Webb to Duke McCall, 1 March 1949, Western Assembly File, SBHC; Duke McCall to Perry Webb, 3 March 1949, Western Assembly File, SBHC. Although the dissidents are never named, certainly Philip McGahey, pastor of the First Baptist Church and Stagg's pastor, was one of them. C. Vaughn Rock, the Arizona representative and Stagg's brother-in-law, was likely the other.

19. SBC and BCNM officials, interview transcript, 21.

20. Ibid.

21. Dale Danielson and Betty Danielson, *Glorieta and Northern New Mexico Discovery Tours,* vol. 1 (Colorado Springs, Colo.: Great Western Press, 1985), 17.

22. Stagg, interview, 4 April 1991.

23. Harry Stagg to Duke McCall, 5 September 1949, Western History File, SBHC. No one to this day knows what those thirty-three points were. In the group interview of SBC and BCNM officials by Smothers in August 1967, Holcomb mentioned climate; latitude; water supply; accessibility; adaptability of site for an assembly; beautification of terrain; and location of highways, railroads, and nearby cities. Presumably, the remaining criteria were subpoints of the above considerations.

24. SBC and BCNM officials, interview transcript, 19–20.

25. Stagg, interview, 4 April 1991.

26. T. L. Holcomb to Harry Stagg, 26 September 1949; Duke McCall to Judge Frank Hooper, 18 October 1949, Western Assembly File, SBHC.

27. Stagg, interview, 4 April 1991.

28. SBC and BCNM officials, interview transcript, 14.

29. Duke McCall to Harry Stagg, 20 December 1949, Western Assembly File, SBHC.

30. Press release, News Service of the Southern Baptist Convention, 31 October 1949, Western Assembly File, SBHC; J. W. Middleton, "Our Ridgecrest in New Mexico," *BNM,* 12 December 1949, 12.

31. "Glorieta Development Outlined in Resort Conference," *BNM,* 4 May 1950, 3.

32. SBC and BCNM officials, interview transcript, 23–24.

33. Prospectus for solicitation of funds for Glorieta Baptist Conference Center, Historical and Informational Material AR 564, SBHC; Baptist Press Release, 31 October 1949, SBHC.

34. Danielson and Danielson, *Glorieta,* 27.

35. E. A. Herron, "Preparation—First Two Years—June 1, 1950–August 7, 1952," 1, 5–6, E. A. Herron File, SBHC.

36. Ibid., 2, 4–5.

37. E. A. Herron, "Pioneer Week—August 7–13, 1952," 1, E. A. Herron File, SBHC. According to Holcomb, the idea for what became Pioneer Week came from C. Vaughn Rock, who suggested such a meeting as a means of manifesting the "pioneering spirit" of the West. SBC and BCNM officials, interview transcript, 4, 41–42.

38. Herron, "Pioneer Week," 4–6.

39. SBC and BCNM officials, interview transcript, 35.

40. Ibid., 33; Herron, "Pioneer Week," 6–9.

41. Danielson and Danielson, *Glorieta,* 59.

42. O'Brien, *Harry P. Stagg,* 146.

43. In the early 1960s, Southern Baptists exchanged 65 acres of land on the Pecos River for 1,200 acres of U.S. Forest Service land surrounding Glorieta.

44. Larry Haslam, interview by author, tape recording, Glorieta, N.Mex., 16 August 1996. Haslam served as manager of the Glorieta facility from 1973 to the time of this writing.

45. Don Carlos Ferguson, "The Garden at Glorieta," 13 September 1982, 5–6, 9, E. A. Herron File, SBHC.

46. Cecil Pragnell, "Every Lowly Clod a Lyric," *Home Life* (June 1960): 14–15.

---

47. Elizabeth Terry, "Glorieta Gardens," brochure, 5–10, Glorieta File, Dargan Library; "Glorieta Flowers: A Holy Land for Southern Baptists," 4–9, Glorieta File, Dargan Library.

48. Elizabeth Terry, "Glorieta Baptist Assembly," brochure, 8, Glorieta File, Dargan Library; Terry, "Glorieta Gardens," 2, 6.

49. Terry, "Glorieta Gardens," 2; Wayne S. Scott, "Cecil Pragnell to Retire from Post at Glorieta," *Albuquerque Journal,* 8 June 1962.

Chapter 5

1. *Annual* (1952), 21.

2. *Annual* (1945), 18, 19.

3. *Annual* (1952), 28; *Annual* (1953), 24.

4. *Annual* (1945), 29; *Annual* (1950), 69.

5. *Annual* (1938), 35; Myers, *History of New Mexico Baptists,* 420.

6. "The Lottery Crowd Is Still at Work," *BNM,* 11 February 1960, 4; *Annual* (1950), 72.

7. *Annual* (1946), 16.

8. *Annual* (1947), 49.

9. "Baptist Relations," *BNM,* 2 August 1951, 12, 13; "Church Union," *BNM,* 21 February 1952, 7.

10. "Baptist Relations," *BNM,* 2 August 1951, 12, 13; Joe W. Burton, "Why Do Baptists Remain Aloof?" *BNM,* 29 June 1944, 6.

11. Mrs. Leo Woods, "Baptists a Separated People," *BNM,* 12 June 1952, 16.

12. "Revelatory Facts . . . It Is Happening in New Mexico," *BNM,* 11 December 1947, 6.

13. Janice E. Schuetz, "A Rhetorical Approach to Protestant Evangelism in Twentieth-Century New Mexico," in *Religion in Modern New Mexico,* eds. Ferenc M. Szasz and Richard W. Etulain (Albuquerque: University of New Mexico Press, 1997), 135–39.

14. The incident transcended state boundaries. Protestants and Others United for the Separation of Church and State provided counsel, and sent a representative who acted in the capacity as "friend of the court." The American Civil Liberties Union also offered assistance.

15. "School Religion Suit Will Name 200 Defendants," *Albuquerque Journal,* 10 March 1948, 1, 2.

16. "Suit Would Oust Catholic Teachers," *Albuquerque Journal,* 11 March 1948, 1, 11.

17. "No Appeal Dixon School Case," *BNM,* 20 December 1951, 10.

18. Myers, *History of New Mexico Baptists,* 587.

19. William D. Wyatt, "The Church and the White House," *BNM,* 3 November 1960, 4–5.

20. "We Would Be Fair," *BNM,* 9 January 1959, 5; "A Roman Catholic President," *BNM,* 11 February 1960, 12–13.

21. Numerous articles, editorials, and sermons appeared in the *BNM* during the late 1940s and throughout the 1950s contrasting Baptist and Catholic theology. The 3 September 1952 issue is especially noteworthy as the newspaper editors published a chart illustrating nine "distinctions" or differences in the beliefs held by the two groups.

22. Joseph B. Underwood, "In this Present Crisis," *BNM,* 11 December 1941, 1.

23. A. C. Miller, "God and Us in Race Relations," *BNM*, 15 August 1946, 4.

24. Lewis A. Myers, "Race Relationship Reported Improving," *BNM*, 8 June 1950, 2; Myers, "The Negro, Too, Is My Brother," *BNM*, 28 September 1950, 2; Myers, "Intolerance: Actions Belie Words," *BNM*, 29 March 1951, 2; Myers, "Chicago Convention Curtails Support to Negro Theological Education," *BNM*, 8 June 1950, 4; Myers, "Negro God-Called May Enter Seminaries," *BNM*, 4 May 1951, 2.

25. "Segregation Ban Raises Questions for Baptists," *BNM*, 15 July 1954, 6.

26. Bernice Elliott, "Inlow International Camp," *BNM*, 28 May 1953, 21; Myers, *History of New Mexico Baptists*, 585; "Pastor Brown is Elected," *BNM*, 12 January 1956, 1; Ralph S. Hogue, "Racial Prejudice," *BNM*, 24 April 1958, 2.

27. Danielson and Danielson, *Glorieta*, 17.

28. Danielson and Danielson, interview.

29. Danielson and Danielson, *Glorieta*, 58.

30. "Christian Hospitality in Fruitage," *BNM*, 16 September 1954, 3.

31. Bill Hunke to author, 7 August 1996.

32. Gerald B. Palmer, "Spanish Missions in New Mexico," *BNM*, 10 September 1959, 11.

33. J. B. Parker, "Baptist Work Among the Spanish-Speaking People of New Mexico," *BNM*, 4 March 1937, 1; *Annual* (1947), 26; *Annual* (1951), 43.

34. Myers, *History of New Mexico Baptists*, 471–72.

35. "Spanish Missions," *BNM*, 10 September 1954, 11; "Spanish and Indian Missions," *BNM*, 30 May 1957, 15; "Training Program," *BNM*, 7 January 1960, 4; *Annual* (1959), 30, 57; *Annual* (1960), 26–27. These figures do not include Hispanics and Native Americans who were members in predominately Anglo churches, of whom there were very few.

36. Duke McCall, "Storm Warnings," *BNM*, 27 October 1960, 5.

37. Horace F. Burns, "A Serious Indictment," *BNM*, 10 December 1959, 3; Joseph B. Underwood, "The Kind of Revival We Need," *BNM*, 19 February 1959, 10; A. C. Miller, "Social Obligations of the Christian Life," *BNM*, 9 July 1959, 13; *Annual* (1958), 30.

38. *Annual* (1960), 21.

Chapter 6

1. H. Franklin Paschall, "The Gospel of Our Time," *BNM*, 6 July 1963, 6, 7.

2. Ibid.

3. *Annual* (1969), 18.

4. *Annual* (1966), 91.

5. In fact, the changes were quite comprehensible. Southern Baptists had escaped the turmoil of modernization that had plagued other mainline denominations in the earlier part of the century, because of their geographical and cultural isolation from the mainstream of American society. The social convulsions of the 1960s, although impacting all religious groups, were especially difficult for Southern Baptists. In the South, their doctrines and convictions were the "center of gravity." But expansion over the previous two decades had brought them into contact with the modern world, where urbanization and technology had displaced transcendent values and beliefs. According to Bryan Wilson, despite people's personal protestations of belief, they "nevertheless operate in a social space in which their beliefs about the supernatural are rendered in large part irrelevant." Wilson, *Contemporary Transformation of Religion* (Oxford: Oxford University Press, 1976), 6.

6. Horace F. Burns, "A Time for Faith—and Works," *BNM*, 4 May 1961, 2.

7. *Annual* (1966), 12.

8. L. Dewitt Matthews, "What Gets Top Priority," *BNM*, 13 February 1971, 8.

9. *Annual* (1971), 21, 22.

10. *Annual* (1960), 20; *Annual* (1961), 21, 22.

11. A nonresident member is on the church roll, but not actively attending services.

12. *Annual* (1961), 14, 22, 23, 26; Alton Green, "The Church and the Non-Resident Member," *BNM*, 12 January 1961, 16.

13. Horace F. Burns, "Numbers Make a Difference," *BNM*, 13 August 1964, 2.

14. *Annual* (1963), 16, 21.

15. *Annual* (1964), 22.

16. *Annual* (1964), 102, 107.

17. *Annual* (1963), 37, 38.

18. *Annual* (1964), 23.

19. *Annual* (1964), 24, 25; *Annual* (1965), 30.

20. "State Board Asks Dr. Stagg to Delay Retirement Date," *BNM*, 27 January 1966, 3; *Annual* (1967), 27, 30.

21. *Annual* (1968), 25.

22. *Annual* (1968), 19.

23. *Annual* (1969), 27.

24. *Annual* (1969), 32, 124.

25. At the state level, programs included the Sunday School convention, teaching clinics, adult institutes, and Sunday School week at Glorieta. Association-wide activities included pastor-led enlargement campaigns, director-led enlargement campaigns, pastor-led soul-winning campaigns, network campaigns, associational planning meetings, preparation week in September, October group schools, January Bible study week, the commencement training banquet, and additional specialized training for individual churches.

26. Edward E. Storm, "Sunday School Reaches Out," *BNM*, 24 January 1963, 13; *Annual* (1964), 31.

27. *Annual* (1966), 28; Edward E. Storm, "Is Your Church Overlooking an Opportunity?" *BNM*, 29 June 1967, 10.

28. *Annual* (1962), 36; *Annual* (1964), 34.

29. *Annual* (1961), 37.

30. Vanita Baldwin, "Baptist Women Announce Revised Organization Plan," *BNM*, 16 March 1968, 13.

31. *Annual* (1963), 94.

32. *Annual* (1965), 111; H. C. Sivells, "Objectives of R.A. Camping," *BNM*, 28 February 1970, 12.

33. *Annual* (1969), 56; *Annual* (1970), 67; *Annual* (1966), 37.

34. *Annual* (1961), 27; *Annual* (1974), 58.

35. *Annual* (1968), 111.

36. *Annual* (1968), 30.

37. Ibid.

38. The genius behind Baptists' successes was in their ability to mobilize the entire congregation. This methodology was very effective in rural and marginally urban areas with close community ties.

39. *Annual* (1968), 41; C. Eugene Whitlow, "The Editor's Page," *BNM*, 3 May 1969, 2.

40. "Hobb's First Church Breaks State Baptism Record," *BNM*, 16 October 1971, 15.

41. Larry Jerden, "Baptists Find Ski Areas Good Places for Witness," *BNM*, 9 February 1974, 1.

42. *Annual* (1969), 46; *Annual* (1970), 57.

43. *Annual* (1973), 52.

44. *Annual* (1965), 31, 32; *Annual* (1966), 34.

45. *Annual* (1967), 31, 32; *Annual* (1968), 27.

46. *Annual* (1963), 14, 15.

47. "Church Withholds Funds from Cooperative Program, Southern Baptist Convention," *BNM*, 26 September 1970, 9; *Annual* (1973), 42, 43.

48. *Annual* (1971), 58.

49. *Annual* (1961), 40; *Annual* (1973), 44.

50. *Annual* (1961), 39; *Annual* (1963), 32; *Annual* (1964), 22.

51. *Annual* (1965), 35; *Annual* (1969), 28; *Annual* (1970), 65, 66.

52. *Annual* (1965), 21.

53. The convention was not in debt for that amount. The committee wanted to impress on their colleagues the fact that if items had not been cut from projected expenses, this amount of debt would have occurred. Actual indebtedness amounted to 12 percent of that figure.

54. *Annual* (1970), 33, 34.

55. Ibid., 30–32, 35–36.

56. Jin Newton, "Peace, Harmony Reign at State Convention," *BNM*, 5 December 1970, 5.

57. The Lottie Moon and Annie Armstrong offerings are collected throughout the Southern Baptist Convention. The former is used for foreign missions and the latter for home missions. Both are named after women missionaries. The State Mission offering is only for New Mexico. It is used to support outreach projects. All three offerings are taken once a year and are in addition to the normal tithing and gifts to the local church.

58. *Annual* (1970), 68; *Annual* (1971), 33.

59. Whitlow, "The Editor's Page," *BNM*, 3 February 1973, 2, 3.

60. *Annual* (1974), 37, 64.

61. R. Y. Bradford, "Bradford Notes State Progress From 1968–1974," *BNM*, 17 October 1987, 5, 6.

62. This phenomenon was not unique to New Mexico, although the reorganization enhanced it. For a more detailed treatment regarding the development of a "headquarters mentality" in the Southern Baptist Convention, see Paul D. Brewer, "The State Convention: Is It Headquarters?" *BHH* 16 (July 1979): 41–51. On the idea that the development of denominational headquarters parallels major industries in their desire to be professional and effectively deliver a product, see Charles Kegley, "God Is Not Dead But Theology Is Dying," *Intellect* 103 (December 1974): 177–81. David Martin argues in *The Religious and the Secular: Studies in Secularization* (New York: Schocken Books, 1969) that the trend to bureaucracy is secularizing religion.

63. *Annual* (1971), 29, 30.

64. W. Albert Hinckley, "What of the Association," *BNM*, 2 December 1972, 4; Horace F. Burns, "What Are We to Do With the Association?" *BNM*, 9 September 1965, 2.

65. For a more detailed examination of what has become known as the post-Christian, or at least post-Protestant, era in American history, see Sydney E. Ahlstrom, *A Religious History of the American People* (New Haven, Conn.: Yale University Press, 1972).

Ahlstrom contends that the idea of America as a chosen nation and a beacon to the world is expiring. In part, the decline of this notion has occurred because of widespread rejection of the Puritan ethic and simultaneous questioning of Judeo-Christian beliefs. Developments that converged in the events of the 1960s are bringing the Puritan epoch in American history to a close.

Chapter 7

1. *Annual* (1964), 21.

2. *Annual* (1965), 14, 15.

3. Samuel H. Lester, Jr., "Conscience and Community," *BNM*, 29 June 1967, 4.

4. T. B. Matson, "Theological Conservatism and Social Liberalism," *BNM*, 19 October 1968, 16.

5. Whitlow, "The Editor's Page," *BNM*, 6 January 1968, 2.

6. Howard O. Marsh, "Arrogancy or Orthodoxy," *BNM*, 4 May 1967, 8.

7. "Albuquerque Weekday Ministries," *BNM*, 7 June 1969, 9–13.

8. The issue of racial prejudice came to a head in 1964 when the Southern Baptist Convention met in Atlantic City. The Christian Life Commission placed a recommendation before the messengers on race relations, which set off a floor fight. Thirteen years later in the pages of *Home Life*, a Home Mission Board publication, the denomination chose to celebrate its heterogeneity in a series of two hundred photographs taken on 2 October 1977 that portrayed its diversity. Foy Valentine, "Baptist Polity and Social Pronouncements," *BHH* 14 (July 1979): 57, 58; Lee N. Allen, "Southern Baptist Home Mission Impact on American Ethnics," *BHH* 18 (July 1983): 11.

9. Harry D. Marsh, "Race and Christian Fellowship," *BNM*, 14 August 1971, 15; "Overcoming Prejudice," *BNM*, 7 August 1971, 14; "Christian Love and Race Relations," *BNM*, 21 August 1971, 14; "Foundations of Racial Harmony," *BNM*, 31 July 1971, 14.

10. Whitlow, "The Editor's Page," *BNM*, 3 August 1968, 2.

11. Whitlow, "The Editor's Page," *BNM*, 17 February 1973, 2.

12. Doyle K. Combs, "The Christian Confronts Abortion," *BNM*, 17 February 1973, 5, 12.

13. R. C. Sherman, "Abortion and Contraception," *BNM*, 10 March 1973, 3, 14.

14. *Annual* (1973), 29.

15. *Annual* (1962), 20.

16. Dale Danielson, "What the New Constitution Will Do for Separation of Church and State," *BNM*, 6 December 1969, 3.

17. Ibid.

18. Ibid.

19. J. R. Burnett, "What Almost Happened to Religious Liberty in New Mexico," *BNM*, 27 January 1970, 3.

20. His recommendation was not implemented. Burnett and Danielson then took it upon themselves to function in that capacity. They alerted the membership through articles in the *BNM* of when the legislature was in session under the title, "Christian Attention to Public Affairs."

21. "Parochiad Becomes Hot Political Issue," *BNM*, 1 August 1970, 16; "Southern Baptist Convention Executive Committee Opposes Voucher Aid, Sets Organizational Structural Study," *BNM*, 3 October 1970, 5.

22. Whitlow, "The Editor's Page," *BNM*, 19 April 1969, 2, and "The Editor's Page," *BNM*, 17 April 1971, 2.

23. John H. Parrott, "Religious Liberty," *BNM*, 21 November 1963, 8, 9.

24. J. Wayland Edwards, "God and Government," *BNM*, 2 November 1968, 5, 9.

25. Horace F. Burns, "The Rights of Minorities," *BNM*, 3 October 1963, 2.

26. Dr. A. Hope Owen, "Teachings of the Church," *BNM*, 31 May 1962, 6, 7.

27. *Annual* (1969), 127.

28. "Alliance in North America Suggested," *BNM*, 12 January 1961, 10.

29. John H. Parrott, "The Baptist Position on Cooperation," *BNM*, 19 December 1963, 4, 5.

30. Horace F. Burns, "Beliefs Do Matter," *BNM*, 26 May 1966, 2.

31. *Annual* (1966), 16.

32. Dallas Lee, "Baptist Participation Urged in Evangelical Ecumenicalism," *BNM*, 8 June 1967, 9.

33. "Baptist Editor Attacks New Ecumenical Plan," *BNM*, 5 August 1967, 5.

34. Whitlow, "The Editor's Page," *BNM*, 2 November 1968, 2.

35. "Rules for Baptist-Catholic Encounter Recommended," *BNM*, 13 April 1967, 5. This dialogue represents a major transition in Southern Baptist thinking. Only a decade before, if a person claimed to be a Christian but was not a Baptist, the church prayed for his or her conversion.

36. SBC and BCNM officials, interview transcript, 44.

37. *Annual* (1962), 15, 16.

38. *Annual* (1961), 18, 19; *Annual* (1962), 20.

39. R. A. Long, "A Sufficient or an Insufficient Religion," *BNM*, 7 December 1961, 4, 5.

40. R. A. Long, "Danger Signs," *BNM*, 6 December 1962, 4, 5, 10.

41. *Annual* (1967), 17, 18.

42. *Annual* (1968), 21.

43. "Convention Reelects Ransdell, Refuses Alien Immersion Amendment," *BNM*, 29 November 1969, 5, 6.

44. Whitlow, "The Editor's Page," *BNM*, 21 February 1970, 2; 21 March 1970, 2, 3; and 23 May 1970, 2.

45. John H. Parrott, "A Plea for a Plan, Patience and Prayer," *BNM*, 10 July 1971, 9; Morris Ashcraft, "Theological Implications of Denver Convention," *BNM*, 17 October 1970, 8; Whitlow, "The Editor's Page," *BNM*, 17 July 1971, 2.

46. *Annual* (1973), 43; *Annual* (1974), 44.

47. Horace F. Burns, "The Ordination of Women," *BNM*, 27 August 1964, 2.

48. Glenn McCoy, "Paul's Concept of Woman," *BNM*, 10 June 1972, 4, 15.

49. John H. Parrott, "The Christian in the Social Order," *BNM*, 12 December 1963, 4, 5.

50. R. A. Long, "The Gospel," *BNM*, 10 August 1968, 10.

51. G. A. Magee, "I Believe in Regularly Scheduled Revival Meetings," *BNM*, 9 November 1969, 10.

52. Ibid.

53. J. F. Hopkins, "The Tongues Heresy," *BNM*, 21 November 1963, 6, 7.

54. John H. Parrott, "An Open Letter to the Disciples of the Current Movement Called 'Glossolalia,' 'Speaking in Tongues,' or 'Baptism of the Holy Spirit,'" *BNM*, 24 February 1968, 4.

55. G. A. Magee, "The New Pentecostalism," *BNM*, 9 June 1973, 3.

56. Whitlow, "The Editor's Page," *BNM*, 5 May 1973, 2. What Whitlow saw in practice is what Martin Buber observed as occurring intellectually in *The Eclipse of God: Studies in the Relation Between Religion and Philosophy* (New York: Harper

and Row, 1965). Buber identified what he perceived as a transition in thought from an emphasis on God to an emphasis on the self.

57. *Annual* (1969), 19.

Chapter 8

1. *Annual* (1975), 30.
2. *Annual* (1974), 26, 27.
3. "From Stagg to Cone: Years of Progress for Baptist Work," *BNM,* 17 October 1987, 6.
4. *Annual* (1975), 30.
5. *Annual* (1977), 64, 65.
6. *Annual* (1978), 59, 60.
7. *Annual* (1981), 76, 77; *Annual* (1982), 72.
8. *Annual* (1983), 67.
9. "Vietnamese Orphans Will Be Admitted to Children's Home," *BNM,* 19 April 1975, 1; *Annual* (1980), 68.
10. *Annual* (1976), 62; *Annual* (1977), 64; *Annual* (1980), 68.
11. *Annual* (1975), 59, 60; *Annual* (1976), 63; *Annual* (1979), 53, 54; *Annual* (1983), 55.
12. Financial data for Inlow and Sivells camps have been extrapolated and compiled from *Annuals* for the 1975–1984 period.
13. *Annual* (1983), 59.
14. "Billy Graham Evangelism School Will be Held in Albuquerque Next Week," *BNM,* 15 March 1975, 1; "Overflowing Crowds at Billy Graham Crusade in Albuquerque," *BNM,* 22 March 1975, 1, 3; Witlow, "The Editor's Page," *BNM,* 8 April 1975, 8.
15. "Growth Rate Slowing Planning Expert Says," *BNM,* 5 August 1978, 3.
16. "Carter Speaks Out on Southern Baptist Convention Condition," *BNM,* 22 September 1984, 1, 7; "From Stagg to Cone: Years of Progress for Baptist Work," *BNM,* 17 October 1987, 6.
17. *Annual* (1978), 33; *Annual* (1979), 35; *Annual* (1984), 70; Whitlow, "The Editor's Page," *BNM,* 26 February 1980, 8.
18. *Annual* (1980), 38, 39, 53; *Annual* (1981), 42, 43; Michael V. Summers, "Northeastern, Tucumcari Area Pastors Plan North Dakota Trip," *BNM,* 25 April 1981, 1.
19. *Annual* (1982), 39; *Annual* (1983), 38.
20. *Annual* (1984), 64; *Annual* (1976), 56; *Annual* (1977), 55.
21. *Annual* (1978), 53; *Annual* (1984), 69.
22. *Annual* (1976), 33, 34; Chester O'Brien, "New Update," *BNM,* 20 March 1976, 4; *Annual* (1977), 55.
23. *Annual* (1979), 63.
24. *Annual* (1978), 52; *Annual* (1979), 65; *Annual* (1981), 86; *Annual* (1982), 78.
25. *Annual* (1980), 63; *Annual* (1983), 63.
26. Chester O'Brien, "Take a Look at New Mexico Baptists," *BNM,* 3 March 1984, 5.
27. *Annual* (1979), 44; *Annual* (1984), 54.
28. Statistical data extrapolated from *Annuals* for the 1975–1984 period.
29. Judy Edwards, "A History of the WMU in New Mexico" [late 1980s], BCNM Archives.
30. *Annual* (1975), 46; *Annual* (1979), 55, 56.
31. *Annual* (1981), 78.

32. Numerical data extrapolated and compiled from *Annuals* for the 1974–1984 period.

33. Charles F. Polston, interview by author, tape recording, Fayetteville, Ark., 22 August 1996. At the time of the interview, Polston was a former associate director of the BCNM's Education Ministries Division.

34. Dayton King, interview by author, tape recording, Albuquerque, N.Mex., 7 May 1998. At the time of the interview, King was director of the BCNM's Education Ministries Division.

35. In this regard, Southern Baptists followed the path taken by other evangelicals. For a discussion of this shift from teaching the great biblical doctrines to an emphasis on "life application," see Robert Brow, "Evangelical Megashift," *Christianity Today* (19 May 1990): 12–14. See also Carl F. H. Henry, "The Church in the World or the World in the Church? A Review Article," *Journal of the Evangelical Theological Society* 34 (September 1991): 381–83; David Wells, *No Place for Truth: Or Whatever Happened to Evangelical Theology?* (Grand Rapids, Mich.: Eerdmans, 1993); and Wells, *God in the Wasteland: The Reality of Truth in a World of Fading Dreams* (Grand Rapids, Mich.: Eerdmans, 1994).

36. W. A. Bradshaw, interview by author, tape recording, Albuquerque, N.Mex., 29 April 1998. At the time of the interview, Bradshaw was associate director of the BCNM's Education Ministries Division.

37. *Annual* (1982), 40.

38. *Annual* (1983), 54, 55; *Annual* (1984), 60, 61.

39. *Annual* (1984), 56.

40. *Annual* (1979), 43.

41. Billy J. Foster, "Church Staff Salaries," *BNM*, 3 May 1975, 2.

42. "Southern Baptist Convention Growth Keeps Up With U.S. but Falters Behind Growth in Sun Belt," *BNM*, 5 September 1981, 6.

43. *Annual* (1982), 76.

44. Presnall Wood, "14 Million Southern Baptists, Where Are They?" *BNM*, 11 February 1984, 2.

45. "Cooperative Giving Tops $8 Million in November," *BNM*, 7 January 1984, 1.

46. Statistical data extrapolated and compiled from *Annuals* for 1975–1984 period.

Chapter 9

1 J. B. Fowler, "Cone Accepts Convention's Call," *BNM*, 19 January 1985, 1.

2. *Annual* (1985), 49, 57, 58, 64.

3. *Annual* (1990), 60; *Annual* (1991), 57.

4. *Annual* (1993), 51; *Annual* (1994), 80; *Annual* (1995), 73.

5. *Annual* (1985), 41; "From Stagg to Cone: Years of Progress for Baptist Work," *BNM*, 17 October 1987, 6. Ironically, three years later the building was put up for sale, primarily for security reasons. It was sold in 2001 for slightly more than it cost to renovate.

6. *Annual* (1986), 41; *Annual* (1990), 45; *Annual* (1995), 48, 49.

7. *Annual* (1986), 49; *Annual* (1988), 56.

8. *Annual* (1985), 58; *Annual* (1986), 41, 42; Claude Cone, "Claude's Comments," *BNM*, 25 October 1986, 5; *Annual* (1987), 44, 53; *Annual* (1988), 43; *Annual* (1990), 45; *Annual* (1995), 48, 49.

9. *Annual* (1985), 64; *Annual* (1986), 41, 50, 56; *Annual* (1987), 56; *Annual* (1988), 59; "Executive Board Recommends Honors For Roberts and Stagg," *BNM*,

12 November 1988, 2; J. B. Fowler, "As I See It: Missions Big Business," *BNM*, 26 August 1989, 2; *Annual* (1990), 60.

10. Claude Cone, "Cone Emphasizes Importance of Supporting Mission Offering," *BNM*, 24 August 1991, 1, 2; *Annual* (1992), 69; M. V. Summers, "10 New Mexico Baptist Projects Will Be Funded by State Mission Offering," *BNM*, 29 August 1992, 1; "1993 Harry P. Stagg Mission Offering," *BNM*, 28 August 1993, 3; *Annual* (1995), 61, 73; John Loudat, "Low Attendance, Funds Cancel BCNM Camps," *BNM*, 20 May 1995, 1.

11. Cone, "Cone Emphasizes Importance of Supporting Missions Offering," 1, 2.

12. M. V. Summers, "91 Stagg State Mission Offering Goal is $191,000.00," *BNM*, 24 August 1991, 1; "1995 Harry P. Stagg State Mission Offering," *BNM*, 26 August 1995, 1.

13. Lee Black, interview with author, tape recording, Albuquerque, N.Mex., 29 April 1998 (at time of interview Black was director of the BCNM's Baptist Foundation); *Annual* (1995), 35.

14. *Annual* (1985), 43; *Annual* (1995), 52.

15. *Annual* (1993), 78.

16. *Annual* (1994), 59, 93.

17. *Annual* (1994), 40, 41.

18. Judy Edwards, interview by author, tape recording, 28 April 1998. At the time of the interview, Edwards was director of the BCNM's Women's Missionary Union.

19. *Annual* (1986), 57, 58.

20. *Annual* (1989), 61, 62.

21. This perceived breakdown of the family reflects the impact of the larger culture on Baptists. Degeneration of the nuclear family in post-1960s America has been the subject of several scholarly studies, two of which are especially appropriate for this work: Christopher Lasch, *Haven in a Heartless World: The Family Besieged* (New York: Basic Books, 1979); and Arlene Skolnick and Jerome H. Skolnick, *Family in Transition: Rethinking Marriage, Sexuality, Child Rearing, and Family Organization* (Boston: Little, Brown, 1980).

22. *Annual* (1986), 59; *Annual* (1987), 60; *Annual* (1992), 22.

23. *Annual* (1995), 77. Recent studies have shown that if new members are not assimilated within six weeks, the church will probably lose them.

24. L. E. "Chief" Lawson, "The History of Simultaneous Crusades," *BNM*, 30 November 1985, 2; *Annual* (1986), 40, 41, 64; *Annual* (1989), 44, 45.

25. Bradshaw, interview, 29 April 1998.

26. *Annual* (1994), 45, 46.

27. Glenn McCoy, interview by author, tape recording, Portales, N.Mex., 25 April 1998. At the time of the interview, McCoy was director of the Baptist Student Union at Eastern New Mexico University.

28. *Annual* (1982), 67; *Annual* (1986), 49. Wayland did establish a two-year school at the Glorieta facility with classes beginning in fall 1996. The school ran for three years, ending the spring semester of 1999. The Texas-based university moved its operation to Albuquerque beginning with the fall 1999 semester. Instead of a junior college format, however, Wayland chose to offer the bachelor of science in occupational education program.

29. Cone, "Claude's Comments," *BNM*, 24 July 1993, 5; J. B. Fowler, "Southwestern Seminary a Possibility," *BNM*, 24 April 1993, 1; Cone, "Claude's Comments," *BNM*, 2 October 1993, 5; Cameron Crabtree, "Golden Gate Seminary Pursues Western

Expansion with Albuquerque Center," *BNM,* 18 June 1994, 1.

30. *Annual* (1992), 81; J. B. Fowler, "1064 Register for 75th Celebration," *BNM,* 14 November 1987, 1–3, 6, 7.

31. *Annual* (1985), 55, 56, 71; *Annual* (1989), 68; *Annual* (1993), 77, 78.

32. *Annual* (1991), 75; *Annual* (1994), 90; Gustavo Suarez, interview by author, tape recording, Albuquerque, N.Mex., 4 May 1998. At the time of the interview, Suarez was director of the BCNM's Missions Ministries Division.

33. Cone, "Claude's Comments," *BNM,* 27 August 1988, 6; Redford Hutcheson, "Rio Grande Association Looks at Work East of Las Cruces," *BNM,* 27 August 1988, 6.

34. Donald Seigler, "Central Association Sees Need to Expand in Metropolitan Area," *BNM,* 27 August 1988, 7.

35. Increasing government intrusion into religious affairs has become a regular feature in the post-1960s period as it has in virtually every area of society. For an analysis of how this factor has impacted religious development nationally, see Robert Wuthnow, *The Restructuring of American Religion: Society and Faith Since World War II* (Princeton, N.J.: Princeton University Press, 1988), 6–8, 114–17, 319–22. Convention leaders have had to inform pastors that under the rubric of "public policy," a church could lose its tax-exempt status should the pastor make "overt" political statements from the pulpit. Some Baptist officials have expressed concern that this same provision may be used in the future to prohibit religious groups from expressing some of their traditional beliefs. Francis Wilson, interview by author, tape recording, Albuquerque, N.Mex., 28 April 1998. At the time of the interview, Wilson was BCNM's business manager.

36. John Loudat, interview by author, tape recording, Albuquerque, N.Mex., 27 April 1998. At the time of the interview, Loudat was editor of the *BNM.*

37. M. V. Summers, "Summers: Beginning Churches Expensive but Still Possible," *BNM,* 26 August 1989, 3; Thomas Eason, "Two Groups Use Same Facilities in Cruces," *BNM,* 26 August 1989, 3; Edward Laughlin, "88 State Mission Funds Were Helpful in Erecting New Facility," *BNM,* 25 August 1990, 3; *Annual* (1990), 58.

38. "Mission New Mexico Outreach Program Is Discussed by Cone," *BNM,* 26 January 1991, 3, 6.

39. Claude Cone, interview by author, tape recording, Albuquerque, N.Mex., 28 April 1998. At the time of the interview, Cone was executive director of the BCNM.

40. Loudat, interview; Wilson, interview.

41. Cone, interview; *Annual* (1994), 64, 74.

42. McCoy, interview.

43. Cone, interview.

44. John Embery, "New Congregations Need Help in Purchasing Church Sites," *BNM,* 27 August 1994, 2; Black, interview.

45. Cone, interview.

46. BCNM, "Associational Task Force Committee Report 1993," BCNM Archives.

47. Ibid.

48. McCoy, interview.

49. *Annual* (1995), 60.

50. Black, interview; Bobby Renfro, interview by author, tape recording, Glorieta, N.Mex., 28 October 1998. At the time of the interview, Renfro was pastor of the First Baptist Church in Roswell.

51. BCNM, "Strategic Planning Task Force Report 1995," BCNM Archives.

52. Renfro, interview.

53. M. V. Summers, interview by author, tape recording, Clovis, N.Mex., 25 April 1998. At the time of the interview, Summers was a former director of BCNM's Missions Division.

54. *Annual* (1994), 43.

55. Although virtually all denominations increased their memberships in the fifteen years following World War II, the impact of the 1960s caused most mainline denominations' rolls to plummet. Southern Baptists did not follow this trend. Even though the rate of increase slowed, it continued upward. The actual drop in membership by the BCNM during the Cone era has ominous overtones. Dean M. Kelley has argued in *Why Conservative Churches Are Growing: A Study in the Sociology of Religion* (New York: Harper and Row, 1972) that denominations with rigid belief structures and practices continue to attract members because they give order and meaning to people's lives in a culture that is in flux. This certainly would apply to the Southern Baptists. Two other works have extended Kelley's thesis: David A. Roozen and Jackson W. Carroll, "Recent Trends in Church Membership and Participation: An Introduction," and Dean R. Hogue and David A. Roozen, "Some Theological Conclusions About Church Trends," in *Understanding Church Growth and Decline, 1950–1978,* ed. Dean R. Hogue and David A. Roozen (New York: Pilgrim Press, 1979), 21–41, 315–33. These authors maintain that religion has prospered at the expense of theology. In the 1950s, a desire for community brought people into the mainline denominations. Attempting to accommodate this desire, churches began to de-emphasize their doctrinal beliefs. In the 1960s, membership began to subside as people searched for community outside the churches. It is possible that the recent plateau and even decline in the BCNM are due to these factors. Beginning in the 1970s, Baptists began to jettison doctrinal training to accommodate the needs of the "new" member. In the process, not only did they fail to train new converts in Baptist theology, but the "individualized" lifestyle programs also began to work against the community life of the church.

56. Statistical data extrapolated and compiled from *Annuals* for the 1985–1995 period.

57. The BCNM's concern regarding stagnation, and in some cases decline, in baptisms, membership, program attendance, and finances is paralleled by the Southern Baptist Convention. For more information on this issue, see J. B. Fowler, "As I See It: Facts That Should Concern Us," *BNM,* 12 March 1988, 2; Mary Knox, "Zero-Increase CP Budget Approved by Committee," *BNM,* 8 October 1988, 1, 5; Fowler, "As I See It: Baptist Churches and Baptisms," *BNM,* 17 November 1992, 2. William O'Brien, executive director of public affairs for the Southern Baptist Convention, blamed the problem on "rurbanity," or the practice of people with a rural mind-set who live and work in urban areas. Betsy Whaley, "O'Brien Says Southern Baptists Are Suffering from 'Rurbanity,'" *BNM,* 2 March 1991, 3.

Chapter 10

1. Even though the Dixon case galvanized New Mexico Baptists' resolve to enter the battle over their cherished principles of religious freedom and separation of church and state, this action by Burnett and Danielson began to politicize the convention. Robert Wuthnow in *The Restructuring of American Religion,* 198–99, notes that in the early 1970s the most conservative denominations were also the least socially active, but later in the decade this pattern began to change. In this respect, New Mexico Baptists fit the emerging national trend. However, Wuthnow states that the issues conservative pastors engaged in were opposition to the Equal Rights Amendment, abortion, and favoring school prayer.

This was not the case for New Mexico Baptists. Although these issues were of concern (except for school prayer, as Baptists have never supported this movement), it was the prospect of government involvement in education that spurred the BCNM to take a more active role in political affairs. For more information on the rise of conservative evangelical involvement in the public arena, see Peggy L. Shriver, *The Bible Vote: Religion and the New Right* (New York: Pilgrim Press, 1981); and James A. Reichley, *Religion in American Public Life* (Washington, D.C.: Brookings Institute, 1985). See also Anson Shupe and William Stacey, "The Moral Majority Constituency," *The New Christian Right*, ed. Robert C. Leibman and Robert Wuthnow (New York: Aldine, 1983), 104–17.

2. J. R. Burnett, interview by author, tape recording, Aztec, N.Mex., 4 May 1998. At the time of the interview, Burnett was pastor of the La Plata Valley Baptist Church in Aztec.

3. Dale Danielson, "State Support of Parochial College Moves Nearer," *BNM*, 15 March 1975, 3.

4. Burnett, "Christian Attention to Public Affairs," *BNM*, 22 March 1975, 4.

5. Burnett, "Christian Attention to Public Affairs," *BNM*, 31 January 1976, 3; Stan Hastey, "Supreme Court Will Not Hear Tuition Grant Case," *BNM*, 1 January 1977, 1.

6. Burnett, "Christian Attention to Public Affairs," *BNM*, 21 January 1978, 5.

7. *Annual* (1977), 30, 31, Whitlow, "The Editor's Page," *BNM*, 6 August 1977, 8, and 13 August 1977, 8.

8. Whitlow, "The Editor's Page," *BNM*, 20 August 1977, 8.

9. "Advertisers Drop Soap," *BNM*, 3 September 1977, 1; Whitlow, "The Editor's Page," *BNM*, 3 September 1977, 8.

10. J. B. Fowler, "Marquez Maneuvers Bill But Committee Tables It," *BNM*, 26 February 1983, 1, 2.

11. "O'Brien on State Lottery," *BNM*, 26 February 1983, 2.

12. Fowler, "As I See It: Sen. Marquez Does It Again," *BNM*, 4 February 1984, 2.

13. *Annual* (1989), 53, 55, 56; *Annual* (1990), 55.

14. *Annual* (1984), 38; Fowler, "As I See It," *BNM*, 21 February 1987, 2; Jim Gardner, "New Mexico's Most-Deadly Crime," *BNM*, 23 January 1993, 2.

15. Carl R. Scott, "The Dreams They Dreamed Too Late," *BNM*, 21 October 1978, 3.

16. Cone, interview.

17. R. A. Long, "Should We Have Women Deacons?" *BNM*, 28 June 1975, 6; Fowler, "As I See It," *BNM*, 12 September 1981, 2.

18. Chester O'Brien and Bonnie O'Brien, interview by author, tape recording, Amarillo, Tex., 21 August 1996. At the time of the interview, Chester O'Brien was a former executive director of the BCNM.

19. *Annual* (1984), 37; Judith Edwards, interview by author, tape recording, Albuquerque, N.Mex., 28 April 1998. At the time of this interview, Edwards was director of the BCNM's missions education/promotion program.

20. O'Brien and O'Brien, interview; Edwards, interview.

21. In *The Restructuring of American Religion*, 319, Wuthnow maintains that after World War II church involvement with public welfare institutions such as hospitals, homes for the aged, and schools declined as the role of the government increased, leading to a more privatized social work producing therapeutic offerings. Southern Baptist social ministry development in New Mexico fits this pattern.

22. Karen Stith, "Rio Grande Literacy Ministry Celebrates 25 Years," *BNM*, 20 February 1993, 6.

23. *Annual* (1977), 55; *Annual* (1982), 80.

Notes   207

24. Chester O'Brien, "By All Means Win Some," *BNM*, 18 February 1978, 4; *Annual* (1979), 64; *Annual* (1984), 62; *Annual* (1981), 86.

25. *Annual* (1986), 62, 69; *Annual* (1988), 69, 70.

26. John Embery, "Youth Not Overlooked in Offering Plan," *BNM*, 29 August 1992, 5; *Annual* (1994), 91.

27. This trend is not solely a Baptist one, but is possibly part of a larger movement in which the individual, as opposed to the religious organization, is providing the impetus for ministry. For example, one of the fastest growing and ecclesiastically "successful" churches in New Mexico, Calvary Chapel in Albuquerque, is actually structured around this concept of individualized ministry. This congregation does not have members nor institutionally designed programs for constituents to support. Rather, ministries are initiated by members of the congregation. The church provides a place to meet, but the curriculum, funding, scheduling, and staffing are the responsibility of those engaged in the work.

28. Dennis Lihte, interview by author, tape recording, Albuquerque, N.Mex., 29 April 1998. (At the time of this interview, Lihte was director of the BCNM's Noonday Ministries program.) Calvin Horn said the name for the ministry came from Isaiah 58:10: "If you spend yourself on behalf of the hungry your night will become like the noon day." In Fowler, "Horn is Honored For 11-Year Noon Day Ministry," *BNM*, 24 July 1993, 1, 5.

29. Ken Goode, interview by author, tape recording, Albuquerque, N.Mex., 4 May 1998. At the time of the interview, Goode was a consultant on church and community for the BCNM.

30. Chester O'Brien, "Neighborhood Center," *BNM*, 6 March 1976, 5.

31. Some observers have perceived this type of ministry response as going down the road of an earlier "liberalism."

32. Goode, interview.

33. Frank William White, "Ethnic Presence Is Increasing in Southern Baptist Literature," *BNM*, 1 April 1989, 3; "Ethnic Church Development Stressed by Mission Leader," *BNM*, 24 March 1984, 5.

34. "Executive Director Cone Addresses Convention on the Priority of Prayer," *BNM*, 14 November 1987, 1, 7; Abel Becerra, "Ethnic Congregations to Benefit From Offering," *BNM*, 26 August 1989, 6.

35. *Annual* (1992), 34.

36. *Annual* (1993), 47.

37. *Annual* (1983), 70, 71.

38. Ibid.

39. Edwards, interview.

40. Suarez, interview.

41. Ibid.

42. Summers, interview.

43. Gustavo Suarez, "Ethnic Ministries Reach Out to Young Adults in New Mexico," *BNM*, 28 August 1994, 6.

44. Baptists in New Mexico, like many evangelical denominations and religious groups, in their desire for growth and expansion, have adopted principles and methods advocated by "church growth movement" practitioners. Their actions are based primarily on the research and writings of two specialists: Donald McGavran, *Understanding Church Growth* (Grand Rapids, Mich.: Eerdmans, 1970), and George Barna, *Marketing*

the *Church: What They Never Taught You About Church Growth* (Colorado Springs, Colo.: Navpress, 1988). McGavran advocated the "homogenous unit principle" that emphasized building churches around common characteristics of the targeted parishioners, such as distinctive economic, social, educational, or racial characteristics, and subgroups within these larger groups. Barna uses modern methods of business marketing to package the product (Christ) attractively within a redesigned "user-friendly" environment (the church) that places no demands on the consumer (the potential member). This approach is not new. During the 1920s, several books glorified the American business model and advocated its adoption by religious organizations, and many did adopt the model. See Ben Primer, *Protestants and American Business Methods* (Ann Arbor, Mich.: UMI Research Press, 1979).

45. In *The Constitution of Society* (Chicago: University of Chicago Press, 1982), Edward Shils argues that mass society is unable to fulfill the function that communities and families once filled, forcing individuals to look to themselves for meaning in life. The loss of the church as a community reflects at a corporate level this same capitulation to the surrounding culture. The new "segmented" format may simply be an evangelical adaptation to modernity.

46. Fowler, "As I See It: Where Is The Southern Baptist Convention Today?" *BNM,* 26 March 1983, 2.

47. Whitlow, "The Editor's Page," *BNM,* 17 May 1980, 8, and 24 May 1980, 8.

48. *Annual* (1980), 35.

49. Fowler, "As I See It: Draper's Mistake," *BNM,* 17 December 1983, 2.

50. Fowler, "As I See It: Pressler and the Executive Committee," *BNM,* 26 May 1984, 2; John H. Parrott, "Commentary: Fundamentalists Upset Pastor," *BNM,* 21 July 1984, 2.

51. Fowler, "As I See It: One Baptist's View," *BNM,* 21 June 1986, 2.

52. "Peace Committee Report Receives Convention OK," *BNM,* 4 July 1987, 1, 3, 5–7. This citation contains a complete transcript of the Peace Committee's report.

53. O'Brien and O'Brien, interview; Cone, interview.

54. Bill Ware, interview by author, tape recording, Las Vegas, N.Mex., 23 November 1996 (at time of interview, Ware was a former pastor of the First Baptist Church in Las Vegas); Stagg, interview, 21 May 1996.

55. Cone, interview.

56. Fowler, "As I See It: The Dilemma that Southern Baptists Face," *BNM,* 16 May 1992, 2.

57. John Loudat, "A New Challenge For Southern Baptists," *BNM,* 19 March 1994, 2.

58. McCoy, interview.

59. Black, interview.

60. King, interview.

61. For more information regarding this trend among evangelicals, see Wells, *No Place for Truth.* Chapter 3, "Things Fall Apart," contains the author's argument that although theology remains on the outer edges of evangelical life, it has been dislodged from its center.

62. King, interview.

63. *Annual* (1979), 29.

64. *Annual* (1990), 39.

65. Fowler, "As I See It: Doctrinal Preaching," *BNM,* 12 April 1986, 2.

66. Fowler, "Cold Weather, Warm Spirit Mark 79th State Convention. Theme: Celebrating the Word," *BNM,* 9 November 1991, 2. Biblical illiteracy is not confined to

Baptists. Pollster George Gallup, Jr., described the religious condition of America as one of gaps. According to Gallup, on the surface Americans claim to be religious. "But when you start to probe a little bit deeper, you become less impressed. . . . Religion does not change peoples' lives to the degree one would expect. . . . There is a tendency to assume we know much more about the Bible than we do. . . . The Sunday School and religious education system in this country is not working. . . . The lack of biblical knowledge in this country is tragic. . . . We revere the Bible but don't read it." In "Poll Shows Wide Gap Between Americans' Faith and Practice," *BNM*, 8 June 1991, 7.

67. For a more in-depth analysis of this phenomenon, see Martin Marty, *A Nation of Behavers* (Chicago: University of Chicago Press, 1976). Marty contends that people are using religion as a means to maintain individual identity by confirming what they are, rather than to inspire them to become something else. Marty sees a militant narcissism molding American religion, in which people embrace a faith that promises them the most personal success.

68. Milford Meisner, interview by author, tape recording, Belen, N.Mex., 7 May 1998. At the time of the interview Meisner was pastor of the First Baptist Church in Belen.

69 Ibid. The combined loss of doctrinal distinctiveness and the function of the church as a community of believers is privatizing the faith of many Baptists. No longer sharing a common set of beliefs, or a corporate expression of them, has sundered the public from the private in the individual's life. Some scholars, such as James Davison Hunter in *American Evangelicalism: Conservative Religion and the Quandary of Modernity* (New Brunswick, N.J.: Rutgers University Press, 1976), see this development as a succumbing of the church to modernity by making belief a private matter shorn of a distinctive worldview and withdrawn from public expression. For more information on this issue in its broader cultural context, see Arthur Brittan, *The Privatized World* (London: Routledge and Kegan Paul, 1977), and Christopher Lasch, *The Culture of Narcissism: American Life in an Age of Diminishing Expectations* (New York: W. W. Norton, 1978).

70. *Annual* (1993), 34.

71. In addition to preaching, teaching, pastoring, and administrating church finances and programs, the modern pastor has taken on a sociological dimension that includes management of conflict, professional/client relations, and application of Christian ideas to a changing world. David S. Schuller, Merton P. Strommer, and Milo L. Brekke, *Ministry in America* (San Francisco: Harper and Row, 1980), 25, 26.

72. Frank W. Wheeler, "Church Discipline," *BNM*, 4 May 1975, 6.

73. Whitlow, "The Editor's Page," *BNM*, 4 June 1975, 8.

74. C. R. Daley, "Pressures that Plague Ministers," *BNM*, 16 August 1980, 8.

75. Jerilynn W. Armstrong, "Rowalt Urges Increased Attention to Families," *BNM*, 2 February 1980, 5; Dayton King, "Smaller Membership Church Training," *BNM*, 27 August 1994, 3.

76. "First Church Artesia Will Sponsor Congress on Family," *BNM*, 20 February 1988, 7.

77. On this transition from an emphasis on God to the self from a sociological view-point, see Robert Bellah, et al., *Habits of the Heart: Individualism and Commitment in American Life* (Berkeley: University of California Press, 1985). On the impact of this shift on human identity, see Christopher Lasch, *The Minimal Self: Psychic Survival in Troubled Times* (New York: W. W. Norton, 1984). For its impact on American religion, see Philip Rieff, *The Triumph of the Therapeutic: Uses of Faith After Freud* (New York: Harper and Row, 1968). Rieff argues that the turning to the self as the source

of mystery and meaning is the key to understanding religion in America. Wade Clark Roof, in *A Generation of Seekers: The Spiritual Journeys of the Baby Boomer Generation* (San Francisco: Harper Collins, 1993), argues that this turn to the self has led to a generation that wants to experience God but without the interference of inherited beliefs. Inward experience, not transcendent truth, is what determines authenticity. As a result, religious authority has moved from an external source (the Bible or even the church) to the internal dimensions of feelings or conscience.

78. Meisner, interview.

79. Loudat, interview, 27 April 1998.

80. Cone, interview.

81. King, interview.

82. Ibid.

83. "Church Members Face Citizenship Dilemma," *BNM*, 4 September 1976, 2.

84. Danielson and Danielson, interview.

85. Bradshaw, interview; "Executive Director Cone Addresses Convention on the Priority of Prayer," *BNM*, 14 November 1987, 1, 7; Chester O'Brien, "New Pastors in the State," *BNM*, 26 August 1978, 4.

86. King, interview; *Annual* (1992), 73.

87. *Annual* (1975), 23.

88. *Annual* (1982), 64.

89. Danielson and Danielson, interview.

90. Summers, interview.

91. O'Brien, interview.

92. Ibid.

93. Black, interview.

94. Summers, interview.

Chapter 11

1. See Will Herberg, *Protestant, Catholic, Jew: An Essay in American Religious Sociology* (Garden City, N.Y.: Doubleday, 1955).

2. William L. O'Neill, *American High: The Years of Confidence, 1945–1960* (New York: Macmillan, 1986), 212–15. O'Neill argues that religious expression during this era was noticeably free of doctrinal conflict, indicating that Americans were learning to "put up" with diversity, contributing to the "high" that characterized the period.

3. Fuller Seminary became an evangelical "think tank" that made fundamentalist theology respectable. For more information, see Richard W. Etulain, "Regionalizing Religion: Evangelicals in the American West, 1940–1990," in *Religion and Culture*, ed. Richard W. Etulain and Raymond M. Cooke (Albuquerque, N.Mex.: Far West Books, 1991).

4. In *Restructuring of American Religion*, 11, Wuthnow argues that the denominations displayed a sense of uncertainty and foreboding after the war and cautiously launched their programs. This characteristic was definitely not true of Southern Baptists. Renouncing the comity agreements with American Baptists on the grounds that their Northern brethren were failing to evangelize their field, Baptists in the South launched the greatest period of expansion in their history.

5. Harry P. Stagg, interview by author, tape recording, Albuquerque, N.Mex., 20 August 1993.

6. A survey of the theological content of *Christianity Today* conducted by David Wells parallels the same development in the *BNM*. Wells found that since its inception in the 1950s, articles dealing with evangelical beliefs had steadily declined from a doctrinally formed faith to psychological survival. By 1989, he claims that *Christianity Today* had become little more that a pious news magazine. Wells, *No Place For Truth*, 208–10.

7. See Harvey Cox, *Turning East: The Promise and Peril of the New Orientalism* (New York: Simon and Schuster, 1977).

8. Richard John Neuhaus contends that the void this lack of a center has created is pushing society toward extreme options: anarchy or totalitarianism. Neuhaus, *The Naked Public Square: Religion and Democracy in America* (Grand Rapids, Mich.: Eerdmans, 1984), 78–93.

9. See Harry Blamires, *The Christian Mind: How Should a Christian Think?* (Ann Arbor, Mich.: Servant Books, 1978), 3–43.

10. Sociologist Peter L. Berger in *The Heretical Imperative: Contemporary Possibilities of Religious Affirmation* (Garden City, N.Y.: Doubleday, 1980), argues that this current state of affairs is caused by secularism, which has produced pluralism. Pluralism in turn increases the process of secularization, but it is pluralism that is the greatest threat to religion.

11. Ware, interview.

12. Ibid.

13. Sociologist Robert Bellah in *Habits of the Heart* made use of this phrase used by a woman he interviewed named Shela. She claimed to have designed her own spirituality by picking and choosing elements from religions that appealed to her. Its use is extended here to refer to a growing trend among churches that are shaping their ministry around demographics rather than commonly held beliefs.

14. The seriousness of this trend attracted denominational attention in the 1990s. Pastor Richard Jackson of North Phoenix Baptist Church addressed this problem at the BCNM's state evangelism conference in 1991. "We are critical of churches that have a hierarchical form of government—bishops, archbishops, pope—but we have the same things in Baptist life." In "Hoffmantown Hosts State Evangelism Conference," *BNM*, 26 January 1991, 1, 6.

15. The writings of Reinhold Niebuhr in America and Dietrich Bonhoeffer in Germany attempted to fill this void, but their influence never reached down to the level of the typical Sunday morning sermon.

Epilogue

1. John Loudat, interview by author, tape recording, Albuquerque, N.Mex., 10 July 2001. At the time of this interview, Loudat was editor of the *BNM*.

2. John Embery, interview by author, tape recording, Albuquerque, N.Mex., 17 July 2001. At the time of this interview, Embery was a former specialist in church planting for the BCNM.

3. Ibid.

4. Statistics compiled from *Annuals* for the 1996–2000 period.

5. *Annual* (2000), 109.

6. Financial data compiled from *Annuals* for the 1996–2000 period.

7. *Annual* (1996), 46; *Annual* (2000), 73.

8. *Annual* (1996), 47; *Annual* (1997), 51, 52; *Annual* (1999), 72.

9. Loudat, interview, 10 July 2001.

10. Jenny Rogers, "Worldwide, Church-Planting Movements Catching Like Wildfire," *BNM*, 21 July 2000, 1, 3.

11. Statistics on membership, churches, baptisms, and core church programs compiled from *Annuals* for the 1996–2000 period.

12. Embery, interview.

13. John Loudat, "Churches Need Small Groups that Work," *BNM*, 26 May 2001.

——————Selected Bibliography

Primary Sources

Archives

Baptist Convention of New Mexico. Historical Archives, Albuquerque, N.Mex.
Danielson, Dale and Betty. Private Collection, Albuquerque, N.Mex.
E. C. Dargan Research Library, Sunday School Board of the Southern Baptist Convention, Nashville, Tenn.
Southern Baptist Historical Commission, Nashville, Tenn.

Interviews

Black, Lee. Interview by author. Tape recording. Albuquerque, N.Mex., 29 April 1998.
Bowes, C. E. Interview by author. Tape recording. San Jon, N.Mex., 26 April 1998.
Bradshaw, W. A. Interview by author. Tape recording. Albuquerque, N.Mex., 29 April 1998.
Burnett, J. R. Interview by author. Tape recording. Albuquerque, N.Mex., 4 May 1998.
Collins, Steve. Interview by author. Tape recording. Albuquerque, N.Mex., 7 April 1998.
Cone, Claude. Interview by author. Tape recording. Albuquerque, N.Mex., 28 April 1998.
Danielson, Dale, and Betty Danielson. Interview by author. Tape recording. Albuquerque, N.Mex., 30 March 1991.
Edwards, Judy. Interview by author. Tape recording. Albuquerque, N.Mex., 28 April 1998.
Embery, John. Interview by author. Tape recording. Albuquerque, N.Mex., 17 July 2001.
Goode, Ken. Interview by author. Tape recording. Albuquerque, N.Mex., 4 May 1998.
Graham, Bill. Interview by author. Tape recording. Albuquerque, N.Mex., 21 February 1996.
Haslam, Larry. Interview by author. Tape recording. Glorieta, N.Mex., 16 August 1996.
King, Dayton. Interview by author. Tape recording. Albuquerque, N.Mex., 7 May 1998.
Lihte, Dennis. Interview by author. Tape recording. Albuquerque, N.Mex., 29 April 1998.
Long, R. A. Interview by author. Tape recording. Los Lunas, N.Mex., 7 May 1998.
Loudat, John. Interview by author. Tape recording. Albuquerque, N.Mex., 27 April 1998.
———. Interview by author. Tape recording. Albuquerque, N.Mex., 10 July 2001.
McCoy, Glenn. Interview by author. Tape recording. Portales, N.Mex., 25 April 1998.
Meisner, Milford. Interview by author. Tape recording. Belen, N.Mex., 7 May 1998.
O'Brien, Chester, and Bonnie Ball O'Brien. Interview by author. Tape recording. Amarillo, Tex., 21 August 1996.
Polston, Charles F. Interview by author. Tape recording. Fayetteville, Ark., 22 August 1996.
Renfro, Bobby. Interview by author. Tape recording. Glorieta, N.Mex., 28 October 1998.
Sheriff, Truett. Interview by author. Tape recording. Albuquerque, N.Mex., 9 April 1991.
Short, Mark. Telephone interview by author. Albuquerque, N.Mex., 9 October 1996.

Southern Baptist Convention and Baptist Convention of New Mexico officials. "History of Glorieta." Group interview by Hubert B. Smothers. Transcript and tape recording. Nashville, Tenn. Historical Commission of the Southern Baptist Convention, August 1967.

Stagg, Harry P. Interview by author. Tape recording. Albuquerque, N.Mex., 2 April 1991.

———. Interview by author. Tape recording. Albuquerque, N.Mex., 4 April 1991.

———. Interview by author. Tape recording. Albuquerque, N.Mex., 21 May 1996.

———. Interview by J. B. Fowler. Videotape. Albuquerque, N.Mex., 26 September 1990.

Storm, Ed. Interview by author. Tape recording. Albuquerque, N.Mex., 21 May 1996.

Suarez, Gustavo. Interview by author. Tape recording. Albuquerque, N.Mex., 4 May 1998.

Summers, M. V. Interview by author. Tape recording. Clovis, N.Mex., 25 April 1998.

Ware, Bill. Interview by author. Tape recording. Las Vegas, N.Mex., 23 November 1996.

Welch, Hoyt. Interview by author. Tape recording. Clovis, N.Mex., 25 April 1998.

Wilson, Francis. Interview by author. Tape recording. Albuquerque, N.Mex., 28 April 1998.

Published Primary Sources

Albuquerque Journal, 1 January 1938–31 December 1995.

Baptist Convention of New Mexico. *The Baptist Convention of New Mexico Annual.* Albuquerque, N.Mex., 1912–1995.

Baptist New Mexican (Albuquerque), 1 January 1912–31 December 1995.

New Mexico Baptist Convention. *New Mexico Baptist Annual.* Albuquerque, N.Mex., 1900–1911.

New Mexico Historical Records Survey. *Directory of Churches and Religious Organizations in New Mexico, 1940.* Prepared by New Mexico Historical Records Survey, Division of Professional and Service Projects, Works Progress Administration, and sponsored by University of New Mexico. Albuquerque: New Mexico Historical Records Survey, 1940.

U.S. Bureau of the Census. *Census of Population.* Washington, D.C.: Government Printing Office, 1940, 1950, 1960.

Secondary Sources

Books

Ahlstrom, Sidney. *A Religious History of the American People.* New Haven, Conn.: Yale University Press, 1972.

Ammerman, Nancy Tatom. *Baptist Battles: Social Change and Religious Conflict in the Southern Baptist Convention.* New Brunswick, N.J.: Rutgers University Press, 1990.

Baker, Robert A. *The Southern Baptist Convention and Its People: 1607–1972.* Nashville, Tenn.: Broadman Press, 1974.

———, ed. *A Baptist Source Book with Particular Reference to Southern Baptists.* Nashville, Tenn.: Broadman Press, 1966.

Balmer, Randall. *Mine Eyes Have Seen the Glory: A Journey into the Evangelical Subculture in America.* New York: Oxford University Press, 1989.

Banker, Mark T. *Presbyterian Missions and Cultural Interaction in the Far Southwest, 1850–1950.* Urbana: University of Illinois Press, 1993.

Barna, George. *Marketing the Church: What They Never Taught You About Church Growth.* Colorado Springs, Colo.: Navpress, 1988.

Barnes, William Wright. *The Southern Baptist Convention: 1845–1953.* Nashville, Tenn.: Broadman Press, 1954.

Bibliography

Barnhart, Joe Edward. *The Southern Baptist Holy War.* Austin: Texas Monthly Press, 1986.

Barr, James. *Beyond Fundamentalism: Biblical Foundations for Evangelical Christianity.* Philadelphia: Westminster, 1984.

———. *Fundamentalism.* Philadelphia: Westminster, 1977.

Barr, Linda S., ed. *Southern Baptist Handbook.* Nashville, Tenn.: Convention Press, 1993.

Belknap, Helen O. *Church on the Changing Frontier: A Study of the Homesteader and His Church.* New York: George H. Doran, 1922.

Bellah, Robert N. *Beyond Belief: Essays on Religion in a Post-Traditional World.* New York: Harper and Row, 1970.

———. *The Broken Covenant: American Civil Religion in Time of Trial.* New York: Seabury, 1975.

Bellah, Robert N., et al. *Habits of the Heart: Individualism and Commitment in American Life.* Berkeley: University of California Press, 1985.

Bellah, Robert N., and Frederick E. Greenspahn. *Uncivil Religion: Interreligious Hostility in America.* New York: Crossroad, 1987.

Berger, Peter L. *The Heretical Imperative: Contemporary Possibilities of Religious Affirmation.* Garden City, N.Y.: Doubleday, 1980.

———. *The Sacred Canopy: Elements of a Sociological Theory of Religion.* Garden City, N.Y.: Doubleday Anchor, 1967.

Blamires, Harry. *The Christian Mind: How Should a Christian Think?* Ann Arbor, Mich.: Servant Books, 1978.

Bloesch, Donald G. *The Evangelical Renaissance.* Grand Rapids, Mich.: Eerdmans, 1973.

Blumhofer, Edith L., Russell L. Spitler, and Grant A. Walker, eds. *Pentecostal Currents in American Protestantism.* Urbana: University of Illinois Press, 1999.

Brackenridge, Douglas R., and Francisco O. Garcia-Treto. *Iglesia Presbiteriana: A History of Presbyterians and Mexican-Americans in the Southwest.* San Antonio, Tex.: Trinity University Press, 1974.

Brittan, Arthur. *The Privatized World.* London: Routledge and Kegan Paul, 1977.

Bruce, Steve. *The Rise and Fall of the New Christian Right: Conservative Protestant Politics in America, 1978–1988.* Oxford: Clarendon Press, 1990.

Cairns, Earle E. *Christianity Through the Centuries: A History of the Christian Church.* Rev. ed. Grand Rapids, Mich.: Zondervan Publishing House, 1970.

Carnes, Ralph, and Beverly Carnes. *The Road to Damascus.* New York: St. Martin's Press, 1986.

Carroll, J. M. *The Trail of Blood.* Lexington, Ky.: Ashland Avenue Baptist Church, 1931.

Chandler, Russell. *Racing Toward 2001: The Forces Shaping America's Religious Future.* Grand Rapids, Mich.: Zondervan, 1992.

Conn, Harrie M. *The American City and the Evangelical Church: An Historical Overview.* Grand Rapids, Mich.: Baker Books, 1994.

Cox, Harvey. *Religion in the Secular City: Toward a Postmodern Theology.* New York: Simon and Schuster, 1984.

———. *The Secular City.* New York: Macmillan, 1965.

———. *Turning East: The Promise and Peril of the New Orientalism.* New York: Simon and Schuster, 1977.

Curtis, Nancy A., and Kay Weldon Madaris. *In the Shadow of Giants: The Early Days of Inlow Youth Camp.* Kingston, N.Y.: Tri-State Litho, 1997.

Danielson, Dale, and Betty Danielson. *Glorieta and Northern New Mexico Discovery Tours.* Vol. 1. Colorado Springs, Colo.: Great Western Press, 1985.

Dayton, Ronald W., and Robert K. Johnston. *The Variety of American Evangelicalism.* Downers Grove, Ill.: Intervarsity Press, 1991.

Dollar, George W. *A History of Fundamentalism in America.* Greenville, S.C.: Bob Jones University Press, 1973.

Dorough, Dwight C. *The Bible Belt Mystique.* Philadelphia: Westminster Press, 1974.

Draper, James T., Jr. *Authority: The Critical Issue for Southern Baptists.* Old Tappan, N.J.: Revell, 1984.

Eighmy, John Lee. *Churches in Cultural Captivity.* Knoxville: University of Tennessee Press, 1972.

Elwood, Robert S. *Alternative Altars: Unconventional and Eastern Spirituality in America.* Chicago: University of Chicago, 1979.

———. *The Sixties Spiritual Awakening: American Religion Moving from Modern to Postmodern.* New Brunswick, N.J.: Rutgers University Press, 1994.

Erickson, Millard J. *The Evangelical Left: Encountering Postconservative Evangelical Theology.* Grand Rapids, Mich.: Baker Books, 1997.

Etulain, Richard W. "Regionalizing Religion: Evangelicals in the American West, 1940–1990." In *Religion and Culture,* edited by Richard W. Etulain and Raymond M. Cooke, 79–103. Albuquerque, N.Mex.: Far West Books, 1991.

———, comp. *Religion in the Twentieth-Century American West: A Bibliography.* Albuquerque: Center for the American West, University of New Mexico, 1991.

Farley, Edward. *Theologia: The Fragmentation and Unity of Theological Education.* Philadelphia: Fortress Press, 1983.

Ferm, Deane William. *Contemporary American Theologies: A Critical Survey.* New York: Seabury, 1981.

Filts, Leroy. *Lott Cary: First Black Missionary to Africa.* Valley Forge, Pa.: Judson Press, 1978.

Finke, Roger, and Rodney Stark. *The Churching of America, 1776–1990.* New Brunswick, N.J.: Rutgers University Press, 1992.

Flake, Carol. *Redemptorama: Culture, Politics, and the New Evangelicalism.* Garden City, N.Y.: Doubleday, 1984.

Flowers, Ronald B. *Religion in Strange Times: The 1960s and 1970s.* Macon, Ga.: Mercer University Press, 1984.

Gallup, George, Jr., and Jim Castelli. *The People's Religion: American Faith in the 90's.* New York: Macmillan, 1989.

Garrett, James Leo, ed. *Baptist Relations with Other Christians.* Valley Forge, Pa.: Judson Press, 1974.

Garrett, James Leo, Jr., E. Glenn Hinson, and James E. Tull. *Are Southern Baptists "Evangelicals"?* Macon, Ga.: Mercer University Press, 1983.

Gaustad, Edwin S. *Historical Atlas of Religion in America.* Rev. ed. New York: Harper and Row, 1976.

Griffith, R. Marie. *God's Daughters: Evangelical Women and the Power of Submission.* Berkeley: University of California Press, 1997.

Guarneri, Carl, and David Alvarez, eds. *Religion and Society in the American West: Historical Essays.* Lanham, Md.: University Press of America, 1987.

Hadden, Jeffrey K., and Anson Shupe. *Televangelism: Power and Politics on God's Frontier.* New York: Henry Holt and Co., 1988.

Hamilton, Robert. *The Gospel Among the Red Men: The History of Southern Baptist Indian Missions.* Nashville, Tenn.: Sunday School Board of the Southern Baptist Convention, 1930.

Handy, Robert T. *A Christian America: Protestant Hopes and Historical Realities.* New York: Oxford, 1972.

Harrell, David Edwin, Jr. *All Things Are Possible.* Bloomington: Indiana University Press, 1975.

———, ed. *Varieties of Southern Evangelicalism.* Macon, Ga.: Mercer University Press, 1981.

Hatch, Nathan O. *The Democratization of American Christianity.* New Haven, Conn.: Yale University Press, 1989.

Hatch, Nathan O., and Mark A. Noll, eds. *The Bible in America: Essays in Cultural History.* New York: Oxford University Press, 1982.

Herberg, Will. *Protestant, Catholic, Jew: An Essay in American Religious Sociology.* New York: Doubleday, 1955.

Hobbs, Hershel. *Fundamentals of Our Faith.* Nashville, Tenn.: Broadman Press, 1960.

Hogue, Dean R., and David A. Roozen. "Some Theological Conclusions About Church Trends." In *Understanding Church Growth and Decline, 1950–1978,* edited by Dean R. Hogue and David A. Roozen, 315–33. New York: Pilgrim Press, 1979.

Hudson, Winthrop S. *American Protestantism.* Chicago: University of Chicago Press, 1961.

———. *Religion in America: An Historical Account of the Development of American Religious Life.* 4th ed. New York: Macmillan, 1987.

Hunke, Edmund William, Jr. *Southern Baptists in the Intermountain West: 1940–1989.* Franklin, Tenn.: Providence House Publishers, 1998.

———. *Southern Baptist Jubilee in the West: 1940–1989.* 4 vols. Alpharetta, Ga.: Home Mission Board of the Southern Baptist Convention, 1996.

Hunter, James Davison. *American Evangelicalism: Conservative Religion and the Quandary of Modernity.* New Brunswick, N.J.: Rutgers University Press, 1983.

———. *Culture Wars: The Struggle to Define America.* New York: Basic Books, 1991.

———. *Evangelicalism: The Coming Generation.* Chicago: University of Chicago Press, 1987.

Hutcheson, Richard G., Jr. *Mainline Churches and the Evangelicals: A Challenging Crisis?* Atlanta, Ga.: John Knox Press, 1981.

Hutchison, William R. *Between the Times: The Travail of the Protestant Establishment in America, 1900–1960.* New York: Cambridge University Press, 1989.

———. *The Modernist Impulse in American Protestantism.* Cambridge, Mass.: Harvard University Press, 1976.

Johnson, Douglass. *Contending for the Faith: A History of the Evangelical Movement in the Universities and Colleges.* Leicester, England: Intervarsity Press, 1979.

Johnston, Robert K. *Evangelicals at an Impasse: Biblical Authority in Perspective.* Atlanta, Ga.: John Knox, 1979.

Jordan, Winthrop. *White Over Black.* Baltimore: Penguin Books, 1969.

Jorstad, Erling. *Holding Fast/Pressing On: Religion in America in the 1980s.* New York: Praeger, 1990.

Kelley, Dean M. *Why Conservative Churches Are Growing: A Study in the Sociology of Religion.* New York: Harper and Row, 1972.

———, ed. *Government Intervention in Religious Affairs.* New York: Pilgrim Press, 1982.

Lasch, Christopher. *The Culture of Narcissism: American Life in an Age of Diminishing Expectations*. New York: W. W. Norton, 1978.

———. *Haven in a Heartless World: The Family Besieged*. New York: Basic Books, 1979.

———. *The Minimal Self: Psychic Survival in Troubled Times*. New York: W. W. Norton, 1984.

Leonard, Bill J. *God's Last and Only Hope: The Fragmentation of the Southern Baptist Convention*. Grand Rapids, Mich.: Eerdmans, 1990.

Lindsell, Harold. *The Battle for the Bible*. Grand Rapids, Mich.: Zondervan, 1976.

———. *The Bible in the Balance*. Grand Rapids, Mich.: Zondervan, 1979.

Lotz, David W., ed. *Altered Landscapes: Christianity in America, 1935–1985*. Grand Rapids, Mich.: Eerdmans, 1989.

Lumpkin, William L. *Baptist Foundations in the South*. Nashville, Tenn.: Broadman Press, 1961.

Malone, Michael P., and Richard W. Etulain. *The American West: A Twentieth-Century History*. Lincoln: University of Nebraska Press, 1989.

Marsden, George M. *The Evangelical Mind and the New School Presbyterian Experience: A Case Study of Thought and Theology in Nineteenth-Century America*. New Haven, Conn.: Yale University Press, 1970.

———. *Evangelicalism and Modern America*. Grand Rapids, Mich.: Eerdmans, 1984.

———. *Fundamentalism and American Culture: The Shaping of Twentieth-Century Evangelicalism, 1870–1925*. New York: Oxford University Press, 1980.

———. *Reforming Fundamentalism: Fuller Seminary and the New Evangelicalism*. Grand Rapids, Mich.: Eerdmans, 1987.

———. *Religion and American Culture*. San Diego, Calif.: Harcourt, Brace and Jovanovich, 1990.

Martin, David. *A General Theory of Secularization*. New York: Harper and Row, 1978.

———. *The Religious and the Secular: Studies in Secularization*. New York: Schocken Books, 1969.

Martin, William. *With God on Our Side: The Rise of the Religious Right in America*. New York: Broadway Books, 1986.

Marty, Martin. *The Fire We Can Light: The Role of Religion in a Suddenly Different World*. New York: Doubleday, 1973.

———. *A Nation of Behavers*. Chicago: University of Chicago Press, 1976.

———. *Pilgrims in Their Own Land: Five Hundred Years of Religion in America*. Boston: Little, Brown, 1984.

———. *Protestantism in the United States: Righteous Empire*. 2d ed. New York: Scribner's, 1986.

———. *The Public Church: Mainline-Evangelical-Catholic*. New York: Crossroad, 1981.

———. *Religion and Republic: The American Circumstance*. Boston: Beacon Press, 1987.

———, ed. *Fundamentalism and Evangelicalism*. Munich: K. G. Saur, 1993.

Marty, Martin, and R. S. Appleby, eds. *Fundamentalism Observed*. Chicago: University of Chicago Press, 1990.

McBeth, Leon. *Women in Baptist Life*. Nashville, Tenn.: Broadman Press, 1979.

McGavran, Donald. *Understanding Church Growth*. Grand Rapids, Mich.: Eerdmans, 1970.

McNamara, Patrick, ed. *Religion American Style*. Belmont, Calif.: Wadsworth, 1984.

Mead, Sidney S. *The Lively Experiment: The Shaping of Christianity in America*.

Bibliography   219

New York: Harper and Row, 1963.

Morgan, David T. *The New Crusades, the New Holy Land: Conflict in the Southern Baptist Convention, 1969–1991*. Tuscaloosa: University of Alabama Press, 1996.

Myers, Lewis A. *A History of New Mexico Baptists*. Albuquerque: Baptist Convention of New Mexico, 1965.

Nash, Arnold S., ed. *Protestant Thought in the Twentieth Century: Whence and Whither?* New York: Macmillan, 1951.

Nash, Ronald H., ed. *Evangelical Renewal in the Mainline Churches*. Westchester, Ill.: Crossway Books, 1987.

———. *Evangelicals in America: Who They Are, What They Believe*. Nashville, Tenn.: Abingdon Press, 1987.

Neely, Alan, ed. *Being Baptist Means Freedom*. Charlotte, N.C.: Southern Baptist Alliance, 1988.

Neuhaus, Richard John. *The Naked Public Square: Religion and Democracy in America*. Grand Rapids, Mich.: Eerdmans, 1984.

———. *Unsecular America*. Grand Rapids, Mich.: Eerdmans, 1986.

Niebuhr, H. Richard. *The Purpose of the Church and its Ministry*. New York: Harper and Row, 1965.

Noll, Mark A. *Between Faith and Criticism: Evangelicals, Scholarship, and the Bible in America*. San Francisco: Harper and Row, 1986.

———. *A History of Christianity in the United States and Canada*. Grand Rapids, Mich.: Eerdmans, 1992.

———. *One Nation Under God? Christian Faith and Political Action in America*. San Francisco: Harper and Row, 1988.

———. *The Scandal of the Evangelical Mind*. Grand Rapids, Mich.: Eerdmans, 1994.

———, ed. *Religion and American Politics from the Colonial Period to the 1980's*. New York: Oxford University Press, 1990.

Noll, Mark A., David W. Bebbington, and George A. Rawlyk, eds. *Evangelicalism: Comparative Studies of Popular Protestantism in North America, the British Isles, and Beyond, 1790–1990*. New York: Oxford University Press, 1994.

Noll, Mark A., et al., eds. *Eerdmans' Handbook to Christianity in America*. Grand Rapids, Mich.: Eerdmans, 1983.

O'Brien, Bonnie Ball, *Harry P. Stagg: Christian Statesman*. Nashville, Tenn.: Broadman Press, 1976.

———. *Promises Kept*. Nashville, Tenn.: Broadman Press, 1978.

O'Neill, William L. *American High: The Years of Confidence, 1945–1960*. New York: Macmillan, 1986.

Primer, Ben. *Protestants and American Business Methods*. Ann Arbor, Mich.: UMI Research Press, 1979.

Quebedeaux, Richard. *By What Authority? The Rise of Personality Cults in American in Christianity*. San Francisco: Harper and Row, 1982.

———. *The Worldly Evangelicals*. New York: Harper and Row, 1978.

———. *The Young Evangelicals*. New York: Harper and Row, 1974.

Ramm, Bernard. *After Fundamentalism: The Future of Evangelical Theology*. San Francisco: Harper and Row, 1983.

———. *The Evangelical Heritage*. Waco, Tex.: Word Books, 1973.

Reichley, James A. *Religion in American Public Life*. Washington, D.C.: Brookings Institute, 1985.

Reisman, David. *The Lonely Crowd*. New Haven, Conn.: Yale University Press, 1950.

Rieff, Philip. *The Triumph of the Therapeutic: Uses of Faith After Freud*. New York: Harper and Row, 1968.

Roof, Wade Clark. *A Generation of Seekers: The Spiritual Journeys of the Baby Boomer Generation*. San Francisco: Harper Collins, 1993.

Roozen, David A., and Jackson W. Carroll. "Recent Trends in Church Membership and Participation: An Introduction." In *Understanding Church Growth and Decline, 1950–1978*, edited by Dean R. Hogue and David A. Roozen, 21–41. New York: Pilgrim Press, 1979.

Rosenberg, Ellen M. *The Southern Baptists: A Subculture in Transition*. Knoxville: University of Tennessee Press, 1989.

Rosman, Doreen. *Evangelicals and Culture*. Dover, N.H.: Croom Helm, 1984.

Sandeen, Ernest R. *The Roots of Fundamentalism: British and American Millenarianism, 1800–1930*. Chicago: University of Chicago Press, 1970.

Schuetz, Janice E. "A Rhetorical Approach to Protestant Evangelism in Twentieth-Century New Mexico." In *Religion in Modern New Mexico*, edited by Ferenc M. Szasz and Richard W. Etulain, 125–43. Albuquerque: University of New Mexico Press, 1997.

Schuller, David S., Merton P. Strommer, and Milo L. Brekke. *Ministry in America*. San Francisco: Harper and Row, 1980.

Shelley, Bruce. "Isaac Backus." In *Eerdmans' Handbook to Christianity in America*, edited by Mark A. Noll, et al., 117–18. Grand Rapids, Mich.: Eerdmans, 1983.

Shelley, Bruce, and Marshall Shelley. *The Consumer Church*. Downers Grove, Ill.: Intervarsity Press, 1992.

Shils, Edward. *The Constitution of Society*. Chicago: University of Chicago Press, 1982.

Shriver, Peggy L. *The Bible Vote: Religion and the New Right*. New York: Pilgrim Press, 1981.

Shupe, Anson, and William Stacey. "The Moral Majority Constituency." In *The New Christian Right*, edited by Robert C. Leibman and Robert Wuthnow, 104–17. New York: Aldine, 1983.

Shurden, Walter B. *Not a Silent People: Controversies That Have Shaped Southern Baptists*. Nashville, Tenn.: Broadman Press, 1972.

Skolnick, Arlene, and Jerome H. Skolnick. *Family in Transition: Rethinking Marriage, Sexuality, Child Rearing, and Family Organization*. Boston: Little, Brown, 1980.

Smith, Christian, with Michael Emerson, et al. *American Evangelicalism: Embattled and Thriving*. Chicago: University of Chicago Press, 1998.

Smith, H. Shelton. *In His Image But. . . .* Durham, N.C.: Duke University Press, 1972.

Spain, Rufus B. *At Ease in Zion: A Social History of Southern Baptists, 1865–1900*. Nashville, Tenn.: Vanderbilt University Press, 1967.

Stratton, David H. *The First Century of Baptists in New Mexico, 1849–1950*. Albuquerque: Women's Missionary Union of New Mexico, 1954.

Sweet, Leonard I., ed. *The Evangelical Tradition in America*. Macon, Ga.: Mercer University Press, 1984.

Szasz, Ferenc M. *The Divided Mind of Protestant America, 1880–1930*. Tuscaloosa: University of Alabama Press, 1982.

———. *The Protestant Clergy in the Great Plains and Mountain West, 1869–1915*. Albuquerque: University of New Mexico Press, 1988.

―――. *Religion in the Modern American West*. Tucson: University of Arizona Press, 2000.

―――, ed. *Religion in the West*. Manhattan, Kans.: Sunflower University Press, 1984.

Szasz, Ferenc M., and Richard W. Etulain, eds. *Religion in Modern New Mexico*. Albuquerque: University of New Mexico Press, 1997.

Thompson, James J., Jr. *Tried as by Fire: Southern Baptists and the Religious Controversies of the 1920s*. Macon, Ga.: Mercer University Press, 1982.

Torbet, Robert G. *A History of the Baptists*. Philadelphia: Judson Press, 1950.

Tull, James E. *Shapers of Baptist Thought*. Valley Forge, Pa.: Judson Press, 1972.

Wald, Kenneth D. *Religion and Politics in the United States*. New York: St. Martin's Press, 1987.

Walker, Randi Jones. *Protestantism in the Sangre de Cristos: 1850–1920*. Albuquerque: University of New Mexico Press, 1991.

Watts, M. R. *The Dissenters: From the Reformation to the French Revolution*. Oxford: Clarendon Press, 1978.

Weber, Timothy P. *Living in the Shadow of the Second Coming: American Premillennialism, 1875–1982*. Rev. ed. Chicago: University of Chicago Press, 1987.

Wells, David F. *God in the Wasteland: The Reality of Truth in a World of Fading Dreams*. Grand Rapids, Mich.: Eerdmans, 1994.

―――. *No Place for Truth: Or Whatever Happened to Evangelical Theology?* Grand Rapids, Mich.: Eerdmans, 1993.

Wells, David F., and John D. Woodbridge, eds. *The Evangelicals: What They Believe, Who They Are, Where They Are Changing*. Grand Rapids, Mich.: Baker Book House, 1977.

Wiley, Tom, ed. *Montezuma Memories: An Anthology*. N.p.: Montezuma Club, 1972.

Wills, Gary. *Under God: Religion and American Politics*. New York: Simon and Schuster, 1990.

Wilson, Bryan. *Contemporary Transformation of Religion*. Oxford: Oxford University Press, 1976.

Wuthnow, Robert. *Christianity in the Twenty-First Century: Reflections on the Challenges Ahead*. New York: Oxford University Press, 1993.

―――. *The Consciousness Reformation*. Berkeley and Los Angeles: University of California Press, 1976.

―――. *The Restructuring of American Religion: Society and Faith Since World War II*. Princeton, N.J.: Princeton University Press, 1988.

―――. *The Struggle for America's Soul: Evangelicals, Liberals and Secularism*. Grand Rapids, Mich.: Eerdmans, 1989.

Yohn, Susan Mitchell. *A Contest of Faiths: Missionary Woman and Pluralism in the American Southwest*. New York: Cornell University Press, 1994.

Zwier, Robert. *Born-Again Politics: The New Christian Right in America*. Downers Grove, Ill.: Intervarsity Press, 1982.

Journal Articles

Allen, Lee N. "Southern Baptist Home Mission Impact on Ethnics." *Baptist History and Heritage* 18 (July 1983): 11–20.

Begaye, Russell. "The Story of Indian Southern Baptists." *Baptist History and Heritage* 18 (July 1983): 30–39.

Brewer, Paul D. "The State Convention: Is It Headquarters?" *Baptist History and Heritage* 14 (July 1979): 41–51.

Brow, Robert. "Evangelical Megashift." *Christianity Today* (19 May 1990): 12–14.

Carpenter, Joel L. "Fundamentalist Institutions and the Rise of Evangelical Protestantism." *Church History* 49 (March 1980): 62–75.

Carter, James E. "The Bible and 20th Century Southern Baptist Confessions of Faith." *Baptist History and Heritage* 19 (July 1984): 2–3.

———. "A Review of Confessions of Faith Adopted by Major Baptist Bodies in the United States." *Baptist History and Heritage* 12 (April 1977): 75–91.

Danielson, Dale, and Betty Danielson. "New Mexico's First Protestant Preacher." *Impact* (*Albuquerque Journal* magazine), 30 June 1981, 9.

Flynt, J. Wayne. "The Impact of Social Factors on Southern Baptist Expansion, 1800–1914." *Baptist History and Heritage* 17 (July 1982): 20–31.

———. "Southern Baptists: Rural to Urban Transition." *Baptist History and Heritage* 16 (January 1981): 24–34.

France, R. T. "Evangelical Disagreements About the Bible." *Churchman* 96 (January/February 1982): 226–40.

George, Timothy. "Southern Baptist Relationships with Other Protestants." *Baptist History and Heritage* 25 (July 1990): 24–34.

Halbrooks, G. Thomas. "Growing Pains: The Impact of Expansion on Southern Baptists Since 1942." *Baptist History and Heritage* 17 (July 1982): 44–54.

Henry, Carl F. H. "The Church in the World or the World in the Church? A Review Article." *Journal of the Evangelical Theological Society* 34 (September 1991): 381–92.

Hinson, E. Glenn. "Southern Baptists and the Liberal Tradition in Biblical Interpretation, 1845–1945." *Baptist History and Heritage* 19 (July 1984): 16–20.

Howe, Claude L., Jr. "Southern Baptists and the Moderate Tradition in Biblical Interpretation, 1845–1945." *Baptist History and Heritage* 19 (July 1984): 21–28.

Iglehart, Glenn A. "Southern Baptist Relationships with Roman Catholics." *Baptist History and Heritage* 25 (July 1990): 35–42.

Kegley, Charles. "God Is Not Dead But Theology Is Dying." *Intellect* 103 (December 1974): 177–81.

Land, Richard L. "Southern Baptists and the Fundamentalist Tradition in Biblical Interpretation, 1845–1945." *Baptist History and Heritage* 19 (July 1984): 29–32.

McBeth, Leon. "Expansion of the Southern Baptist Convention to 1951." *Baptist History and Heritage* 17 (July 1982): 32–43.

McCall, Emmanuel M. "Home Mission Board Ministry in the Black Community." *Baptist History and Heritage* 16 (July 1981): 29–40.

McSwain, Larry, and Walter B. Shurden. "Changing Values and Southern Baptists, 1900–1980." *Baptist History and Heritage* 16 (January 1981): 45–54.

Nettles, Tom J. "Southern Baptists: Regional to National Transition." *Baptist History and Heritage* 16 (July 1981): 13–23.

Nord, David Paul. "The Evangelical Origins of Mass Media in America." *Journalism Monographs* 88 (1984): 1–30.

Pragnell, Cecil. "Every Lowly Clod a Lyric." *Home Life* (June 1960): 14–15.

Sapp, W. David. "Southern Baptist Response to the American Economy, 1900–1980." *Baptist History and Heritage* 16 (January 1981): 3–12.

Sullivan, James L. "Polity Developments in the Southern Baptist Convention (1900–1977)." *Baptist History and Heritage* 16 (July 1979): 22–31.

Szasz, Ferenc M. "The Clergy and the Myth of the West." *Church History* 59 (December 1990): 497–506.

Bibliography

Valentine, Foy. "Baptist Polity and Social Pronouncements." *Baptist History and Heritage* 14 (July 1979): 52–61.

Wheeler, Edward L. "An Overview of Black Southern Baptist Involvements." *Baptist History and Heritage* 16 (July 1981): 3–11.

Dissertations

Neely, H. K., Jr. "The Territorial Expansion of the Southern Baptist Convention, 1894–1959." Ph.D. diss., Southwestern Baptist Theological Seminary, 1963.

Todd, Willie Greer. "The Slavery Issue and the Organization of a Southern Baptist Convention." Ph.D. diss., University of North Carolina at Chapel Hill, 1964.

Valentine, Foy. "A Historical Study of Southern Baptists and Race Relations: 1917–1947." Th.D. diss., Southwestern Baptist Theological Seminary, 1949.

Index

urban membership, 166; vision and sense of purpose lacking within churches of, 159–60, 177; women's roles in, 142

Baptist Dollar Days program, 38

Baptist Faith and Message, 81; 1925 statement, 15; 1963 statement, 16, 100, 152

Baptist Foundation, 39, 82, 109, 168

Baptist Friendship Centers, 90, 143

Baptist Jubilee Advance, 14

Baptist New Mexican, 24, 33, 39–40, 46, 58–61, 64–66, 69–71, 85, 113, 128, 141, 142, 164, 167; declining circulation, 73, 123; and proactive resolutions, 140; and social issues, 88–105

Baptists, 2, 19; as anarchists, 1; creation of collective consciousness, 164; defense of church/state separation, 61–64, 138; differences between Southern and Northern, 6; division over slavery, 6; establishment of schools, 19; expansion and growth, 2–4, 21, 28, 154; as only true church, 9; persecution of, 2, 3; and politics, 3; relations with Catholics, 97–98, 163; silent years, 19. *See also* National Baptist Convention; Northern Baptists; Primitive Baptists; Southern Baptist Convention

Baptist Student Unions (BSU), 38, 40–41, 80–81, 115, 119, 126, 165–66; at Eastern New Mexico University, 21

The Baptist Workman, 22

Baptist World Alliance, 14

Barrick, C. R., 22, 38, 41

Becerra, Abel, 146

Begaye, Andrew, 128

Bible: deification of, 152; and Genesis, 15, 148; inerrancy issue, 14, 101, 149, 151–52, 161, 167

Bible chairs, 40, 41, 80, 81, 82, 142, 165, 167, 168; abandonment of, 115, 126

biblical authority, 14, 16, 183

Black, Lee, 109, 123

Bowes, C. L., 159

Bradford, R. Y., 26, 65, 74, 86

Brewer, Viola, 10

Broadman Bible Commentary, controversy over, 15, 100, 101, 110, 148

Brooks, Harry D., 91

Brotherhood, 38, 39, 73, 113, 124, 181; reorganization of, 77

Brown, Acquilla, 124

Brunner, J. W., 25–26

Burnett, J. R., 93, 94, 137–39

Burns, Horace, 71, 86, 95–97, 102

Calvin, John, 1

Calvinism: and Baptist theology, 2

Camack, Pauline, 14

campaigns: 8.5 by 85, 114, 124; Bold Mission Thrust, 109, 110, 125; Crusade of the Americas, 79; Enlargement Campaign, 35, 36; Good News America, 125; Here's Hope, Jesus Cares For You, 125; Hope for Humanity, 144; Jubilee Revivals, 79; Simultaneous Revivals, 35, 79; Ten Weeks campaign, 35

Care and Share project, 110

Carey, William, 4

Carpenter, B. I., 33, 38

Cary, Lott, 5

Castillo, Candelario, 28

Catholics and Catholic Church: Archdiocese of Santa Fe, 47, 69; Baptist dialogue with, 14, 97–98; and church/state separation, 61–64, 138; relations with Baptists, 19, 63, 163; selling of Montezuma College to, 27; selling of University of Albuquerque, 138; use of Baptist facilities, 141

Chama Valley Medical Center, 9

Chavez, Blas, 19

Children's Home, 2, 26, 41, 82, 108, 113, 120–21, 163, 168, 179

Christian Life Commission, 15, 65, 139, 165

Christian Social Ministries program, 112

churches, Baptist: and affiliation, 20; and eastern border, 33; Hispanic, 28; and pastoral vacancies, 159

churches, Baptist, cited: Alb. Crestview, 112; Alb. Edith Street, 90, 145; Alb. First, 28, 36, 62, 112; Alb. Fruit Avenue, 112, 128; Alb. Heights, 142; Alb. Hoffmantown, 36, 110; Alb. Parkview, 65; Alb. Rio Rancho, 128; Alb. Riverside, 65, 90; Artesia First, 156; Belen First, 143; Bloomfield First, 112; Clovis Central, 128; Clovis First, 110; Clovis Sandia, 112; Gallup First, 112, 144; Hobbs Calvary, 143; Hobbs Castle Avenue, 128; Hobbs First, 79–80; Las

Cruces First, 129; Las Cruces Mesilla Park, 143; Portales First, 26; Roswell Calvary, 81; Roy First, 142; Santa Fe First, 59; Socorro First, 81, 143
Church Training program, 76, 114, 125; declining participation in, 124
Civil War: effect on missions and SBC, 8
Coleman, Lucien, 89
colleges, 29, 40–41, 81, 166; in Alamogordo, 3; as means to evangelism, 27; nonadmission of Blacks, 65; purging of liberals from, 14–15
colporteurs, 19, 23
Combs, Doyle, 92
comity agreements, 10, 24
communion: closed, 9; open, 25
community canvassing, 35
Cone, Claude, 24, 119, 120, 126, 150
Cooperative Program, 12, 16, 69, 70, 72, 74, 84, 85, 107, 119, 168, 171, 179; withholding of funds from, 81, 149
creedalism, 16, 100, 102, 149
Criswell, W. A., 54, 100

Danielson, Dale, 66, 93, 126, 137, 138, 139, 159
Davies, Gene Henton, 15, 101, 148
deaconesses, 142
debt, 31–32, 75, 85, 107, 116, 120
Discipleship Training program, 115, 125, 153, 181
Dixon, A. C., 14
Dixon, New Mexico, 61–62, 137, 163
Dougherty, Bernard, 75
Draper, Jimmy, 149

Eastern New Mexico University, 41, 80, 81, 115, 126
Eaton, Betty, 147
ecumenism, 59–61, 96–98, 141
Edwards, J. Wayland, 95, 96, 105
Elliott, Bernice, 72–73
Elliott, Ralph, 15, 148
Embery, John, 127, 130, 179
Estes, Joseph R., 71, 96
ethnic missions, 11, 29, 36, 84, 109–112, 146–48; Hispanics, 67–68, 78–79; Native Americans, 7, 22, 28, 67–68, 78, 146
evangelism, 6, 34–37, 79, 184; to Blacks,

Indians, and immigrants, 9, 36, 63; and driving out sin, 8; ethnic, 22, 111–12; and growth, 43; hindered by anti-mission forces, 7; intense, 111; literacy classes as tool for, 77; school of, 109; and Second Great Awakening, 4; at ski resorts, 80; social aspect of, 36
Everett, Mina, 20–21, 28
exclusivity, doctrinal, 59
Executive Committee, 13, 69; and Glorieta, 46

Filmore, Annie, 66
Foreign Mission Board, 12, 69; and African-American missionaries, 7; Landmarkist opposition to, 9
Fortress Monroe Agreement, 10, 23, 44
Foundation Ventures, 123
Fowler, J. B., 140, 142, 149–50, 152
fundamentalists: charges of liberal takeovers, 15; and purging of modernism, 14

General Baptists, 1
Glorieta Conference Center, 6, 7, 43; and African-Americans, 66; and carpenter strike, 53–54; Catholic use of, 141; as conservation project, 55; construction of, 51–57; gardens of, 55–57, 163; and music, 83; as outdoor cathedral, 55–56; and Penitente crosses, 98; site selection, 44–51; and tax issue, 54–55
glossolalia, 103, 104
Graham, Billy, 14, 80, 94, 98, 109; crusades of, 141, 161
Great Awakenings: First, 2–3; Second, 4
Great Get Together Meeting, 24
Gross, Bob, 145

Hanks, A. B., 13
Harrell, W. A., 50
health clinics, 12
Helwys, Thomas, 1
Henry, Carl F. H., 14, 80, 97, 98
Hensley, E. T., 62
Herron, E. A., 8, 30, 36, 52, 53
higher criticism: rejection of, 15
Hispanics: outreach to, 146–48, 169; resistance to evangelism, 68
Hobbs, Herschell, 104
Holcomb, T. L., 47, 50–52, 54, 165

Holcomb, Tillie, 10
Home Mission Board, 7, 12, 29, 34, 35, 37, 38, 127, 133, 145, 151, 166; appropriations for New Mexico reduced, 25; and destitute South, 7; evangelism in non-English languages, 11, 67, 167; friendship centers, 65; and Navajo Indians, 28; opposed by Landmarkists, 9; pastoral salary supplements from, 26; relocation to Atlanta, 8; and rural missions, 33
Home Mission Society (Northern Baptist), 18–21; end of operations in New Mexico, 24
homesteading, 25; and church growth, 21
Hopkins, J. F., 103
hospitals, 26–27; in Clovis, 4

Impact program, 123
individualism, 4, 125–26, 137, 157, 173
Ingraham, Harold, 50
Inlow, Eva, 20, 41–42, 72, 77
Inlow Camp, 41, 65, 73, 74, 84, 107, 108, 113, 121, 179; Catholic use of, 141; Native Americans at, 18; White Bible ceremony, 19
Inlow Lodge, 17
Irwin, Clint, 47

Jester, David, 126
Jojola, Seferino, 28

Kennedy, John F., 63–64, 98
Key 73 movement, 80, 98
Killough, Charles, 100
King, Charles M., 13

Lamy, Jean Baptiste, 19
Landmarkism, 9, 25, 60
Lester, Samuel, 89
liberalism, 15, 98–99, 103
liberals, 81, 152; purging of, 14–15, 148; and seminaries, 149
literacy programs, 12, 77, 112, 143, 145
Lites, W. J., 36, 45, 72
local church autonomy, 3, 4, 16, 24, 25, 40, 100, 131, 133, 167, 184; ecumenism as threat to, 60
Long, R. A., 98, 102, 142
lotteries, 139, 141

Magee, G. A., 103, 104
Matson, T. B., 89, 104
McCall, Duke, 45–49, 51, 54, 69, 165
McGahey, Philip, 46, 49
Meacham, Edwin L., 53, 58
The Message of Genesis (Elliott), 15
Miller, A. C., 64
ministers. *See* pastors
missionaries, 11, 18, 22, 29, 41, 78, 166; banning of, 63; catalytic, 147; first female, 21; to non-English speaking people, 67; Northern Baptist, 20; speaking in Catholic churches, 19; traveling, 23
Mission New Mexico, 119, 122, 130, 131, 136, 176, 178–79
The Mission of Our Nation (Love), 23
missions, 6, 7, 10–11, 22, 184; and anti-missionary movement, 5, 7; cessation of, 29; expansion of, 109; Fortress Monroe Conference and, 10; lay workers, 78; rural, 33; and Second Great Awakening, 4. *See also* ethnic missions; Foreign Mission Board; Home Mission Board
mission societies, 5
modernism, 14, 39, 157
Montezuma College, 27, 29, 30, 40
Moody, Jess, 79, 97
Moore, Marcia, 142
Moore, Milford, 83
Morrow, Duane, 114
Mullins, E. Y., 15
Myers, Lewis A., 39–40, 58, 65, 66, 70

Naranjo, Rose, 10
National Baptist Convention, 6, 7
Native Americans, 10; evangelizing of, 7, 28, 36, 63, 78, 146, 169; resistance to evangelism, 68
Neighborhood Centers, 90, 145
New Hampshire confession, 15
New Mexico: constitution of, 93–94; effect of economy upon Baptist development, 23; lack of educational system, 19; population growth, 32
The New Mexico Baptist, 22
New Mexico Baptist Builders, 124
New Mexico Baptist College, 21
New Mexico Baptist Convention: division

Smith, Bailey, 79–80
Smyth, John, 1
social concerns, 88–105
social gospel, 102, 103, 107, 174
Social Service Committee, 59
soul competency, 4, 15, 16, 152, 167, 184
soul winning, 43, 154, 167, 170
Southern Baptist Convention (SBC):
    African-Americans in, 6, 13, 28; and
    boycotts, 139; changes in subject matter
    of sermons, 153; changes in worship
    form and values, 12; conservative take-
    over of, 16–18; and cooperation with
    other churches, 96–97; diversity within,
    17; downplaying doctrine to appeal to
    greater numbers, 154, 173; effect of
    Civil War upon, 8; and expansion, 10,
    162; financial contributions, 11, 29, 32;
    first confessional statement, 15; forma-
    tion of, 6–9; furnishing missionaries to
    work in Black churches, 7; Glorieta and
    unity, 50; growth of, 9, 10, 29, 43, 154,
    170; polarization of, 101, 149; relations
    with other Christian denominations,
    13–14; roles for women in, 13; shift
    from rural to urban membership, 12,
    32; similarities and differences with
    BCNM, 164–65; and state conventions,
    11, 40, 160
Southern Baptist Journal, 17
Southern mind-set, 147
The Southwestern Baptist, 22
Stagg, Harry P., 27, 30–43, 60, 70, 71, 73,
    98, 163, 165; and civic involvement, 42;
    and Glorieta, 45, 47–52, 55; growth
    under leadership of, 34; opposition to
    lottery initiative, 59; personal interest
    in others, 31; retirement of, 74; use of
    air transportation, 42, 166; with wife,
    Alma, 1
Start Something New program, 178
State Mission Board, 29, 38, 72, 73, 74,
    116, 166; and Glorieta, 47, 48
State Mission Offering, 84, 122, 129
Storm, Ed, 36, 75–76, 114
Strategic Planning Task Force recommen-
    dations, 133–35
Student Union Department, 38
Stumph, C. W., 12, 29, 31
Suarez, Gus, 146, 179

Sullivan, James, 54, 100, 165
Summers, M. V., 130, 147, 179
Sunday School Board, 9, 11, 12, 15, 34, 37;
    and Glorieta, 47, 49–52
Sunday School Department, 36
Sunday School program, 34, 36, 75, 164,
    181; declining numbers, 76, 124
Sutton, Roy, 31–32

Tichenor, I. T., 8
Tingley, Clyde, 59
Training Union program, 34, 36–37, 152,
    164; declining participation in, 76;
    name changed to Church Training, 76
Truett, George W., 44, 150
trustees: replacement of, 16–17
Two-in-One plan, 129

Underwood, Joseph B, 64, 72

Vacation Bible School (VBS), 34, 36, 164;
    Catholics and, 141
Valentine, Foy, 139

walkouts, convention, 24
Western Assembly Committee, 47–49
Wheeler, Frank, 100, 155
Whistle Stop Workshops, 114
Whitlow, Eugene, 84, 90, 91, 94, 97, 101,
    104–105, 139, 148–49, 150
Wilson, Francis, 115, 119
women: changing roles for, 13; first
    female Baptist missionary, 21; and
    mission societies, 5; and ordination,
    13, 102, 141–42. *See also* Women's
    Missionary Union (WMU)
Women's Baptist Home Mission Society, 20
Women's Missionary Union (WMU), 9,
    41–42, 66, 113; declining participation
    in, 77, 124, 181
Women's National Indian Association, 22
Worldchange New Mexico program, 144
Wyatt, William D., 63, 93, 109

year of concern, 75, 85

Zellers v. Huff, 62–63, 137, 163